Sport and Society

Series Editors
Benjamin G. Rader
Randy Roberts

A list of books in the series appears at the end of this volume.

Go Big Red!

Go Big Red!

The Story of a
Nebraska Football Player

George R. Mills

Foreword by Randy Roberts

University of Illinois Press

Urbana and Chicago

This book is printed on acid-free paper.

Library of Congress Cataloging-in-Publication Data

Mills, George R., 1953–
    Go Big Red! : the story of a Nebraska football player / George R.
Mills ; foreword by Randy Roberts.
        p.   cm. — (Sport and society)
    Includes bibliographical references.
    ISBN 0-252-01825-7 (alk. paper)
    1. Mills, George R., 1953–   . 2. Football players—United
States—Biography. 3. University of Nebraska—Lincoln—Football—
History. I. Title. II. Series.
GV939.M54A3 1991
796.332′092—dc20
    [B]   91-7577
                                                                          CIP

To the almighty power of God—
may He work through each of us for a better world—
and
to my wife, Diane, and sons, Aaron and Michael.

Contents

Illustrations follow page 112

Foreword

In *The Great Gatsby*, F. Scott Fitzgerald describes Tom Buchanan as "one of the most powerful ends that ever played football at New Haven—a national figure in a way, one of those men who reach such an acute limited excellence at twenty-one that everything afterward savors of anticlimax." Unfortunately, no one ever asks Tom what he thinks. Certainly Fitzgerald, through his narrator Nick Carraway, never inquires whether Tom believes his life is over at the age of twenty-one. Nor does Fitzgerald portray Tom as capable of achieving any nonphysical accomplishments. Rather, Fitzgerald's characterization of Tom draws from crude stereotypes: the quintessential jock—physical, powerful, malignant, twisted, with "arrogant" eyes that give Tom "the appearance of always leaning aggressively forward" and "a cruel body." Even Tom's wife refers to him as "a brute of a man." And true to form, Tom moves through *The Great Gatsby* like a hulking tight end, leaving smashed people and smashed dreams in his wake. Nick last sees Tom prowling through the jungle of New York, "walking . . . along Fifth Avenue in his alert, aggressive way, his hands out a little from his body as if to fight off interference, his head moving sharply here and there, adapting itself to his restless eyes."

Fitzgerald believed that Tom Buchanan, born to play football at Yale and to hurt everyone and everything he touched, was the embodiment of a thoroughly corrupt class and economy in America. He also believed that the one-dimensional character was among his greatest creations. He was sure he *knew* Tom, yet he reduced the character to a syllogism: Tom is big and powerful; Tom played football at the then "football factory" Yale; ergo, Tom is a brutal, simple-minded person, incapable of nonphysical accomplishments or tender feelings. Perhaps Tom would have told a different story— one in which anatomy and destiny were not so cruelly intertwined.

Many of us share this reductionist attitude. We are all too ready to attribute intelligence to the frail little kid with thick glasses and to label the muscular athlete dull. At some deep level we want to believe that the fates are fair, that the physically endowed are not also intellectually blessed. Our popular culture is filled with examples of such thinking—the dumb blond, the stupid jock, the brilliant nerd. In this simplistic world, hybrids are not supposed to exist.

George Mills demonstrates the fallacy of such thinking in *Go Big Red!* He is one of those hybrids. Between 1971 and 1975 he played football at the University of Nebraska, which during those years was the nation's preeminent football power. The six-foot-five-inch, 228-pound defensive tackle entered Nebraska in the fall of 1971, and as a freshman watched the Bob Devaney–coached Cornhuskers defeat rival Oklahoma in one of the greatest football games ever played, finish the season undefeated, and capture a second straight national championship. The 1971 team, which featured future Heisman Trophy winner Johnny Rogers and future Outland Trophy and Lombardi Award winner Rich Glover, was recently named by *The Sporting News* the best college football team of all time. During the next four years, Nebraska rolled to 9-2-1, 9-2-1, 9-3, and 10-2 seasons and played in the Orange Bowl, the Cotton Bowl, the Sugar Bowl, and the Fiesta Bowl. It was an exceptional five years to be a football player at Nebraska.

Judged by Nebraska standards, however, George Mills was not exceptional. He was a shade above average, perhaps a little better when he was not injured—which was seldom. His Nebraska years mixed frustration with joy, pain with exhilaration, failure with triumph. He battled for a starting position but never started. He seemed to be on track to play a major role on the team, but he was usually injured before his hour came. In his senior year he clawed his way to the top rung in his position but fell quickly down the ladder. He left Nebraska in 1976 with memories and a degree. But stardom had eluded him.

Go Big Red! is unique, for it is the exceptional story of an unexceptional player. Most sport autobiographies fall into one of two categories. The first, and by far the oldest, centers on heroic athletic exploits. It details the small failures and large successes of the star athlete. It extols sport as the great teacher of teamwork, discipline, delayed gratification, and manliness. It is reverential: the playing field becomes the temple, spectators become worshipers, players become gods. The heart of these star autobiographies, however, are the games themselves. The games—and the great plays in those games—are recounted in loving detail in prose that resonates "Sportuguese," the patois of sportswriters. This is not surprising, for most of the star autobiographies are written not by the athletes themselves but by a friendly sportswriter.

The second type of sport autobiography emphasizes the brutal reality behind the illusory facade. Betrayal is the theme. Players tell of their betrayal by coaches, by other players, and by society at large. This category of sport autobiography emerged during the late 1960s and early 1970s, at a time when the Vietnam conflict, civil rights struggles, and the Watergate scandal had weakened the bonds of trust in American society. All authority figures seemed suspect, from the president and congressional leaders to teachers and coaches.

Perhaps the first and best example of the sport autobiography as exposé is Jim Bouton and Leonard Schecter's *Ball Four* (1970), the highly popular memoir of a nonconformist major league relief pitcher. Bouton burst baseball's bubble gum. Here was one of the gods, standing outside the temple and throwing rocks through the windows. *Ball Four* recounts the antics of crude players, stupid managers, and insensitive, uncaring owners; it also shows that pressure and instability, not heroics and glory, were the constants of Bouton's sporting experience. One of the few classics in the genre, *Ball Four* is by turns funny and sad but always deeply moving.

The success of Bouton's book, combined with the questioning mood of the times, changed the emphasis and style of the sport autobiography. Gone was the earlier innocence, replaced by the razor edge of controversy. In *Confessions of a Dirty Ballplayer* (1970), Johnny Sample (with Fred J. Hamilton and Sonny Schwartz) exposes the racism of college and professional football. In *Out of*

Their League (1971), Dave Maggyesy exposes illegal recruiting schemes, authoritarian coaches, and drug use in football, and asserts that football reflects the worst aspects of American society. In *Meat on the Hoof: The Hidden World of Texas Football* (1972), Gary Shaw exposes the inhumane way college football players are used by college coaches. He recounts how the legendary Texas coach Darrell Royal employed ritualized humiliation, punishment, and violence to get his players to win for him and for the university. According to Royal, football was nothing more than "meat on meat, flesh on flesh, and stink on stink"; and as Shaw tells it, he was willing to go to great lengths to get "those old trained pigs who'll grin and jump right in the slop for him."

The exposé sport autobiography has now become standard and has even invaded the pages of *Sports Illustrated*. Readers expect upon picking up a sport autobiography to read tales of steroid abuse, criminal behavior, racism, cheating, and every other sort of corruption. Just as once sport autobiographies emphasized purity, now they reinforce the theme of athletic and social shoddiness.

Given this trend, *Go Big Red!* is a refreshing change. It is not an exposé; nor is it a return to the purity theme. Rather, it is an honest inside look at major college football. In several ways Mills is like Bouton; neither was an exceptional player. Bouton, a relief pitcher, spent most of his time on the bench watching others perform; Mills, a substitute who was often injured, occupied a similar position. Both men had time to watch and to contemplate the action on the playing field. Their positions on the sidelines gave them unique perspectives.

Mills and Bouton also share a certain innocence. Bouton was perhaps a little more worldly—he was, after all, a man playing a boy's game—whereas Mills reminds us that even major college football is a boy's game played by (big) boys aged eighteen to twenty-two. Away from home for the first time, many of them are insecure, confused, and desperately trying to fit into their new environment. On television and from the stands they may look like fully developed men, but they are closer, chronologically and emotionally, to grade-school players. Mills and his teammates were groping for maturity—certainly that meant more to Mills than football. And I suspect that his experiences are typical. To be sure, football provided him with important memories, but memories are seldom products of the football field. Instead, they are of the small joys of life—the first sight of an ocean, the camaraderie on the team bus, the feeling of belonging.

George Mills's memoir gives a different view of college football players and challenges the tired stereotypes of both purity and corruption. After reading *Go Big Red!* you'll be less apt to accept Fitzgerald's portrait of Tom Buchanan; in fact, you'll long to hear Tom's story in his own words.

Randy Roberts

Preface

The idea to write this book was given to me on a hot summer day in 1972. I was cruising around town with my cousin John Grandinetti in his little black MG convertible and, as usual, we were talking about sports. All of a sudden John got excited and said, "Do you realize you're on a college team that has a chance to do what no other team in college history has ever done—win three national championships in a row?" He said that if it happened, I should write a book about it. Before the idea gained much momentum, my team, the University of Nebraska (ranked No. 1 in both preseason polls), was upset by UCLA in the opening game of the 1972 season. So much for three national championships.

But the idea stuck with me. Granted, at that point our chances of winning a third national championship seemed remote, but I had only to look back to the 1970 season for encouragement. After being ranked third going into an Orange Bowl game against LSU, we ended up being crowned national champions after the two teams ranked ahead of us were beaten. Anything was possible. Besides, there were other interesting features about our team. It was going to be the last season for Head Coach Bob Devaney, the winningest coach in college football at that time. We had an Outland Trophy candidate in Rich Glover and a Heisman Trophy candidate in Johnny Rodgers. As it turned out, that year Rodgers won the Heisman Trophy, Glover won both the Outland Trophy and the Lombardi Award, and we ended the season ranked fourth in the country after beating Notre Dame 40-6 in the Orange Bowl. We came close.

The notes, diary, and memories from that year marked the beginning of this book. After that year, I didn't give the book more than a passing thought. It wasn't until my senior year in 1975 that I got serious about writing again. Our team was 6-0 and ranked No. 2 in the nation. Believing we were going to be national champions, I began to make notes of the happenings and even began using a tape recorder. I taped conversations with some of the players in which they talked about our team and season. I even sneaked a small tape recorder into team meetings, the locker room on game days, and bus rides to the games. I wanted an accurate source to help me tell the world what a great team we had. We lost our last two games and the story ended.

After graduation in 1976, I felt that my experience of playing college football at Nebraska had been so overwhelming that I wanted to share it with people. I had five years of emotionally intense memories about a popular topic, Nebraska football. Over the next ten years, I tried several times to write about it. I would meet with local writers, we'd talk about the idea for a while, and once I even worked on it for a few months. Then I'd stop. I was stumped because I had not developed a proper perspective for telling the story.

At age thirty-six, married, with one child and another on the way, it finally occurred to me that my career at Nebraska was one of mediocrity. I was an average player in a big-time program. This should have been obvious, but admitting to yourself that you are average is a very difficult thing to do. Accepting this truth created a new perspective. I realized that the majority of guys who play college football never become stars. Most players were, in fact, like me, struggling just to make it. Glory for us was a dream. Someone once told me, after I had explained my career to him, that players like me are similar to stripes on the field: we're barely noticed, but without us they couldn't play the game. With that thought, I finished the book.

As much as my memory would allow, I tried to write from the perspective of how I felt back then, but at times the more mature, conservative thoughts of a thirty-six-year-old fused into the voice. My ambivalence toward playing was probably greater than what comes across in the book. My emotions were stronger, the high points were higher, and the low points were lower than I could ever describe. But what I do present to you is honest and forthright, without anger or malice. I have written about vivid memories aged over time. It is my hope that you come away with a realistic yet balanced perspective of what it was like to play major college football. *Go Big Red!* is my story, but it could just as easily have been the story of any of those padded gladiators, No. 78 or No. 62 or No. 94, that we watch every autumn with fun, vigor, and passion.

George R. Mills

Acknowledgments

I feel very fortunate that throughout the writing of this book I received no negative feedback. All the people in whom I confided were very supportive, and this kept me going during the many times that finishing the book and getting it published seemed hopeless.

I would like to thank the many people who helped me, starting with my cousin John Grandinetti, who gave me the idea to write the book. I owe special gratitude to Bill Pserros, who worked with me one summer on the book and who gave me ideas, confidence, and encouragement. Thanks to Joseph C. Porter and Joseph McGloin, S.J., both of whom are authors. Joe answered my questions about the publishing process and Father McGloin once critiqued a chapter for me and taught me that to be published, one must persevere. He also complimented me, which gave me the confidence I needed to continue. Roberta Hagemann did an outstanding job in typing and preparing the manuscript. She was also very cheerful and encouraging during some of the low points I encountered.

I was blessed to have been entrusted with very patient editors in Ben Rader, Randy Roberts, and Herb Hyde. Ben's phone call informing me he liked the manuscript was something I'll always remember. He patiently answered my questions and gave me advice and encouragement, as did Randy Roberts. Randy also critiqued the manuscript and made dozens of suggestions on how to improve it. With Randy's guidance I was able to add more depth and perspective to the story. Herb meticulously went through each page, correcting my impoverished grammar. He made the book much easier to read and offered several other helpful hints that I used. Ironically, Herb is a graduate of Oklahoma. I also would like to thank the unknown reader whose startling criticism was helpful. I want to thank Dick Wentworth, director of the University of Illinois Press, for being so warm and generous and for giving me the chance to be published. His assistant, Karen Hewitt, made the detail work fun, and she had a hand in creating a suitable title. I'd also like to thank Steve Allard of the *Omaha World-Herald*, who assisted me in obtaining many of the photographs we've used as illustrations.

My relatives got involved too. My sister, Kim Mills, did some typing; my brother, Dave, offered humorous feedback for the parts of the manuscript that he read; and my uncle Don Kelley, who was the first person to read the entire manuscript, offered me a welcome response.

I am grateful for the association with all of my former teammates, especially the freshman class of 1971 and the graduating class of 1976. And I thank the University of Nebraska Athletic Department for making the experience possible and Coach Cletus Fischer for recommending me for a scholarship instead of someone else.

I owe the most gratitude to my wife, Diane. She put up with my mindless ramblings for a year while I was writing this book, nine months of which she was pregnant. In addition to offering me words of encouragement, being patient, and being understanding when I took time off from work, she edited each chapter and did a lot of typing. She was always there to listen when I had problems. She is a wonderful person to be married to, and I love her.

I also thank God for giving me the strength to finish.

To anyone who helped whom I may have overlooked, thank you very much.

Go Big Red!

1

The Neighborhood

The Neighborhood, as we affectionately called it, was a working-class neighborhood in east-central Omaha. It was bordered by Interstate 480 to the west, Leavenworth Street to the north, Twentieth Street to the east, and Hickory Street to the south. The Neighborhood was hilly, with most of the streets paved in red brick and lined with giant elms that created a lush green canopy during the summer. The houses were either small bungalows or small two-stories. They cramped the large Catholic families that dominated the area. Yards were also small and fenced with a variety of materials—metal rods, hedges, wooden pickets, even chicken wire—and some people kept farm animals in their backyards: chickens, goats, geese. There were two large playgrounds in the Neighborhood, Columbus Park and Mason schoolgrounds.

The Neighborhood was ethnic. People had names like Abboud, Rotella, Grandinetti, and Lipari. For a lot of the grandparents, English was their second language. Sundays were reserved for family get-togethers. Grandmas would rise early to prepare the Italian or Syrian dishes for the day's meal; relatives and friends would begin arriving after Mass at St. Ann's Church. I attended Mass on Sundays with my mother until I became an altar boy in sixth grade, and then only when I didn't serve Mass.

My mom, Teresa, was small and comely. She was a dutiful wife and mother who used her vast energies to clean house, shop for groceries, wash clothes, and cook supper every night. She not only kept everything running smoothly for our family, she also worked as a waitress during the day. She had eight brothers and sisters, which served to enrich my life with thirty first cousins that I got to play with on Sundays at Grandma's.

My dad, Max, was an in-town truck driver, so he was always home for dinner. My dad was a quiet man who never pushed me in any direction. Rather, he taught me by example. He was faithful to my mother, rarely cussed, and he went to work every day and handed his paycheck over to my mom on Fridays.

My parents had a good relationship. They went out on Wednesday and Saturday nights. They enjoyed each other's company. I can remember only a couple of times when they had yelling-type arguments. Generally when they were angry, they wouldn't talk to each other. Things would be tense and quiet for a few days until the anger passed.

Most of the things my dad and I did together were home projects, such as shoveling snow, cutting grass, fixing a leaky faucet, or going to his slow-pitch softball games. I used to warm him up playing catch before the games. He was a super athlete, even into his late thirties. He had a muscular build with enough agility to play second base and, as a left-handed hitter, the power to tatter the ball over the fence. He was also a great basketball player, winning several Most Valuable trophies for the teams he played on while he was in military service. I wasn't able to beat him in a game of horse until I was a senior in high school.

My sister, Kim, and brother, Dave, were born after my junior year in high school, so I, for the most part, grew up an only child. I don't think I was overly spoiled. Whatever special attention I received from my mom was tempered with an even hand from my dad. My needs were provided for, with occasional extras. My first bicycle was purchased secondhand. I didn't get a store-bought bike until sixth grade. It was a gold Sting Ray with a white banana seat and knobby tires. With it I roamed the Neighborhood with my friends, looking for adventure, except those times when I was grounded by my mom, usually after bringing home my report card. My subject grades were not the problem because they were average, though I did manage an occasional *A*. My weakness was classroom conduct, in which case I received *D*'s and *F*'s, accentuated in red and written upside down to emphasize the teacher's dissatisfaction.

I was gabby and always talked out of turn. I wore thin the patience of most of my teachers and consequently stayed after school frequently. A typical punishment might have been to write five hundred times "I will not talk out of turn in class," and I wouldn't for a while, but I had much to say and was easily drawn into discussions with teachers and schoolmates. My unbridled enthusiasm was too much. Within a week I'd be in trouble again. My friends were equally rambunctious.

I hung around with a large group of kids. My best friend was Tim Lalley. Tim was a first cousin but was more like a brother, even though we fought a lot. John Grandinetti, another cousin, was a couple of years older and our leader. Ted Lipari, Jr., was the youngest, so we looked out for him. There was also Bill Cullen, Tony Paletta, and Richie Smith; the Nano brothers, Joe and John; Art Abraham; and the Digilios, Steve and Frank. My friends and I, while in grade school during the sixties, devoted most of our time to playing sports; but we also took time out to experience all the crazes that swept the country: we Hula-Hooped, hung ten on our skateboards, drove homemade Sting Ray bicycles, and wore Levi's and Bermuda shorts. We sang Beatles songs and let our hair grow long. We listened to the Beach Boys and tried to build a woody. We went swimming at Peony Park and, on hot summer nights, played kick-the-can and the flashlight game, which was a version of hide-and-seek. Getting caught in the flashlight game meant that you'd get roughed up by the older guys.

St. Ann's grade school was the center of neighborhood activities. St. Ann's sponsored our sports teams in Catholic youth leagues (CYO). While in school, during recess we'd play baseball, basketball, or kill-the-man-with-the-ball. Most often we'd play a variation of soccer in which the ball was advanced by running with it, and we allowed tackling. The games were really rough.

Looking back, I can't emphasize enough how important sports were in our neighborhood. Sport was king. It was for the adults, who bet on college and pro games and anxiously listened to static-filled radios for scores, and it was for the kids, who played the games every day and dreamed of playing in the pros.

As athletes we all had sports we favored or disliked. Hockey was my worst sport. I was too tall and ungainly; I fell a lot on the ice. But I played because everyone else did. Every winter the city workers would haul dirt to Columbus Park and form a border. Then they'd flood it, and we would have a hockey rink. We never knew how the surface would turn out. Sometimes dogs or kids would run through it before it was completely frozen, causing ridges and ruts. If it were windy, there would be frozen waves. The games we played were physical. There was a lot of bodychecking into the cyclone fence that lined one side of the rink. I frequently got hurt because I was a poor skater and a big target.

We were all hot-tempered kids, and the slightest disagreement could explode into fisticuffs. Gloves would fly off and punches were thrown. We'd let the fight go on until someone began to bleed, then we'd stop it. Fights weren't limited to hockey games, either. In the Neighborhood a common question was "Who's the toughest kid in your class?" Consequently there were fights to see who the toughest kid was; being thought of as tough was important. I know I wanted to be thought of as the toughest guy in my class and was willing to prove it if someone said otherwise. There were people in the Neighborhood who I knew could whip me, but I tried never to show fear if confronted by them. Rather than back down, I fought. I usually threw the first punch because that was what the older guys said to do.

Losing a fight or getting beat up was not as bad as being labeled a chickenshit. The people who did back down from fights received that label and were never able to live it down. Even if you weren't the toughest guy, if you fought back, you'd still have some respect. You'd be thought of as a someone with a lot of guts.

Being one of the biggest kids kept me out of some fights. My size probably scared people off. But at other times it wasn't too helpful. It made me a target. On at least three occasions I can remember being picked out of a group because I was the biggest guy and punched and pushed around by older guys. There were also times when I was the bully, using my size to intimidate or push someone smaller around. I knew fighting was wrong and felt guilty afterward, but I was not in total control of my emotions. My frustrations and anger often resulted in my punching someone or something. I acted without thinking.

In spite of the fighting, we were close. My favorite time was spent just sitting around the bonfires we'd build to keep warm. We sat around the crackling flames or smoldering embers and swapped stories, lied, cussed, and bragged. Sometimes after a game we'd sit on split logs for hours staring at the fire, hypnotized.

In the spring our frozen pond became an ugly mud puddle. Then slowly the ground began drying and green patches formed. Birds began to sing. The trees that lined the field began to take on color as buds appeared. A sweet lilac aroma welcomed us to the park, and yellow, blue, and lavender dotted the landscape. Armed with bats, gloves, and balls, we headed for the fields, ready to play baseball.

We played baseball more than any other sport. As soon as you were old enough to walk, someone stuck a bat in your hands and showed you how to hit. We first learned by playing Whiffle Ball at home. When we were old enough, we'd venture to Columbus Park or Mason schoolgrounds to play with the older kids.

There was a natural progression in playing at the schoolgrounds. When I was five or six years old, I watched the older guys play and would shag foul balls for them. I'd roost with my friends on top of the backstop and daydream or climb back and forth between the fence and an old elm tree. Once there was a foul ball, though, we'd all chase after it. It was prestigious to be the one who retrieved it.

When I was old enough to catch a hardball, the older guys would let me shag balls in the outfield while they played home-run derby. Once in a while, if I were lucky, I'd get to fill in while they played their games. It was scary, because if I played badly, the older guys would crow on me. Being embarrassed was serious stuff. No matter what happened, the next day I'd brag to any of my friends who weren't there that I got to play with the big group.

Finally, when I was old enough, I'd play any day I didn't have a league game. There were always pickup games going on. First two guys would show up, and they'd play catch. Then a third guy appeared. One would hit, one would pitch, and one would shag. There would be four guys, then five, and pretty soon the whole neighborhood would show up in cars, on bikes, and walking. We'd play marathon games that lasted for hours.

I first started playing organized baseball in third grade. We played at a small field at Hanscom Park next to a lagoon. Gene Shaffer was our coach; his son Tom was a member of the team. Our jerseys were dark blue with gold letters that had our sponsor's name, Barbara's Beauty Bungalow. Barbara was Gene's wife. We made it to the championship game at Rosenblatt Stadium that year. It was big time for us, even though we lost. Playing in that league was a whole lot of fun, and it helped me develop my attitude about competition. The anticipation of playing well and winning started then.

I also played a lot of basketball. The first games were at my cousin Tim's house. Our basket was a coffee can with the bottom cut out taped to the wall. The ball was a rolled-up sock. When we got older, we played up the alley, where a backboard and hoop had been braced onto the roof of a garage. It was a terrible place to play because the alley was on a hill. You constantly had to adjust your shot to the slope or chase after the ball.

Whenever I played with the high school boys, I was the automatic. I'd automatically take the ball out of bounds. I used to try hard to get a return pass so that I could take a shot, but the older guys did all the shooting in those games. I used to be intimidated by them, so I never went inside for a rebound. My first experience at playing on a league team was at the Christ Child Center when I was in the fourth grade. The gym was tiny, but it seemed big to me. I remember straining with all my might to reach the rim with a shot. The smell from the hardwood floors and the leather balls mixed in the stale air with the stink of sweat and produced a new smell. Whenever I recognized that scent, I'd get butterflies because I knew that shortly I'd be competing.

At St. Ann's I started playing on the school teams in sixth grade. We usually got beat. In seventh grade I sprained the thumb on my right hand. It hurt, but since I was the tallest guy and the team needed me, I played. I taped it as best as I could and learned for the first time what it was like to play with pain.

Not only did we play house basketball at my cousin Tim's, we also played house football. We'd play on our knees. After the grown-ups left, Tim and I would play against his older brother, Tom. We'd push the dining-room table aside and put the lamps out of the way so we had an open area for a field. We'd use a miniature football. The end of the couch was the goal line. Sometimes we'd stand up while Tom played on his knees. When we'd run, he'd knock our feet out from underneath us. We'd get carpet burns, and occasionally we'd hit our head on the furniture. If we did get hurt and cried, Tom would tell us to shake it off. When we had more players, we'd orchestrate goal-line stands and pretend to run plays in slow motion like we saw on TV.

We were always trying to imitate college and professional athletes. When we imitated college players, we would pretend to be Nebraska players like Dennis Claridge, Tony Jeter, or Frankie Solich. When we were pros, we'd always be a Chicago Bear or Green Bay Packer, a Dick Butkus or Jim Taylor. We once made John Grandinetti's basement into a locker room. We each made a stall for our equipment. We also made a bench and brought in a radio. There was even a shower over a wash drain.

One day when it was raining, we put on our helmets, shoulder pads, jerseys, and cleats and hustled over to Mason schoolgrounds. We went through calisthenics and then lined up in a huddle. We broke from the huddle and lined up across from a mudhole that had formed at second base. At the snap of the ball, we ran a play, diving into the mud. We played a whole game, and whenever we could we'd kick, throw, and wipe mud on each other. When we were through, I had a side ache because I'd been laughing so hard. We called the games mud bowls and we played them until we were out of high school.

Of all the different sports I played then, pickup football at Mason schoolgrounds was my favorite. We played regularly every fall through grade school. After school, I'd run home to dress in my favorite pair of jeans, jersey, and stocking cap. I'd run to the field and wait for everyone to show up. We had ten or twelve regulars, all within two or three years of age. Our field was about twenty-five yards wide and forty yards long. The bus-stop sign on Twenty-fourth Street acted as an out-of-bounds marker on one side of the field, and the school's fence was the other. Telephone-pole placements served as goal lines. The footballs we used were smaller balls made out of plastic. On special occasions John would bring out the Duke, a regulation-size leather football. We'd pick captains, who in turn would pick the teams. The oldest guys would always be the quarterbacks. I usually played fullback. The youngest guys, or the least outspoken, played in the line. We played with intensity, gang-tackled, and gave forearm blows to each other. We laughed, we argued, and sometimes we'd fight.

Play calling was an experience. The quarterback would stand with his back to the defense and point on his chest where he wanted everyone to go: "Tim, I'll fake to you here and then pitch it to George over there on two." If the play was too complicated, the quarterback might use a stick and diagram it in the dirt.

As they did in baseball, the high school guys would come by and butt into our games. We liked it, though, because playing with the older guys made us feel older and our game seem important. They would play quarterback, of course, call all the plays, do the officiating, and even pretend to be TV announcers. The greatest thing they did was to encourage and praise us. Whenever we'd make a good play, they'd say simple things like "Way to go" or "That's the way to hustle." I loved praise and always tried hard to get it.

I can't remember when praise from the older guys became important to me, but it was. I think part of the reason was that playing sports was such an integral part of the Neighborhood and a cornerstone for our identities. We were identified as either good athletes or bad ones. I don't think there was ever a day that I didn't participate in at least one activity related to sports. Whether it was playing catch by throwing a rubber ball against a wall, shooting baskets, having a race with someone, or just collecting baseball and football cards, I did something. The older guys represented a closer link to professional sports, which all of us dreamed of playing someday. They weren't professionals, of course, but as sixteen- or seventeen-year-old high school athletes, their athletic skills and abilities were enough to keep us in awe. And they were accessible. They'd take over our games and play with us, joke with us, and tell us how we were supposed to act as athletes. "You gotta be tough." "You gotta tackle hard." "Shake off that pain." "They put jockstraps on the same way you do." "Hustle." "Slide hard." These simple adages were repeated over and over. They became our rules for behavior. Consequently, my outlook and attitude and emotional development with relation to sports was largely shaped by those older guys. As with teachers in a classroom, any praise or criticism from them was received with either elation or despair. Their comments served as a gauge for us to compare ourselves with one another. I was conditioned early to react to coaching commands, to accept or dish out punishment. It helped me when I began to play organized football.

St. Ann's had a team made up of seventh- and eighth-graders

that played in the CYO league, but because the school was small, if you were big enough, you played. I was big enough, so I started playing while I was in the sixth grade. I was the center. Playing with the older guys was scary.

We had an average team. Sometimes we'd get buried like we did when we played Christ the King and lost 44-0. They just kicked our butts. I remember attempting to tackle their big tight end, and he stopped to change directions, throwing me off like a rag doll. After the game I hurt. I had bruises all over my body and was growing weary of football.

I began to question then whether I wanted to play. All the negative aspects of playing football came together in my mind. Organized football was not the same fun game that I had played with my friends at Mason School. The practices were long and monotonous. The equipment was uncomfortable. The helmet squeezed my head, and the shoulder pads pinched my neck whenever I made a tackle or a block. I was always hot and sweaty. I'd have to run until I felt like dropping. It meant doing leg-lifts until my gut hurt and doing so many push-ups that my arms ached. It meant tackling someone bigger than I was and accepting a collision that made my head ring. It meant crushed fingers and charley horses. Organized football turned drinking water into an obsession, the subject of a recurring daydream while standing in line for yet another drill on a hot, humid day.

Yet after dwelling on the negative aspects for a while, my thoughts would shift to the positive. I began to think about all the things I liked about football. Praise. How I loved praise from the coach when he'd compliment me for an aggressive tackle or block. It made me feel special, and I liked feeling special. Just being on the team made me special, if only to my friends and family. In spite of the agony, there was a great inner sensation I experienced after making it through a practice or a game. Plus, I loved talking with my teammates. There was a comradeship that drew us together and made us feel closer.

But the second time we had to play Christ the King that year, I didn't show up for the game. I hid out. I rode my bike around the Neighborhood, avoiding all the places where people who knew I played might be. I didn't want to be asked the embarrassing question "Hey, aren't you supposed to be playing a game today?" I remember seeing my aunt Helen driving toward me from the end of the block. My heart started pounding, and like a fleeing animal I peddled to a nearby house, laid my bike down, and hid behind a large concrete stairwell. She didn't see me as she drove by.

Despite all my arguments against playing, I felt this awful pressure to play, and I don't know why. I guess it was because I was so big for my age that everyone expected me to be a football player. I felt there was something wrong with me because I didn't want to be a football player when everyone else seemed to want to play.

On that day when I drove my bike around until the game was over I didn't show up because I was afraid of getting hurt again. To me, playing would have been like touching a hot iron for the second time. To my surprise, no one really said anything negative about my missing the game. When I turned in my equipment, Coach Chuck Christenson was very nice. All he said was, "We missed you." I think he sensed what had happened. Anyone who has ever played football has experienced some fear.

When I became a seventh-grader, I wanted to play again, so I played for the 240 Club, which was part of the citywide midget football league called Peewees. We practiced at Columbus Park and played our games at Boys Town. We won our first game, and I intercepted a pass from my defensive line position. The quarterback threw it right to me. I returned it about ten yards and got clobbered.

The situation was much better for me here. I was the same age and of equal ability with those I competed against. Playing for the 240 Club was prestigious. My cousin Tim also played. One Sunday before our game, we were in our uniforms and the other guys made a big deal about it. We were the only two of our group playing, and they were kind of envious.

The practices were long and hard and I had that same old debate about playing, but I finished the season. I started every game at offensive and defensive tackle. I did get pulled from a game once because one of the assistants said I wasn't playing well. He told me to get tougher, and I did. I began to charge more aggressively, and I played harder. Then I got the wind knocked out of me. I lay there gasping for air, unable to breathe. One of the coaches came out and administered some aid to me. He told me to lie flat and relax while he pulled up on my belt to ease the pressure on my lungs. Slowly I recovered. Still wheezing, I walked off the field and thought to myself, "This is no fun."

2

High School

The bell rang, and I raced out of study hall to be first in line for lunch. From behind me a heavy hand grabbed my shoulder. I turned and the man spoke. "What year are you?" "A freshman," I said politely. Oh, Oh, I thought, I got caught running in the hall. Then he said, "How much do you weigh?" and I told him 180 pounds. He sized me up and asked, "About six-three?" I nodded. "Yeah." I knew he was a teacher, but what did he want? Then he smiled and asked if I played football; without letting me respond, he kept talking. He thought that because of my size I might make a good football player. He introduced himself as Dick Butolph, chemistry teacher and sophomore football coach. I had just been recruited to play for the Central High School Eagles.

Central was a racially mixed inner-city school with a recent tradition of losing. Its last glory years were when National Football League Hall of Famer Gayle Sayers played there. In 1960 he led a undefeated team that shared the city and state championship with Creighton Prep after they played to a 0-0 tie during the season.

I was a welcome sight for the Central High football coaches. They were trying to reestablish a winning program, so they were looking for new talent, and because of my size I was an automatic prospect. During the first week of school I was stopped at least four times by coaches and asked if I were going to play football.

The recruiting effort paid off for them. I went out for the team when I really hadn't planned on it. They didn't have a freshman team, so I had to try out for the sophomore team. I checked out equipment and made it through the first week of practice. My chances of making the team seemed good, but I wasn't totally committed to the idea. I didn't like the early September heat. The field we practiced on was a dusty cinder bowl with little grass. The dust was suffocating; it mixed with sweat and created a thin layer of mud across my arms and face. The locker room was small and the lockers tiny. Before and after practice the room was so cramped with players that I could hardly move. In addition, none of my friends played. They all got to goof around after school, and I envied them.

All that began to wear on me. It made me question whether I really wanted to play or whether I was playing because of all the attention I had received from the coaches. Their interest made me feel important. One particularly hot and humid day we were getting ready to do some conditioning work. We hadn't been practicing long, but I was desperately in need of a drink of water when a convertible filled with my friends slowed down as it passed the field. They were laughing and Frankie Digilio stood up and yelled, "Quit, Georgie, it's too hot!" They laughed even louder, and the car squealed off. I checked in my gear the next day.

For weeks after I turned in my equipment I tried to avoid the football coaches. I felt guilty because I knew they wanted me to play and I had let them down by quitting. A couple of times I couldn't avoid running into them, and they asked, "How come you didn't want to play?" Defensive, I told them I just didn't feel like it. But it was more than that. It was more than the inconveniences and the unpleasantness of practice. It had to do with a change in attitude of my friends from the Neighborhood.

When I was in grade school, sport was king. Everyone played. As I grew older, the importance of sports diminished. Part of the reason was that in grade school everyone got to play, regardless of how good they were. But in high school you had to make the team to play. The competition was stiff. Many of my friends stopped playing sports because they simply weren't good enough to make the high school teams. Instead they formed bands, went out with girls, and partied. Social events and dates replaced sports. So that fall, instead of playing football, I joined a rock 'n' roll band made up of neighborhood friends and became a stage-crew member. I was into music and girls.

I didn't give up on sports completely, though. I went out for the sophomore basketball team. To make it to practice on time, from November through February I got up every morning during the week at 5:00 A.M. to catch the early bus. Practice was at 6:00 A.M. At practice the coach yelled at me all the time. He told me I had the worst hands he'd ever seen. Nonetheless, I started every game.

It was a real experience making the team. I made new friends, and, for the first time, I got to know some black players, all of whom became friends except one, who happened to be the sophomore star of the team. One day after a game he asked me to pass him a coat hanger so he could hang up his uniform. He was a few feet away, and I tossed it to him. He wasn't ready and the hanger hit the floor. For some reason he was insulted and told me to pick it up. From his tone I could sense a challenge and said no. Then he demanded that I pick it up. I refused. He spent the next week at practice trying to intimidate me. During a shooting drill I was under the basket waiting for a rebound and he purposely shot a ball low and hit me on the side of the face. I didn't say anything, but I stared at him. After practice I was standing in front of my locker when he came up to me; we stood nose to nose. There was a moment of silence, then he pulled off his shirt, threw it down, and said, "Pick it up." I couldn't believe what was happening. I said, "No, man." I took off my glasses and dropped them on a pile of clothes. I came up swinging. We barraged each other with wild punches. After about a minute, the coach appeared and pushed us apart, then took us into his office and let us have it. Coach talked about teamwork and sportsmanship and said we weren't very good examples of either. He made us shake hands. After the fight the player didn't give me any more trouble, which was fine with me, but I was always leery of him.

Despite the fight and despite getting up every morning at 5:00 A.M. to catch a bus, I liked basketball and was determined to be a good player. In the spring I'd give baseball a try, but as for football, I was through, or so I thought.

Over Christmas something happened to change my attitude. I was at a Christmas party with all my relatives and my cousin Tom laughed and pointed at me, saying, "Can you imagine, this big dummy didn't play football!" I was extremely embarrassed and began to wonder what people were thinking of me because I didn't play. I didn't want them thinking I was a wimp. In addition, about a month earlier there had been a story in the *Omaha World-Herald* about my cousin Tim. Tim was still in eighth grade and had been playing midget football. He was the star of the team, playing tackle, center, fullback, or wherever the coach needed him. The article contained a large picture of him with the caption "Tim— Courageous." It explained that, despite the loss of an eye at age seven, he played with a reckless abandon that inspired others. I felt a little jealous and ashamed. Here I was, this big animal, and I didn't play and my little cousin Tim was out there on the field kicking ass. I decided I'd better play again.

Why was I so concerned with what other people thought of me? I think it was because I was a self-conscious fifteen-year-old adolescent and peer pressure for me was real. My cousins and I were like brothers, and what they thought of me was important. If my cousin Tom thought I should be playing football, then maybe I should. Maybe if I gave it another chance, I'd like it the way Tim seemed to. Obviously, if I hated every aspect of playing, I wouldn't have played, but I didn't. I only hated what seemed to me were long, hard practices and pain from contact. But the passing of time made me forget all that. I now thought only of my cousin Tim's success, and I wanted the same. I respected my older cousin Tom and preferred his saying nice things about me to being ridiculed. I guess I also had a competitive spirit that wanted to see if I could make a high school team, play, and possibly be a starter or maybe even a star. So my sensibilities were being attacked on three fronts: peer pressure, visions of grandeur, and a need to compete. Combined, they were a powerful force. I knew I'd have to give football another try.

The following fall, I transferred to Bishop Ryan High School on the urging of a close neighborhood friend, Bill Cullen, and made the junior varsity football team. I went out for quarterback and ended up being the starting fullback. With my new attitude, football was fun. It was a tremendous thrill to run the ball amid the confusion of colliding bodies. I was doing well. I even scored a few touchdowns. Then, in practice one day, someone fell on my knee and it slipped out of place. It swelled up and I had to have it drained a couple of times. I played the following week, but it was still sore and taped so tight I could hardly bend it.

I began questioning again why I was playing. The monotony of practicing and accepting bumps and bruises were aspects of the game I still didn't enjoy but lived with because they were outweighed by the fun elements of playing: winning, camaraderie, status, and praise. But playing with the pain from an injury was something I was not prepared for. Things I took for granted, such as starting, cutting, and stopping, had become tests for my ability to stand pain. During each play a stabbing pain demanded that I stop. I found relief in the referee's whistle or in a slow jog to the sideline. In the offensive huddle, I found myself praying that my running plays would not be called. When they were, I felt panic in anticipation of the forthcoming twinge. The sacrifice of playing in pain was one I wasn't willing to make but made anyway because the coaches said they needed me. With my heart not in it, I played lousy. After that, I couldn't wait for football to end.

When the football season was over, I played on the JV basketball team. I also got to suit up with the varsity, which was a thrill. Our team was winning and school was easy. Bishop Ryan had modular scheduling and a work-at-your-own-pace philosophy, which suited me fine. Transferring to Ryan High had turned out to be a good move for me.

After playing CYO baseball that summer, I began preparing for football by running. It didn't help much because the varsity practices were far more strenuous than I had prepared for, and to make it worse, we had two a day: we practiced in the morning and in the afternoon. Practicing was miserable, but I survived and became a two-way starter. On defense I played end; on offense I played wingback and tight end. It was big time to play on the varsity.

In one game I was getting tired of our quarterback throwing all the passes to our All-State senior split end and team captain, Tim Lackovic. When I went back to the huddle, I kept telling the quarterback I was wide open and that he should throw me the ball. He'd say, "Yeah, OK," and then he'd still throw to Lackovic. This went on the entire first half. Finally, in the third quarter, it was third down and six yards for a first down, a perfect situation to throw me the eight-yard curl pass I had been calling for. He finally called the play. I ran my pattern, forcing my way past defenders. I began to curl back toward him, and as I did he threw a dart that hit my face mask and bounced to the ground. I jogged back to the huddle and somebody said, "Nice catch." Lackovic said, "No more throws to Rock Hands." Everyone joked about the play on the bus ride home.

Before our last game, our coach, Joe Ponseigo, let us know he wasn't happy with our 4-4 record. He was a short, stocky man who had played for the University of Nebraska a decade earlier. We were watching films and he was criticizing us. He was particularly unhappy with me. "Mills," he said, "start playing like a guy six-three and two hundred pounds. Start kicking some ass out there. Get mean." I got mad. I wasn't used to being yelled at. All season long the coaches had been praising me, so his criticism was a shock. Despite his yelling, we lost the last game to a previously winless team. I swore I'd never play football again.

The only bright spot on our team was the All-State performance by Tim Lackovic. He received recruiting letters from all over the country. One day I saw a well-dressed, middle-aged man walk into Coach Ponseigo's office. Curious, I walked by, peeked in, and saw he was talking to Lackovic. I figured he was a college coach. Later I asked Lackovic who the man was. He said it was Cletus Fischer from the University of Nebraska. Tim said Nebraska was really interested in him but he wasn't sure where he wanted to play. Eventually he did sign with Nebraska.

I had a week off and then started practice for basketball. It was good for me to start practice because idle time was bad for me. The group of neighborhood guys I had been hanging around with grew to include some really tough and rowdy dudes. We were influenced by violent action movies, such as *The Wild Bunch*, *The Dirty Dozen*, and *Butch Cassidy and the Sundance Kid*. Much of the music we listened to was from the Woodstock album. Steppenwolf's "Born to Be Wild" was our theme song. It seemed like whenever we went out, we'd either drink, fight, or smoke marijuana. I really didn't like to drink because I got sick; when I smoked pot, I felt disorganized and paranoid; when I fought, I was always afraid I'd hurt somebody. Oh, at the time we did those things it seemed like fun, but the next day I'd realize how wrong it was. Still, I always went along with them because not doing so meant getting mocked. I was caught up with being perceived as cool or tough, so

I succumbed to the peer pressure. Fortunately my mother waited up for me to come home at night. Knowing that she'd be waiting at the door often kept me from getting too wild.

During basketball season I started at center and averaged about ten points and seven rebounds a game for a .500 team. By this time I had a lot of notoriety in school. I was George Mills the jock. I wasn't interested in learning. I only wanted to play basketball and be a star. Consequently, in the classroom I did whatever I had to do to pass. I'd copy notes, copy answers, sweet-talk teachers, and when I couldn't cheat I'd even study, but only just enough to pass.

I really fit the stereotype for the cocky-jock athlete. I thought I was hot stuff. I strutted around like I owned the school. I talked big, acted bad, and was a real clown. One person who wasn't impressed was Father John Vernon, superintendent and disciplinarian deluxe. One day in the cafeteria I was demonstrating my aim, using peas and french fries. Out of nowhere Father Vernon grabbed my shoulder and pulled me up, then led me out of the lunchroom into the adjoining corridor. He pushed me to the wall and said, "If you think we need you around here, young man, you're mistaken. You've been out of line for a long time and I've had it with you. Go home." With that I was suspended for three days. My mother was angry with me, but angrier that I'd miss three days of school. She talked to Father Vernon, and instead of serving the three-day suspension I had to work a month of Saturdays cleaning up the school. After that I didn't throw any more food in the cafeteria and was a little more down to earth.

When summer CYO baseball ended, I began working out regularly for football. In part, my effort was due to my cousin Tim, who also was working out enthusiastically. He inspired me. But it was also because I was a senior and desperately wanted the prestige of being a captain. At captain's practice, the players' informal conditioning workouts that began in August, I played the part of captain by hustling, organizing drills, giving orders, and cracking jokes. It was a great lobbying effort.

My enthusiasm continued into two-a-days. I was always first or second in line for drills. I hustled on and off the field. I ran my sprints hard at the end of practice. I encouraged other players. I yelled and I clapped my hands during drills. On the day of the vote at the end of two-a-days, I tried to muster some last-minute support with the younger guys. I was worried. After the vote, we were told by the coaches that because the vote was so close they had decided to have four co-captains instead of the usual two. I was one of them. I had never been a captain before, and it felt wonderful.

Sometime during the practice before our first game, I noticed Coach Ponseigo talking to two men on the field. Coach was showing them around, pointing and talking. I thought I recognized one of the men as Coach Fischer of Nebraska, but I wasn't sure. I figured that whoever they were, they were college coaches. It was a good opportunity to get noticed, so I stepped up the hustle a notch and was like a madman—sprinting, yelling, clapping. I wanted those coaches to think I was Charlie Hustle.

According to the paper, we were supposed to be one of the top teams in the Metro Conference. We were a big team with a lot of speed. I was to be one of the star linemen at six feet, four inches and 205 pounds. But we struggled in the first game and were tied by Abraham Lincoln 6-6. We rebounded and won the next two games by a combined score of 88-0. We were rated fifth in the newspapers.

Our next game was against perennial power and top-ranked Creighton Prep. Prep, an all-male school, was Omaha's oldest Catholic high school, having opened its doors in 1878. It was run by Jesuit priests, and its name was synonymous with excellence in both academics and sports. Many of Omaha's most prominent men had attended Prep. Its trophy cases filled a large room, with state-title trophies in football, basketball, baseball, and track. Because it was a private school, it attracted a student body from Omaha's more affluent families. There were also some families of more modest means who were willing to make financial sacrifices to send their sons to this prestigious college-preparatory school. Prep's athletes were thoroughbreds, being sons and grandsons of former Prep greats. When I was growing up, I had dreamed of donning the blue and white of the Junior Jays, but the high cost of tuition and a poor score on my entrance exam kept me from being a Prepster.

The only thing my school, Bishop Ryan, and Creighton Prep had in common was that they were both private Catholic schools, except Ryan's tuition was less. Ryan was a new school, barely ten years old. It was run by the School Sisters of St. Francis out of Milwaukee. It was an alternative school, very progressive, using modular scheduling. We had twenty-one twenty-minute periods during the day and no class bells. The school simulated college in that we had large group lectures followed by small group discussions, and we worked at our own pace. The emphasis was on individualized learning and freedom of choice. Develop your God-given talents to the best of your ability was the philosophy behind it.

Prep was structured and traditional, whereas Ryan was nonconforming and self-directed, a perfect environment to produce socially comfortable people. After all, we did spend much of our time talking to each other on the school's gardenlike lawns during free periods, of which there were many. Both schools had their share of misfits, heavy drinkers, drug users, and brawlers. The biggest difference, though, was that Prep had tradition and we didn't. Because Prep always won, our players hated the Prepsters passionately. They were our biggest rival.

At school we had a pep rally; the game was well publicized and was to be played at the Rosenblatt Stadium. I felt pressure. I had butterflies on the bus ride to the game. I was afraid of getting beat, and that fear was my motivation.

The national anthem and the kickoff came and went quickly. I found comfort in the start of the game, and the jitters left. Now all we had to do was play. But Creighton Prep was tough. They hit as hard as we did. The man I was blocking, Jim Sledge, was stronger than I was. I wasn't used to being pushed around. I had to use my quickness to block him and then keep with it. They scored first and led 13-7 at the half. We scored in the third quarter and took the lead, 14-13. With 3:40 left in the fourth quarter, they took over on their own 14 yard line. All we had to do was hold them and let the clock run out. We held them twice. It was third and nine. In the defensive huddle we all were screaming; then eleven muddy, sweaty hands converged as one and someone said, "Let's hold one more time and we'll win this frickin' game." We broke our huddle with the vigor and enthusiasm of a team about to win. The ball was snapped and they gave it to their big fullback, Jim Wingender, who ran low with his shoulders square. He hit the hole and two of our guys hit him hard. I thought it was over, but he bounced off, turning and twisting, both legs pumping as he passed them and bulled his way over another tackler. I tried to scramble off my block to get to him but couldn't. With one more hurdle and lunge, he made the first down. It was a nightmare. We kept struggling to hold them, but that was the play of the game; it had demoralized us. My hands had taken a beating and were swollen with pain, and my body ached. I kept firing into their blockers, hoping somehow to disrupt the play and cause a fumble, but it was useless; they went down the field and scored. During the bus ride home, I agonized over our loss. Except for the mechanical sounds of shifting gears and squeaky breaks, the bus was hushed.

The night air cooled my sweat-soaked body. The chill intensified my brooding. I could find no comforting thoughts in replaying the game over in my mind, except for the discovery that I had played at a new level of intensity. It was a small consolation. The competitiveness of the game forced me into a frenzied effort to win. Never before had I played so hard. I had surprised myself, and all the while I had thought my effort and that of my teammates, who I assumed were trying as hard as I was, would result in our winning. Obviously, I found out that trying hard doesn't always ensure victory. Other forces were involved, such as the quality of the opponent, coaching, officials' decisions, and breaks. Before the game I was confident and felt invincible. Now I felt like a loser.

The next morning at 8:00 A.M. we were supposed to report to a routine practice of stretching and jogging. I didn't show up. I couldn't. My body was beat up and unwilling to move. I was also emotionally drained and angry, and I didn't want to talk to anybody.

The Prep game was an emotional zenith for me. I started out the season wanting to have the best team and be the best player, but the muscular linemen from Prep proved to me that both my team and I were not the best. We had our chance to prove how good we thought we were, but we crumbled in the fourth quarter. That game took the luster off the rest of the season. Coach Ponseigo told us to keep our heads up because we could still win our division and play for the Metro Conference championship. His words didn't register with me. I practiced and played with less enthusiasm after that. We tied our next opponent and won the following week. Our record was 3-1-2, and we were still rated. All I could do, though, was think about the day the season would end. One day after a hard practice, teammate Kenny Jaworski and I were having a conversation about the unpleasantries of football. Everyone else had gone in and we sat alone outside the locker room. I said, "This is the last season I'll ever have to take off shoulder pads. Never again!" as I peeled them off my soaked T-shirt. "Kenny, do you realize we have only eighteen practices left?" Kenny said somberly, "I can't wait, either. This crap's getting old." "Just think," I said longingly, "next year at this time we'll be someplace nice taking it easy." Kenny nodded. No more football practice.

My attitude was reflected in the way I practiced. I no longer had the same intensity I had at the start of the season. I was sluffing off, as Coach Ponseigo would say. I began to come late to practice and not hustle during drills. In an attempt to fire me up, the line coach, Dick Kutlas, kept telling me the other tackle, Bernie Krecji, was playing better than I was. He'd say, "George, you used to be king of the hill. Bernie's done passed you up." Then he'd have us play against each other in practice. It had the temporary effect of making me play hard, but whenever Coach Kutlas didn't watch, I'd loaf.

Other things were also weighing heavily on me. I liked some girl who thought of me as a friend while loving someone else. My bad study habits had caught up with me, and I was behind in several classes. I really needed to study at night but was usually too tired after practice. Life seemed difficult.

I received a shot of adrenaline the week we played my cousin Tim's team, Rummel High. I knew all my relatives would be at the game, and I wanted to play well and outdo my cousin. That was one competitive rivalry I could always count on. On the first play of the game, I sprinted down the field as hard as I could. Out of nowhere some kamikaze took my feet out from underneath me and I went down hard. It was my cousin Tim. Later in the game I speared him in the back while he was trying to break a tackle and got even. The 14-0 win put us in the conference championship game. During that game, with Omaha Tech, I also played hard. I figured it was my last game so I might as well go out a winner. Besides, the quarterback, Jimmy Ramirez, and I had worked out a plan to run a tackle-eligible pass to me. Jokingly, Coach Ponseigo had let us work on it in practice.

On the day of the game, everything went wrong. Our bus broke down on the way to the game and we arrived forty minutes late. Tech ran all over us. They were much quicker than we were. By the time it was 14-0, I was mad and frustrated. I told Jimmy in the huddle to call our play, disregarding the play from the bench. The pass play to me worked and i gained nine yards. In the end, they beat us 33-0, but I had caught three passes for twenty-one yards. Not bad for a tackle on the losing team.

The next two weeks were tumultuous for me. It began with friends and relatives telling me I would make the All-Metro team. At first I thought, What a joke. The more they talked, the more I began to take them seriously, and eventually I convinced myself that I deserved the honor. The day the selections came out in the *Omaha World-Herald,* a teammate stopped me in the hall and said, "Did you see the All-Metro team? Krecji, Meyers, and Smith made it!" I didn't say a word. It was a cold slap in the face. My heart beat fast and fear set in. Why didn't he say my name? I was afraid to ask the obvious question, so I headed for the school office, swiped the newspaper, and took it to study hall. I scanned the All-Metro team and was horrified to discover the truth: my name was absent from the list. It was, however, in a list below the All-Metro team, the one reserved for honorable mention. My heart sank. I was sick. I was angry. I was jealous.

It finally occurred to me later that what the coaches had been saying was true. I had loafed at the end of the season and Bernie had passed me by. He did play better, was more consistent, and deserved to be All-Metro instead of me.

The only redeeming thing about the season was that I had received a few recruiting letters. They were all questionnaires asking about my height, weight, forty-yard time, and grades. I hadn't planned on playing college football, but I felt a certain amount of pride in being considered a prospect. So I filled them out, padding my statistics a bit. Late in the season, three other teammates and I received a letter from the University of Nebraska inviting us to Lincoln to watch the Kansas game. We all planned to go down.

About a week before the game, on my way to a movie to meet some friends, I took a shortcut called Dead Man's Curve. I was coming from a girl's house, where I had had a couple of beers. As I approached the turn, I decided that I'd try it without using my brakes. I collided head on with a tree. When I woke up, some men from a nearby bar were prying open the car door and asking me if I was all right. My head hurt and my knees, which had prevented me from crashing through the windshield, were throbbing with pain. The next time I woke up, I was in a hospital emergency room. Miraculously, nothing was broken. I was bruised and couldn't walk for several days. My left knee, which had absorbed most of the blow, was swollen to the size of a softball. I had to have it drained two or three times.

I was devastated. I had ruined our family car. I couldn't go out for basketball. Plus, in little more than a week I was supposed to visit Nebraska on a recruiting trip. What if I was still on crutches? What would the coaches think? They'd certainly ask me what happened. "Oh, I was just drinking and driving without the use of my brakes, Coach."

By the day of the recruiting trip, I was feeling much better. I could walk without the crutches but was limping. We sat in the south stands, and it was freezing as the north wind blew into our faces. There were at least twenty or thirty other recruits. As I looked around at them, I said to my teammates, Bernie Krecji and Dave Smith, "No way are they going to offer us scholarships. Look at some of those guys, they're huge." Bernie said, "They ain't no better than we are."

It's funny how other people's attitudes can affect your thinking. Even though I was basically tired of football, all the excitement I was experiencing at being recruited made me forget about the unpleasant aspects of playing. I got caught up in the excitement and wanted to get a scholarship offer. But after the recruiting trip, I figured my chances weren't that good. Why would Nebraska offer me a full ride? I wasn't even All-Metro, and some of the other recruits were high school All-Americans.

The next week at school I was still feeling down about the recruiting trip and about the fact that I still couldn't practice my first love, basketball. During a discussion of career plans in a business class taught by Mr. Frenser, I took out my frustration on my classmates, riding them about their career plans. Mr. Frenser then said to me, "Well then, Mr. Mills, what are your fantastic plans after graduation?" "I don't know," I mumbled. "Seriously, Mr. Mills, I want you to tell us what you plan on doing next year." I was caught off guard. I hadn't seriously thought about my future. He had me cornered, so I said confidently, "Oh, I'll probably go to a small college on a football or basketball scholarship. You know, something like that." The incident stressed me out. I was forced for the first time to think about what I would do after high school. What would I do? I didn't really believe anybody would give me a scholarship. Not wanting to dwell on a bad situation, I took the Scarlett O'Hara approach: I told myself I'd worry about it later.

In early December, Coach Fischer visited me at school. We sat in Coach Ponseigo's office and talked. Coach Fischer said Nebraska was still interested in me and wanted to evaluate some game films of me. We chatted a bit and talked about Nebraska's 28-20 win over Oklahoma, which I had listened to on the radio.

I also received recruiting letters from schools like Iowa, Iowa State, South Dakota and Kansas. In fact, an assistant coach from Kansas, Sandy Buda, called me one night at home and wanted to know what my plans were. He told me Kansas was really interested in me. All the recruiting stuff was nice, but until someone offered me a scholarship, it was all rather meaningless.

At that time my only real concern was basketball. I wasn't at full speed yet and was playing sparingly. I wasn't happy. Then one day I came home from practice and found a letter from Nebraska. I figured it was just another questionnaire, but it proved to be special:

December 11, 1970

Dear George:
Enjoyed meeting you while at Bishop Ryan this past week and we had an opportunity to view the film. We feel that you are a Big 8 prospect, but we will have to check your grades because it looks as if you may have a problem qualifying under the NCAA 1.6 rule.

However, we are offering you an NCAA Scholarship. Of course, this is under the condition that you qualify for an NCAA grant. I would suggest you do a great deal of studying and see if you can get your grade point average raised so that you will qualify for the grant and for participation.

I will plan to be in Omaha to visit with you and your parents about the University of Nebraska and the athletic scholarship as soon as time permits. I hope that you have taken or registered to take the SAT and the ACT which are needed for qualification under the 1.6 rule.

As you know, we will be practicing for the Orange Bowl starting immediately, and we will be leaving on the morning of the 24th. I would like to make arrangements for you to visit us here on the campus some weekend that is convenient for you and we would prefer to have it as early in January as possible. I am enclosing a return card for your convenience and a schedule of our athletic events.

Looking forward to hearing from you soon.

Sincerely yours,

Cletus Fischer
Assistant Football Coach

My first reaction was to question what I had just read, so I read it again. The smile on my face was fixed. I walked into the kitchen and handed the letter to my mom. She said, "I'm cooking, just tell me what it says." "They're offering me a scholarship!" I screamed. She looked up from the frying pan. "Who? Who's offering you a scholarship?" "Nebraska!" "You're kidding," she said as she laid down the spatula and wiped her hands with the dish towel that hung over her shoulder. She sat at the kitchen table, put on her reading glasses, and read a moment. The face that reappeared was smiling. "That's great! What about your grades, though?" "I can get them up. I'll just study harder," I promised. My dad's response was the same; he smiled and congratulated me.

I told everyone at school the next day. I was in a cloud, walking on air. The effects were immediate. I was no longer George Mills but "George Mills, he's got a scholarship to NU." At home everybody called to congratulate me and my parents. Teachers and acquaintances who had formerly been indifferent were now friendlier. My immediate friends were not affected by all the hoopla. In fact, they did me a favor by keeping me in place. To them I was still big old George. They joked with me just as they always had. They'd say things like "You're tall, that's all."

As the initial excitement of being offered a scholarship wore off, I began concentrating on getting my grades up. I went around to all my teachers and asked them what I needed to do and began to work in earnest. Also, basketball was in full swing. It was holiday tournament time. I still wasn't 100 percent, but I was close. We got beat in the championship game, but I made the conference All-Star team. Our coach, Joe Neuberger, kept encouraging me and by season's end I was playing well, averaging sixteen points a game.

Then I started getting recruiting letters for basketball. In fact, I was offered a scholarship to play at the University of Nebraska at Omaha. Deep down I wanted to accept, but I couldn't. I was even afraid to tell anybody how I felt, afraid of what the reaction would be. Nebraska had ended up being rated No. 1 after a come-from-behind win over LSU in the 1970 Orange Bowl game, and the state was in a frenzy. People would have thought I was crazy giving up a Nebraska football scholarship to play basketball at UNO. Supposedly, playing at NU was the chance of a lifetime, so the urge to play basketball at UNO passed and I got used to being introduced as "George Mills, he's got a football scholarship to Nebraska."

In January my parents and I attended a recruiting dinner at the ritzy Blackstone Hotel in Omaha. In attendance was Cletus Fischer, along with a couple of other NU assistant coaches, the other four Omaha-area recruits, and our parents. The purpose was to acquaint all of us with the coaches, explain to us the terms of our scholarships, and give us examples of what life would be like playing at NU. I was nervous the entire time and a little bored too. It was a serious affair, except for an occasional joke by a coach or a misdirected question or comment by a nervous parent that drew laughter.

Coach Fischer told us we'd probably be redshirted and then proceeded to explain redshirting, which was a National Collegiate Athletic Association rule that allowed an athlete an extra year of school to save a year of playing eligibility. He told us how redshirting had helped one of Nebraska's current players, six-seven, 245-pound John Dutton. During his redshirt year, Dutton practiced but didn't play, and during that time he was able to develop physically by putting on thirty pounds. It also allowed him to get better established in school. After the dinner, as we were walking to the car, my dad said the scholarship was worth about ten thousand dollars, which made me feel proud.

Like a salesman closing a deal, Cletus Fischer kept in close contact with me. He sent me a letter every couple of weeks telling me what the team and coaches were doing and reminding me of important dates. There were several dinners, an overnight recruiting trip to Lincoln, a Big Eight Conference letter-of-intent signing on February 9, a national letter-of-intent signing in May, and there was the spring game.

Dean Kratz, a booster, hosted a Big Eight letter-of-intent signing party at his home. He was a warm and cordial man. His house was filled with coaches, area recruits, and media people, including an NBC crew, which was filming a piece about Nebraska's successful football program. It was a good time, and I got to meet some of my future teammates.

After dinner, cameras were set up in an upstairs room for interviews. The lights were bright, and it was hot. I was sweating profusely because I was third in line to be interviewed. When it was my turn, I stepped forward between Head Coach Bob Devaney and the interviewer. Coach Devaney introduced me, "This is George Mills from Omaha Rummel. He's a fine tackle." I thought, It's Omaha Ryan, Coach, but I didn't dare correct him. I just smiled and waited for a question. I don't remember the question I was asked by the interviewer, but it was something like "What's it like being headed for the number-one-rated team in the country?" "It's great, it's exciting," I said. Then he wished me luck and the next guy was up. Afterward my mom got dozens of calls from friends and relatives who saw the coverage on the local news. All they could talk about was how Coach Devaney had said the wrong school.

After the signing party, the recruiting process wasn't as exciting. The novelty had worn off. It wasn't fun anymore; it was all business. Even the weekend I spent in Lincoln was dull. My escort, Pat Fischer, Coach Fischer's son and a member of the team, tried hard to show me a good time. He took me around the campus, we visited other football players in the dormitories, and we even went to a big outdoor keg party. There were about one hundred people standing around drinking beer and listening to loud music. Pat introduced me to some of the players who were there. They looked old to me. I felt self-conscious and didn't have much to say. I remember seeing tackles Carl Johnson and All-American Bob Newton and thinking that they were unbelievably big. After an hour or so I wanted to leave, so we did the old reliable and got something to eat. We must have eaten ten times during my two-day stay. It was kind of funny because Pat would always have to ask for a receipt so he could document the cost of the meals. Not a real exciting weekend.

During the two days I was there, I kept thinking how different big-time college football recruiting was from what I had envisioned while reading the sports pages as I was growing up. I was aware that some universities made grand promises and offered money to recruits to attend their schools. But that was not the case with me, and I was somewhat disappointed at the mundaneness of it all. At the time, I failed to realize that I had been reading recruiting stories about stars, which I wasn't. I was a good high school football player with the kind of height and speed that would be needed to play college football, but I was the kind of player who would have to be developed, so I wasn't recruited by many schools. Only three schools, Nebraska, Kansas, and UNO, were willing to offer me a scholarship. I was not in a bargaining position like some Texas or California Blue Chipper; I was fortunate to be offered anything by anyone. I imagine my reality was the reality of most recruits.

I can't say how the star recruits of my class were treated. I do know that once I was in school with them I never heard stories of any of them being offered bribes or any inducement to attend Nebraska. I can't remember anyone driving a new car or wearing flashy clothes. Nebraska had been crowned the national champion the year before, for the 1970 season. I would imagine that most recruits, even stars, would have been excited to be offered a chance to play for the Huskers. But I admit, I grew up a fan of Nebraska football, so my perspective was somewhat skewed.

The only negative element of the recruiting process for me was that my sense of importance was disrupted by all the attention I was receiving. Overnight I became a somebody. My picture was on the sports page, and I was a topic of conversation. The attention created an emotional polarization for me. At times I'd be overly confident, and I came to expect the smiles and pats on the back that I started receiving once it was announced that I'd be attending Nebraska on a football scholarship. Consequently my ego grew, and the attitude that "I'm special because I'm going to be a Nebraska football player" began to dominate my personality. My status became my justification to act out whatever emotional state I was in. Sometimes I was aloof, at other times arrogant, and at still other times gregarious. Whatever mood I was in, in a large way it emanated from my new station in life. But that station at other times caused me to be less than confident. I had doubts about my ability to live up to the automatic expectations a guy has placed on him when he becomes a Nebraska player. I was told I'd have to put on forty pounds, which I didn't want to do. I knew I'd be competing with high school All-Americans, which was scary. Everyone would be able to monitor my progress in the newspaper. And even if I wasn't going to play football, I'd have been nervous about moving away from home and attending college. Everything had happened so fast. I was an unreflective seventeen-year-old who had committed to something that he hadn't thought through. I went along with everything, the scholarship, the notoriety, moving away, and attending college, without being firmly committed to any of it. It was just happening. The process continued relentlessly.

Next I received three letters: one informing me that I had met the requirements for my scholarship, one congratulating me for being named to the South Shrine Bowl team, and one inviting my parents to the NU spring game. We were to sit in the press box. The spring game was a big event, and my parents and I looked forward to it. As we drove by the NU Coliseum, there was a group of players walking over to the stadium. They had on T-shirts and their huge arms bulged. "Look how big! Looks like they've been lugging beef," my dad said, laughing. As we sat in the press box and watched the game, my feeling of uncertainty grew. There were guys on the field who were legends: Johnny Rodgers, Jerry Tagge, Rich Glover. What was I doing there?

3

The Shrine Bowl

Teammate Bernie Krecji and I walked up a driveway that ended in a large gravel parking lot. It was an uncomfortable walk for me. I was loaded down with a heavy suitcase in one hand and shoulder pads and a helmet in the other. It was a Sunday in early August 1971, and the heat and humidity were extreme. I was perspiring, my Levi's sticking to my legs. Heat waves rose up from the lot and made the men sitting at a table in front of a two-story dormitory appear miragelike. Because there was no one else around, the scene had a sense of desolation and loneliness.

One of the men was holding a clipboard as he greeted us. "Hello, I'm Ken Parish, the head coach." We shook hands. He had us sign a roster, and we were assigned a room, given a key, and handed a practice schedule. My room was on the second floor; Bernie's was down the hall. The stairway to the dorms was on the outside, so each room on the second floor opened onto a veranda. I entered the room into a common area that connected to four bedrooms, each having a bunk bed. Since I was the first to arrive, I had my choice of rooms. I took the one to my immediate left, opened my suitcase, and filled up a couple of drawers built into wall desks. I lay claim to the upper bunk.

Rather than wait to see who the other guys were, I went to investigate Doane College, my home for the next two weeks. I crossed a bridge over a small lake. Everywhere I looked there were oak trees. It was pretty. The sidewalk I followed led up a hill to a clearing in which there were several buildings, one of them the cafeteria where we'd be eating our meals. I followed the sidewalk farther until I came to the edge of the campus and looked at the quiet little town of Crete, Nebraska. I headed back to the dorm by a different route and came to a white split-rail fence that enclosed a green field with chalk lines and goal posts. Sprinklers were watering it down in preparation for our practices. We were scheduled for three-a-day practices: 9:30 A.M., 3:00 P.M., and 7:30 P.M. I had always hated two-a-days. Now I wondered how I was going to handle three. Quickly I figured out how many total practices that meant. The countdown would be an everyday ritual until practice was over and we played the game. The game, of course, was the thirteenth annual North-South Nebraska Shrine Bowl, which was scheduled for Saturday, August 21, 1971, at Memorial Stadium in Lincoln, home of the Cornhuskers.

Back at the dorm, my new roommates were filing in. There was Rod Norrie, a 235-pound NU recruit from Geneva, and Bob Decker, a 170-pound end from Holdrege. Others came in from towns that I'd never heard of, such as Milford, Red Cloud, Tecumseh, and Gibbon. Last came Jerry Lloyd, a fellow Omahan and NU recruit whom I had befriended during the recruiting process.

The first evening, we had a meeting and then dinner. We spent our free time talking and getting to know one another. Names and schools were exchanged tentatively at first, but within an hour music was blaring and players were laughing and joking, telling stories. Knowing that my roommates were also dreading practice and that most of them, like me, were away from home for the first time made me feel at ease. Relaxed, I began having a good time.

As athletes, I guess we checked each other out, comparing sports stories with what our eyes saw. I had read and heard a lot about Tom Kropp, a kid from Aurora who the papers were saying was the state's consensus Blue Chipper. I was eager to see him, but when I saw him for the first time at dinner that Sunday, I came away with mixed emotions. He was huge. The paper listed him at six-three and 243 pounds, but he was probably closer to 255. Except for his size, he didn't look like a football player. He had a fuzzy crew cut on top of a baby face. The newspaper described him as muscular, but he was really kind of roly-poly looking. Plus, he was quiet and shy. Kropp was media hype, I concluded.

During our first practice we had a drill where each player would run up and forearm the two-man sled. We formed a line and took turns. Guys would run up to it and, with a mighty grunt, hit it as hard as they could. The front of the sled would lift off the ground a couple of feet, and everyone standing around would cheer and yell. After about ten guys, it was Tom Kropp's turn. He sprinted with an uncanny grace for a man his size, and he hit it with an explosiveness not exhibited by any of the other players. He flipped the sled completely over. There was sudden silence, as everyone was stunned by what they had just seen. Then we whooped and hollered and congratulated Tom as he trotted back to the end of the line. The two coaches conducting the drill looked at each other, shaking their heads, and then they laughed as they walked over to lift the sled. We each got three hits at the sled. Each of the next two times that Tom Kropp exploded into the sled, the result was the same: it overturned.

Once when a heavy rain drove the team into Doane's gymnasium, Tom managed to get a basketball and was shooting baskets. I had heard he was a good basketball player too, making the All-State team. I felt a little testy and began shooting around with him. I thought there was no way he could outplay me, since basketball was my favorite sport and I had played in the tough Metro Conference. I challenged him to a friendly game of one-on-one. The Kropper, as we called him, dribbled the ball effortlessly between his legs a couple of times, then, standing flat-footed, rocketed up and stuffed the ball with two hands. "Oh my," I thought, "I'm in trouble now." But before our competition could begin, the coaches yelled at us to quit playing. They didn't want anyone to sprain an ankle. All through camp Tom demonstrated that he was the best athlete there; he was probably the best athlete I had ever seen. He lived up to and surpassed his billing, and he was one of the nicest guys I met at the Shrine Bowl. He was free from any harshness except when he was in uniform and on a football field.

There were other good players as well. Andy Wilson from Bellevue introduced himself as the guy who broke Johnny Rodgers's scoring records in the Metro Conference. Tony Davis, a running back from Tecumseh, was equally confident, and with just cause. Both were tough football players.

At our first full scrimmage, some of the hardest hits I ever saw were between Kropp and Wilson. They were competing for the same positions offensively and defensively. When Kropp was playing fullback, Wilson would be the linebacker. When Wilson was the fullback, Kropp would be there to meet him at linebacker. They went after each other. The crack of their collisions echoed over the field.

Tony Davis also established himself as a hitter early in the week. During a short scrimmage I kept seeing this guy with a yellow helmet coming up from cornerback and just smacking people. He was like a little tank out there. Later I asked who it was and found out it was Tony. Until I knew the other players' names, I always identified them by their high school helmets.

Practice settled into a miserable routine. Coaches started pounding on doors at 7:00 A.M., and I joined the other players in our zombielike walk over to the cafeteria for a light breakfast. Then we'd go over to the lockers. The morning practice was two hours of torture: drills and more drills. As it turned out, my high school coach, Joe Ponseigo, was the defensive line coach, and I thought that maybe I'd get some preferential treatment. Boy, was I wrong. I guess he wanted to prove that he wasn't playing favorites. Except for a few athletes, we weren't in very good shape. Because there isn't enough time to perfect execution, All-Star coaches tend to simplify the plays, both offensively and defensively, and concentrate on conditioning, believing the team in the best shape will win. Two weeks is enough time to get someone into decent shape, so we ran our butts off—a lot of wind sprints and conditioning drills. After the morning session, I'd shower and head for lunch, where I'd eat some but drink a lot, usually five or six glasses of orange drink or lemonade at a crack. After lunch I went back to the air-conditioned dorm, where I'd listen to some music and try to sleep before the next practice. At 2:00 P.M. I'd get up and go to the locker room for practice and endure more of the same torture. After supper we had practice at 7:30. The evening practice wasn't as long or as hard as the other two. It was cooler too.

I ate, drank, and slept football. The first day, I was excited and fresh. By the second day, all those muscles that had been on summer vacation ached and throbbed. My body took pleasure in small things. Lying in bed and drinking pop was like being in heaven. The evenings were spent watching the one working channel on the TV. Sometimes I'd call home, but mostly I'd sit and talk.

After three days, it was difficult to get up for practice. The Shrine Bowl stopped being an honor and became a curse. After about five days, guys were privately cussing Coach Parish for working us so hard. We survived by joking and jacking around, making our own fun; a team comradeship was developing in the agony. I guess the key individual, the guy that kept us loose by his practical joking, was a player from Omaha South, Mike Wees.

Wees simply tormented my roommate, Jerry Lloyd. The second night, Wees sneaked into our room while Jerry was in the bathroom and began filling up his pillowcase, suitcases, and dresser drawers with shaving cream. Everybody but Jerry knew what was going on, so we were grinning, laughing, and waiting to hear Jerry start screaming for someone's blood. To everyone's surprise, Jerry got into bed and didn't say a word. The guys in our dorm piled into the room, peeking into Jerry's lower bunk to see what had happened and why Jerry wasn't mad. Instead of being mad, Jerry took the pillowcase, pulled it over his head, and started wiping shaving cream all over his body. Everyone just broke up laughing.

In the morning, though, Jerry found the shaving cream in his clothes, and he was hot. He started cussing and yelling. "Who in the !!??##**!! did this?" he said. "I'm going to kill him." Later that day he found out that it was Wees. Jerry went to Wees's room and sprayed his clothes with shaving cream. Wees just laughed.

But Wees kept it up. He gathered all of Lloyd's practice clothes from his locker and dropped them into a toilet, stirred them around, then returned them to Jerry's locker. I don't think Jerry noticed; he must have thought it was sweat.

One night those two had a pillow fight in our room. Then the other guys showed up and joined in. Pretty soon the room was filled with players clobbering each other. One pillow flew out an open window, across the veranda, and onto the parking lot below, where Assistant Coach Paul Wilson happened to be walking by. It was after curfew. He stormed into our room. "Knock it off," he yelled. "Mills and Lloyd, get to sleep." He told Wees and the others to get their butts down to their own rooms.

During the slow walk to breakfast, we were talking and joking about the pillow fight the night before. Coach Wilson's catching us was big news, and we all speculated about what, if any, the punishment would be. All our talking and joking served to egg

Wees on. He ate quickly and hurried over to the locker room. Jerry, who had skipped breakfast to get a few more minutes' sleep, wasn't around. Wees later told us he had sneaked a pair of scissors from the training room, opened Jerry's locker, and cut out all the rigging from inside Jerry's helmet.

Out on the practice field, we kept waiting for Jerry to come out, his helmet hanging down, but Jerry didn't show up. We lined up for calisthenics. Still no Jerry.

"Where's Lloyd?" Coach Parrish said as he was taking roll. No one answered, just muffled laughs and hidden grins. Ten minutes into warmups, Jerry came running out with his helmet flopping. Parish was furious. He immediately took Jerry aside and had him do one hundred push-ups.

Jerry tried to explain, but Parish wouldn't listen. He had heard about the shaving cream and the pillow fight, and he was mad. Coach Parrish had the equipment manager fix the helmet, but during practice we all could see that Jerry was beet red. He kept saying how he was going to get Wees. After practice, Jerry chased Wees all over the practice field. Fortunately for Wees, Jerry didn't catch him. Jerry, in addition to being the strongest guy on the team, was also one of the state's top heavyweight wrestlers.

The next night, the Shriners and townspeople put on a barbecue for us. It came at a good time because in spite of the clowning around we were all a little edgy. We needed to get out and relax. The food was great: steaks, corn on the cob, baked potatoes, and milk. The milk inspired Wees. After we stuffed ourselves, Wees took up a collection and bet Jerry twenty dollars he couldn't chug a gallon of milk. Jerry, with his familiar deep machine-gun style of laughter, said no. Wees got Andy Wilson and Scott McIntosh to cajole Jerry into doing it. One thing Jerry couldn't turn down was attention. He took the bet, even though he had eaten a huge meal.

We all gathered around Jerry to watch. A group of about ten players began chanting, "Jerry, Jerry, Jerry!" Unbelievably, he drank the whole gallon. Milk did spill out and run down his face, but, judging from the way his stomach stuck out, most of it reached his belly. Jerry's face turned white. He ran behind a tree and began heaving. By this time the buses were ready to go back to the campus, so all of us onlookers ran back to the buses. Everyone was afraid of getting in trouble for egging Jerry on. Minutes passed and the bus didn't budge. We sensed trouble. We sensed right.

Coach Parish stormed into the bus. "Wees, Mills, Wilson, and McIntosh!" he said, pointing his finger at each of us as he yelled our names. "One more goof-off and you're all going home."

I felt wronged. I was innocent, I hadn't done anything this time. Being singled out was the price I was paying for always going along in the past. Wees was the instigator; I just happened to be around watching. The bus ride back to campus was quiet. I resolved to stay out of trouble for the balance of Shrine camp. I would be good. For Wees, though, he just turned his attention to other guys.

Mike Fangmeier was his next target. He was one of the biggest guys on the team, a gentle giant. On the first day, he had befriended a small stray cat. From that point on, whenever I saw Fangmeier, there was Kitty. But Wees didn't think football players should be carrying kittens around. One day before practice, Wees got hold of Kitty and hid him in a locker. Fangmeier heard the poor cat meowing and opened every locker in the locker room until he found it and held it in his big arms, caressing it. The next day, Wees got hold of the cat and held it over the second-floor balcony. We were all down below watching. As Fangmeier came out of his room, Wees yelled, "Fangmeier!" and dropped the cat. Fangmeier went nuts and chased Wees. The balcony wasn't very high and the cat was all right. It was more startled then anything, just bounced up and ran away. It never came back, though.

Roger Fix also got Wees's attention. Fix would make unusual sounds when he blocked. Everybody grunts and groans during contact, but Fix sounded like a karate guy breaking a board: "Yeeeeeaahhhhhh!" And he made that sound through the whole play. It drove everybody nuts. We kept asking him to make other sounds, but he couldn't. It irritated Wees, so he hid Roger's football spikes one day to keep him from practicing.

The trip to the Shriners' hospital for crippled children was the one event everyone was looking forward to. We had been practicing what seemed like an eternity, and we needed a break. It was particularly exciting for me because I had never flown before. It was also the first chance I had to look at the opposition, the North squad, which was also making the trip. I didn't know what to expect, so I read some of the brochures about the hospital and the history of the game that were handed to us by some Shriners who went along on the flight. I found out that the Shriners raised money to run nineteen children's orthopedic hospitals and three hospitals for burn victims. The Shrine Bowl games were one way in which they helped to raise money. The first Nebraska Shrine Bowl was in 1959, and the record between the North and South teams was 8-3-1, the South team ahead. It was estimated that if attendance at the game reached twenty thousand, the Shriners would earn seventy-five thousand dollars.

When I walked into the Minneapolis hospital and saw all those little crippled kids, the effect was immediate. I felt sad. Then I perked up when a nurse introduced me to a bright and smiling Teresa Dennison, a four-year-old who was born with clubbed feet. I was to escort her around. At first I didn't know how to act or what to say. Instinctively, I smiled. From her wheelchair, she smiled back. We talked a little, and I wheeled her around the courtyard. We ate cake, mingled, and talked with the other players and kids. Whenever I looked at her tiny feet, bandaged and crooked, I'd hurt, my eyes would moisten, and I'd have to look away. Even the prankster, Mike Wees, was a little red-eyed as he played with a boy in a body cast.

When the few hours had passed and it was time to go, I said good-bye to Teresa and let go of her hand. I vowed never to forget her. Her small, bubbly face, brown eyes, and fine, sandy-colored hair were etched in my memory. During the remaining days of practice, when I was tired, I'd think of her and why I was playing. I now understood the Shrine Bowl theme: "Strong legs run so that weak legs may walk."

The next day, Sunday, our major game-type scrimmage was to begin at 2:00 P.M. I was to play at offensive tackle and defensive end. It was a hot day, as usual, with a lot of people gathered to watch us. I noticed one face in particular, that of NU Coach Cletus Fischer. My stomach knotted up and I felt the sudden pressure to play well. I was told there were other Nebraska coaches there, but Cletus Fischer had recruited me; as far as I was concerned, he was the only coach that mattered. I respected him and wanted to play well. After all, I was recruited by Nebraska, the No. 1 team in the country, and that meant I had to be great. But during the scrimmage I really didn't do anything outstanding. A couple of times when I felt I had made a nice play, I'd look over to see if Coach

Fischer was watching. Toward the end of the scrimmage I got hit in a pileup and thought my knee had slipped out of joint, but it was diagnosed as a slight ligament strain. I limped off the field feeling embarrassed. What would Coach Fischer say? After a few plays he came over to me smiling. "Kind of hot out there, isn't it," he said. "How's your leg?" After a while he said nonchalantly, "Hang in there. We'll see you in a few weeks," and walked away. I thought he'd be critical, but it was business as usual. I didn't know what was expected of me.

The standard I set was to be as good as Kropp, whom Nebraska was desperately trying to sign (after the game he did sign with NU). He dominated the scrimmage and set the level of excellence. Everyone tried to play up to his level. Watching him motor that big body of his with the agility and grace of a premier athlete was unbelievable. At fullback, he would hop, skip, and hurdle runners. If there wasn't an opportunity to do that, he'd crash into a tackler and run over him. I remember trying to tackle him. I tried to wrap my arms around that massive body and haul him down, but it was futile. We had to gang-tackle him to bring him down. He just kept pumping his legs, dragging me and others along until the weight was too much and he'd fall forward, always forward, for the extra yard. At linebacker, Kropp would crouch low behind the defensive linemen he dwarfed. His shoulder pads seemed funny, perhaps a size too small. He reminded me of an old-fashioned ball player, which, in a way, he was. On every play he'd spring to the ball carrier with lithe, catlike quickness. Despite his six-foot-three frame, he'd always get under the ball carrier with a walloping blow that knocked the guy down. He made ferocious tackles play after play. I got the impression that he could play at that high level of intensity forever. Kropp scored two of the five touchdowns in the scrimmage. He popped an 80-yard run off tackle, outrunning the secondary. He also kicked two extra points, and he was a leader defensively. Pure athlete.

The monotony of three-a-day practices went on. After the tenth day, I began to feel a little homesick. I had never been away from home for so long. Calling home every couple of days was something I looked forward to. I'd usually talk about practices and what we were doing. Judging from the number of guys waiting in line to use the phones, I guess homesickness was epidemic.

One night after the team had seen a movie, *10,000 Leagues Under the Sea*, a few guys and I were walking back to campus from downtown Crete, talking about sneaking out after bed check to rendezvous with some girls we had met one day outside the cafeteria. Somebody had written down these girls' names and telephone numbers. So Wees, Krecji, Wilson, McIntosh, and I called the girls to arrange a meeting. The Kropper overheard our plans and asked what we were up to. At first he wanted to come, but he changed his mind. We tried to persuade him to come. We wanted to corrupt him and bring him to a mortal level. I said, "It will be great, Tom. We will meet the girls, get some beer, and have fun." He just shook his head and said, "No, you guys are crazy."

After bed check, I crawled out my window, which I had left open. I didn't want to wake the other guys by opening and closing a door; besides, climbing out a window seemed neater. I knocked on Kropp's window, hoping he'd change his mind and come. After a few minutes of exhorting whispers, I gave up and met the other guys at the end of the dorm. It was an incredible feeling trucking around that campus at night to meet the girls. The night air was refreshing. I felt free; I felt alive.

A late-model car was waiting at the edge of the campus. There were three girls in the front seat. We piled in back and suggested other seating arrangements, but the girls giggled and said they liked where they were sitting. We rode around town, talking and laughing. They asked us questions about camp and football. We told some tall stories. Someone suggested beer, but we couldn't figure out a way to get it. We settled for Cokes from a gas station. We felt nervous pulling into the station, fearing that the attendant would go tell the coaches. I guess after twelve Shrine Bowls, the people of Crete were used to seeing players sneaking out. After a couple of hours, we were all tired and the girls dropped us off. The next day we let it out that yeah, we had sneaked out and met some chicks and partied. The story had the imaginations of the other guys on the team soaring.

During the course of our stay I had also been talking to one of the girls who worked in the cafeteria. She too was going to be a freshman at NU in the fall, so we had something in common. One night toward the end of camp, I met her outside the cafeteria. We walked and talked and eventually settled on the steps of a building.

It was a beautiful night, a breeze was up, and the sky was lighted with stars. I really felt good because the hard part of camp was behind me; the big game was near, and it looked like I would be a starter. We sat talking for a couple of hours. I kissed her good night and promised to call her once we started school. I was lonely and needed a friend, and she was nice. As I walked back to the dorm, I thought how lucky I was to be experiencing so much.

During the last days of camp, our team made final preparations. The coaches ran us through drills designed to polish our skills. We repeated over and over the few plays we had learned. It was two days before the game, and we thought all the playing positions were settled. In other words, we all knew where we'd be playing. Wrong. Jerry, who had by now become the team's mascot, was confused about his plays. He had initially been prepared to play offensive tackle, but he had trouble remembering whom to block on the plays. Coach Parish then moved him to defensive tackle, a position that had fewer assignments and less responsibility. In the course of polishing up for the game, Defensive Line Coach Ted Mills of Hebron (no relation), found out that Jerry didn't know the plays; he was still confused and making mistakes. Jerry was such a talent that Coach Mills wanted to get him into the game, so on the day of the game Coach Mills shifted Jerry to middle guard. At middle guard he had only three things to remember: charge straight ahead, charge left, or charge right. To ensure that Jerry didn't become confused, a coach marked an *R* on Jerry's right hand and an *L* on his left hand. It was hilarious. I don't believe Jerry was really that confused. I think playing dumb was his way of being part of the team: to make us laugh and keep us relaxed and loose for the game.

On our bus ride to Memorial Stadium I was antsy and walked around talking to the guys. Our captains, quarterback Don Osvog from Lincoln Southeast and the Kropper, were smiling but quiet. I spent most of the time going over my assignments with Scott McIntosh, the other defensive end. I was nervous, and talking with McIntosh helped ease the butterflies.

One thing I really like about football is the esprit de corps before a game. We were once thirty-three strangers, but now we were teammates on a mission. In a few hours we'd be relying on one another to do a job. I had confidence in the other players. I only hoped I'd be able to live up to my part.

The game had been billed as our size and muscle versus the North squad's finesse and quickness. Many people thought the game was even. We had Tom Kropp, but they had a talented Nebraska recruit from Fremont, running back Ritch Bahe.

During our first defensive series, I tipped a pass, which fell incomplete. The play gave me some confidence. That was it, though. For the rest of the game I was locked in a battle with their tight end, Dave Redding. He stuck me all afternoon. I didn't know it then, but Redding was also a Nebraska recruit, and even though he was only 190 pounds, he was the best tight end I had ever played against. He'd fire out hard every play and try to block me. I'd stop his charge, but he'd continue to pump his legs, clawing and scratching until the whistle had blown. In high school, if you whipped a guy, he'd quit. That wasn't the case with Redding. He never quit. He was a fighter, hungry and mean. I respected him immediately.

The heat during the game was a very real factor. The temperature was in the nineties, and the artificial turf was several degrees hotter. Conditioning played an important part in the game. By halftime I was exhausted, drained of both fluids and energy.

In the second half, the personal battle between Dave and me continued much as it had in the first. I'd beat him for a play or two, and he'd beat me for a play or two. Late in the game, I loafed on a play and paid for it. The North ran a screen pass away from me, and as I lackadaisically pursued the play, I got blindsided by a block that leveled me. The world turned upside down and I lay flat on my back with the wind knocked out of me. One of the trainers had to help me off the field. "Did anybody get the number of that Mack truck?" I asked? A trainer said it was No. 79. When I went back into the game, I looked for the guy. It was Larry Honke, a future Husker. I wanted to get even, but the game ended before I had any chances. For the rest of the game, although I was tired, I remained alert.

As people predicted, it was a game of our muscle against their finesse. We scored with two minutes left in the first quarter. After Tony Davis broke some long runs, the Kropper flattened a cornerback on a short run to score our first touchdown. In the second quarter the Kropper kicked a 29-yard field goal that gave us a 10-0 lead at halftime.

In the second half, the North kept us off balance with passing and flashy runs by Ritch Bahe and took the lead, 13-10. With about three minutes remaining, we were sixty-two yards away from a score. We had gained yardage on short runs, but we needed a big gainer because time was running out. Fortunately, we caught the North's secondary asleep with a pass to Brad Bryant. With time ticking away, Kropp high-stepped over a defender for fifteen yards to the two. Then, with :49 remaining in the game, Osvog gave the ball back to Kropp for the score. The North tried some Hail Mary passes, but Kropper ended the game with an interception and we ran out the clock. The final score was South 16, North 13.

I was relieved when the gun went off. Everyone was too tired to jump up and down and holler. We just took off our helmets and quietly congratulated the other team.

The headlines read, "Aurora Ace Cream of the Kropp," and that was right. Kropp was the most dominant player in the game, despite other fine performances. Ritch Bahe had gained 106 yards rushing, breaking Gale Sayers's record, and Tony Davis reeled off 99 yards. But it was the Kropper's performance that I remember most. He scored all of our points. He intercepted a pass, and he was one of the defensive leaders in tackles. I doubt that his performance will ever be duplicated. North Coach Dallas Dyer called him the finest high school football player he'd ever seen. Amen.

As for me, I was just happy we had won and it was over. After the game I went with my parents and relatives, including my grandma Mary Abboud, to a restaurant to eat. All I did was drink fluids and squirm around, hyper with excitement. My cousin Mick Lalley, Tim and Tom's brother, told me that after the tipped pass I didn't do too much. I told him he was right but that I had learned a lot.

The guys I played with and against showed me the level of intensity that was necessary to compete at the college level. I learned that at that level of competition you had to be ready to play hard every play. That's every play. No rests, no fatigue. Tony Davis taught me, Ritch Bahe taught me, Dave Redding taught me, and Larry Honke the Mack truck sure taught me, but mostly the Kropper taught me. I would definitely have to adjust and raise my level of intensity if I were to succeed at Nebraska.

4

Frosh

I pulled up to the intersection at Sixteenth and Vine streets in my blue 1966 Catalina convertible that my aunt Adelaide ("Ace") Lalley, Tim's mom, had given me as a graduation present; it was September 1971. My car was loaded with all my clothes and worldly belongings. The campus was swarming with activity: everywhere I looked there were students. Some of them were moving belongings into the fraternities that faced the intersection, while others were standing in groups, just watching, talking, and laughing. As I waited for the light to change, panic set in. All the people, the unfamiliar surroundings, and the bumper-to-bumper traffic made things confusing. I also realized I didn't know where my dorm was. "Hey," I yelled to a group of guys, "where's Abel Hall?" They pointed in the direction of immense twin buildings a block away.

There was a large driveway in front of the dorm. I double-parked and waited impatiently for a parking space. Then I loaded up with as much as I could carry and struggled into the building to get my room assignment. I opened the door to room 715 and was pleasantly surprised that it was not too bad. The belongings of my new roommate were there, but he wasn't, which was a relief. It gave me a chance to unpack, check out his things, and try to figure out what he might be like.

The room had two of everything: two beds, two built-in desks, two closets, and two medicine cabinets with mirrors. The walls were concrete blocks painted white, and the floors were covered with dark green tiles. What impressed me about the room was the view from the large picture window, which overlooked a parking lot and an athletic field that was used for intramural sports.

While I unpacked, I noticed two large stereo speakers and an expensive-looking amplifier and turntable. A large stack of albums was tilted against the base of the wall, including a lot of my favorites, such as the Doors, the Rolling Stones, and the Beatles' "White" album. I thought my new roommate must be OK. The door opened and I was greeted by a smiling face. His name was Larry. We talked and found out we had a lot in common. Larry was also from Omaha, we liked the same music, and he was a big fan of football, especially Nebraska football. He said he was proud to have me as a roommate and that I could use his stereo as long as I didn't scratch the records and I put them back in their jackets. He also said I could use the small refrigerator he had rented and could drink his grape juice. In return, he said jokingly, "You have to protect me in case anyone gives me trouble." Unlike some schools, NU didn't have a separate football dormitory. Athletes were housed with the general population. I found that student reaction to football players varied from awe and curiosity to resentment. Whatever people thought, one thing was certain: the other students living in the dorms knew who the football players were.

The next morning, I woke up an anxious freshman. My goal for the day was to get all my school business finished by 12:30 P.M. so I could eat lunch and then head over to the field house by two o'clock for equipment checkout and physicals. It was a beautiful morning, with students wandering everywhere. Every few blocks or so I'd ask someone for directions to my adviser's office. When I got there, the reality of college life set in; I found a long line of students ahead of me and had to wait for an hour and a half. The red-carpet treatment I had received while being recruited was over. After I was given an explanation of the College of Business requirements, I made out my schedule and was sent to registration, where I encountered an enormous line of students and mass confusion. After a long wait without much movement in line, I took some initiative and went around to the exit, walked into the registration room, pulled my class cards, and got into the cashier's line. Proudly I told the cashier that I was a scholarship athlete and that the athletic department was footing the bill. The older ladies at the desk seemed impressed that I was a ball player. They asked me where I was from and what kind of team we were going to have. It wasn't much in the way of attention, but it was enough to make me feel special again.

I was running late, so I skipped lunch at the training table and headed for the locker room. As I approached the field house, I saw two big, ugly guys. I assumed they were varsity players and was shocked when they walked into the freshman locker room. My stomach knotted as I entered. The air was cool and stale, and the room was filled with players in all sizes and shapes. Everyone was sitting on benches or leaning against the walls. Some were talking, but no one smiled; they all looked tense. I felt their eyes size me up when I walked in; feeling self-conscious, I straightened up. I walked to the far end and was grateful to sit down and get out of the center of attention. Then I too became an observer of the rest of the unsuspecting freshmen who entered. The two big uglies that I had seen coming in were leaning against the wall near the entrance. They had shaved their heads into mohawks and both had a grizzly three-day-old growth of whiskers. They were also two of the biggest guys in the room—both at least six-four and 250 pounds.

The room filled with players, and eventually the equipment checkout began. The tension eased and players began to talk, then joke and laugh. I too felt at ease and began talking to some of my new teammates.

I put my equipment into my locker and went to a mirror, put on my helmet, and adjusted the chin strap. Seeing the familiar red *N* on the white helmet did something to me. Yes, I was really a Husker. I looked like a Husker, anyway. I whacked myself on the helmet with the palm of my hand a few times. It felt good.

When I arrived at the Student Health Center, the line for physicals already stretched out of the building. By now I was extremely sick of waiting in line. Once inside, though, I was moved from examining room to examining room quickly. In each room there was a different physician or nurse, each testing for something different. I was squeezed, prodded, and probed. I was weighed and measured. I gave a urine sample and coughed while the doctor examined my testicles. I had to bend over while a rubber-gloved hand inspected my insides. The doctors and nurses were friendly, but the fact that I was one of sixty big, hot, sweaty bodies standing in line for the battery of tests made it seem impersonal. I couldn't help but feel like a cow or horse being examined for auction. I was glad when it was over.

The next day was more of the same: finding buildings and classrooms. My teachers didn't waste any time, and we were given assignments. Then there were more long lines at the bookstore. After a nice lunch at the training table, I stopped at the Nebraska Union for an emergency pit stop. I walked into the restroom and didn't see any of the usual white porcelain wall urinals. Instead there was only a huge round basin in the center of the room. I thought for a moment, then decided that must be it, and began urinating into it. As I did, a man entered the room and stepped on a metal ring that circled the basin. Water shot out of a metal piece set in the middle, and he began washing his hands. He looked at me, smiled, and said, "I guess you could use it for that." Blood rushed to my head. When I realized what I was doing, I tried to hurry up and escape the embarrassment of the moment before someone else could see my freshman mistake. I ducked out and headed for the field house, laughing to myself. On a return visit the next day, I found the urinals on the inside walls of the restrooms.

At practice, there wasn't to be any contact work the first three days, so, except for helmets, we practiced without equipment. The purpose of the practices was to get us into the proper condition so we'd be physically ready to start contact work. The practice was organized and disciplined. We ran wind sprints and had agility drills, along with running over ropes and bags. It was exhausting. When the final whistle blew, we looked like a herd of horses heading for the barn. As I lumbered up the steps that led to our locker room, I looked up and saw Coach Fischer standing at the top. He was smiling as he said in his scratchy voice, "A little different from Ponseigo's program, eh?" I was happy he spoke to me. It felt good having a varsity coach talk to me in front of the other freshmen. I didn't even mind his sarcasm.

After dinner and a nap, I had to report back to the training table for a two-hour mandatory study hall that was conducted three nights a week for freshman scholarship athletes. Boyd Epley, the strength coach, was the proctor for the study hall. He was aided by an elderly woman named Miss Hagge, who tutored English and helped us whenever we'd have to write a term paper. After a long, hard day I was not in the mood to study, so I pretended to study. Once in a while, someone would crack a joke or get smart with Boyd, but basically it was all business and quiet. The two hours passed slowly.

I daydreamed and thought about how different the reality of being a Nebraska football player was from how I had imagined it when I was little and pretended to be a Nebraska player. Back then, Nebraska football was a collection of fun, exciting sights and sounds. They consisted of radio announcer Lyell Bremser's familiar voice screaming, "Holy man, woman, and child, we've scored again!" being drowned out by the roar of the home crowd. I always relished reading the Sunday sports page, seeing the action photos of the game, and watching the Huskers play in bowl games on TV with family and friends. It was all fun, cheering crowds, winning games, and jubilant players on TV. I could pretend to be a Nebraska player, but once I left the field, the act was over. I could turn it off and on like a TV.

My new routine of school, football practice, and study was overwhelming and nonstop. I had to perform every day. Being a college athlete was also different from high school, where I could loaf in practice and still be one of the best guys on the team. I could also put off studying and still pass. From what I could tell, the classes I was taking would require my best effort just to be average.

At the end of the first week I was so unhappy that I was asking myself what I was even doing there. Why would anyone continue to play football when it produced such a festering ambivalence as it did for me? How did it happen? I think for me my size was my destiny. "You're a big kid. Do you play football?" was a question I was asked often. That, coupled with being raised in a strong sports environment, pointed out the direction of my future. It was all part of a socialization process, and I emerged from it assuming the role of a football player. Once I received the scholarship offer to play in Lincoln, the role became even more pronounced: Nebraska football player.

The socialization started at home with my parents. My dad was a good athlete; we played catch and shot baskets together. He was someone I could try to emulate. My mother was also athletic. She and I had footraces at the schoolgrounds, and she always encouraged me to try out for the sports teams. At home the TV was always tuned to a football, basketball, or baseball game. When I read the newspaper, I read only the sports page. When I read a magazine, it was *Sports Illustrated.* I collected football and baseball cards. I knew every player on the Green Bay Packers and Chicago Bears football teams. My most prized personal possessions were sports equipment: a baseball glove, a bat, and a miniature plastic football.

My grade school promoted participation in team sports by sponsoring teams. My church created a Catholic youth league for our teams to participate in. My friends were equally turned on by sports; they played sports every day. Together we acted as an informal support group to encourage one another to participate. We had two large playgrounds on which to play and practice and act out our dreams of being professionals.

I realized early on that playing organized football was not as much fun as our pickup games, but I kept playing anyway because I did enjoy certain aspects of playing. The aspects I didn't like—practicing, the monotony of repetition, the pain from contact—were enough to make me think about quitting. But by eighth grade or even earlier, the particular sport ethos of my neighborhood had been internalized. I was taught that winners never quit and quitters never win. So even thinking of quitting, despite whatever intense displeasure I may have been experiencing at the time, brought on an enormous feeling of guilt.

By my freshman year of high school, most of my grade-school friends had stopped playing football to pursue other interests or had stopped playing for lack of size or athletic ability. It was easier to quit, but I still felt ashamed about it. During the year I didn't play, I had forgotten about the negative aspects of playing. In part, my cousin Tim's success on the field and my cousin Tom's insults for not playing motivated me to play again. Each fall for the next three years, I followed a pattern of being excited to play at the beginning of the season and then by midseason began counting the number of days of practice I had left, always vowing never to play again. I probably wouldn't have, either, except I had the misfortune or good fortune, depending on what my attitude for football was that day, of being six-four and being able to run forty yards in less than five seconds. Those physical attributes attracted college football recruiters, one of whom happened to be with the No. 1 team in the country, the University of Nebraska. Not being a particularly reflective teen, I did not thoroughly examine what was happening to me. I was, instead, swept away by the emotion of the moment and accepted a football scholarship and everything else that was to be a part of it. So my commitment to playing was more than just saying yes; it was the manifestation of a long socialization process. How does one undo that? I knew only that I was unhappy and that quitting football would bring me only temporary relief. The resulting anxiety and guilt I would feel for doing so were more dominating feelings. I'd stay and play and hope things would get better.

I know other freshmen felt the same way because some guys did quit. Committing to playing at a big university was a big decision for seventeen- and eighteen-year-olds. Even Tom Kropp was unsure. Less than three weeks after accepting a scholarship, he left Nebraska and enrolled at Kearney State College. Rumors had circulated that both Coach Devaney and Coach Osborne had gone to his dorm room to try to persuade him to stay. Before he left, I ran into him under the north end of the stadium. I said, "Kropper, how come you're leaving?" He said, "George, Kearney had always been my first choice, but I felt a lot of pressure to come here." "Why Kearney?" I asked. "Oh, I guess I feel more comfortable on a smaller, more quiet type of campus." He was a big man and he made a tough choice. Going his own way, he showed he wasn't a follower. He had gained a lot of respect from me during the Shrine Bowl, but I respected him even more because he had the courage to tell people how he really felt, courage that I didn't have.

Kropp ended up being a National Association of Intercollegiate Athletics All-American at Kearney State in both football and basketball. In 1975, while breaking numerous school records, he was named Nebraska's State College Athlete of the Year. That same year, he was drafted in both football and basketball. The Pittsburgh Steelers made him their eighth-round pick. In basketball, he was drafted in the third round by both the Chicago Bulls and Denver Nuggets. He played one year with the Bulls, then played several years in Europe. In 1990 he was named co–head basketball coach at Kearney State.

When I went home on the weekends, it was always to a lot of fanfare. Friends and relatives asked what it was like being a player and how the varsity looked. The attention lifted my spirits. Most of my high school friends seemed to be scrambling to find out who they were; everyone was searching for an identity. Some grew long hair and became hippie types and got into drugs, some learned trades and drank beer, some got married and started families, and some attended college. I didn't have to search for my identity; it was given to me in the form of a scholarship. I was Mr. Nebraska Football Player. But I wasn't sure it was the right identity.

Time has a way of healing, of soothing situations. Fortunately for me, as the weeks passed I became more settled and more confident. I was coping better with my new life and I began to look for fun. I was hanging around with two high school friends, Kenny Knoblauch and Don Moriarty. After study hall, Kenny would pick me up on his Kawasaki 500 motorcycle, which was one of the fastest production bikes made. We'd zip around campus at dangerous speeds, find Donny and go walking through the dorms, talking to girls and friends, or we'd stop and eat at the snack bars. We'd do anything but study.

Once, Kenny got us some tickets to see Grand Funk Railroad, a popular rock group, at Pershing Auditorium. The concert was on Wednesday, the same time as my study hall. On the preceding Monday I asked Boyd Epley, the proctor, if I could skip the study hall. He said no. So I begged him. He still said no. I then got smart with him and said, "I'm going no matter what you say." We exchanged some words and it got tense. All eyes in the study hall were on us. I thought to myself, I'd better shut up. On Wednesday night I attended the concert with my friends. We had a great time.

After practice on Thursday, the freshman coach, Jim Ross, called me and two other guys who had also skipped to the side. He informed us that we had broken a rule by skipping study hall and that we would now have to accept our punishment: grass drills. We lined up on the goal line. A graduate assistant blew his whistle and we dived to the ground, landing on stomachs, then bounced up quickly. We did that five times. Then we jogged ten yards and did five more grass drills. We did five grass drills every ten yards until we reached the goal line at the other end of the field. Gasping for air, I began to walk away. "No, no, no," the assistant said, "You're not finished. Let's go back." We all grumbled, and he laughed. By the time we had made it back to our starting point, we were all staggering to get up. I didn't miss any more study halls after that.

At practice we were given positions. I was to play defensive end and offensive guard. I didn't like playing offensive guard because I had to play against defensive linemen who were usually bigger than I was. I figured I would try harder at defensive end, which was a stand-up position, and make the coaches realize that was the best position for me. I liked my position coach, graduate assistant Al Larson; knowing he was a former player made him special. Plus, he was a good coach, real easygoing. Sometimes he'd show up for practice needing a shave, something I could relate to. He was also dating one of the sharpest girls on campus, which made all of us freshmen envious.

During our first intrasquad scrimmage, we were all nervous. We found out who the hitters were. The All-Conference, All-State, All-American honors didn't mean a thing. We were judged on how we did against each other. I did well enough to earn a starting spot at defensive end; I was also second-team offensive guard.

Our next test was to scrimmage the redshirt sophomores, an annual event. I was nervous. Seeing the twenty-five of them coming down from the stadium to our practice field below was scary. They came like a conquering horde. They were confident, laughing and joking. We stood quietly and watched. The coaches lined us up in two separate groups, one on offense and the other defense. They broke some long runs against us, but we more than held our own. Coach Ross spoke to us after the scrimmage and said he was proud of us. We all felt a little closer after that. We were developing confidence in one another, unity, and spirit—all the things important for a winning team.

Our first game was against Missouri in Columbia. After five weeks of practice, it was exciting finally to be playing a game. The bus ride was fun. I felt special, especially after I read an article in the newspaper about our team the day before the game. The article said we were the best recruits in America and were going to help keep Nebraska rated No. 1. Seeing my name listed in the newspaper was awesome.

We jumped to an 18-0 lead. Terry Luck, our quarterback, threw two touchdown passes to Tom Ruud, and Tony Davis scored on a 6-yard run. In the second half, Missouri came back to take the

lead, 23-18. With time running out we recovered a fumble and
Terry Luck passed for a 10-yard touchdown, then scored on a
2-yard sneak. At the game's end, we erupted with cheers, and
carried Coach Ross off the field. The 32-23 come-from-behind
victory was a great way to start a career.

On the following Monday I went to practice feeling good about
my performance. But after reviewing films with the coaches, I saw
I really didn't play that well. I had played hard, but that's not
enough at Nebraska; you also have to play disciplined, which I
didn't. Assistant Coach Jim Walden said, "There were two defenses
being played here, Mills, the one we called and yours." I didn't do
my assignments. I would pursue a play when I was supposed to
stay home, or I'd stay home when I was supposed to drop back
into pass coverage. I even went offside twice. When the team left,
Coach Walden asked me to stay. He showed me a play in which I
eluded several blockers and put pressure on the quarterback, forcing him to throw a bad pass. He said the play showed I was a good
athlete but that I'd have to work on being more disciplined and
concentrate on my specific assignment once the defense was called.
"Tomorrow we're going to put you at a position where you can
mix it up without worrying about a lot of defensive calls. We're
going to move you to right defensive tackle." I didn't like moving
to the defensive line. I was skinny compared to the linemen I'd be
playing against. Plus, I thought defensive end was a much more
prestigious position than defensive tackle. The idea of getting
down in a three-point stance and wallowing around in the trenches
with big uglies was not thrilling. At one point during practice the
next day, I was loafing, angry about being switched, and graduate
assistant Ben Gregory told me to hustle. I shot back sarcastically,
"For what? So they can move me to a new position?" He let it slide
and just said, "Get going."

In our next intrasquad scrimmage the coaches were anxious to
see how those of us in new positions would perform. About
midway through the scrimmage, Coach Ross said, "Mills, get in
there and take some plays at right defensive tackle." Still angry
about being switched, I said, "How about quarterback instead."
That was a mistake. At Nebraska you don't talk back to coaches,
especially the head freshman coach, who also happened to be the
assistant athletic director. He blew up and yelled, "Get off this field

right now!" As I trotted off, I was the most embarrassed person who had ever lived. I felt like a jerk; my big mouth had gone too far. Coach Ross was a mild-mannered person who rarely got angry, so for him to explode meant I was in big trouble.

I stood off to the side and watched, wondering what I should do. After the scrimmage, Coach Walden called me over for a few words. Everyone else had already gone in to shower. The huge walls of the field house were above us, blocking the last rays of the day's light. There was a golden cast on the field, and the air was crisp: distinctly fall. Coach Walden was wearing a baseball cap, an oversize red nylon jacket, and sweats; his lower lip was filled with chew, and sincerity was in his eyes and compassion in his voice as he said, "Son, I know you're upset about being switched to a new position, but the coaches feel it's the best move. Life is full of doing things you don't like, but you've got to be a man and do it. I want you to look at this as a challenge that you have to learn a new position and try to excel at it. Here at Nebraska we don't have individuals, we only have a team, and we feel your being switched is going to help the team, and that's what's important. Now I know you're a good ball player and you can make this move. So you go apologize to Coach Ross and tomorrow you came out here and start all over." He spit off to the side and then, looking me in the eye, said, "OK?" I nodded. I felt selfish. After I apologized, I made up my mind to try to be the best I could be at my new position.

That weekend I got into a wreck with my Catalina in Omaha. It was Sunday afternoon and I was daydreaming when I stopped at an intersection, looked both ways, then pulled out in front of a car. My front end was totaled, but no one was hurt. After that, I had to bum rides and hitchhike. I was mad at myself.

On my eighteenth birthday I registered for the draft. As I rode my bike across campus to downtown Lincoln to register, I thought of how weird it was to be getting a draft card. All through high school I had watched the news and live film footage of fighting in Vietnam and had listened as the TV anchorman gave the casualty count for the day. I had seen the protests, Kent State, draft-card burning, and college administration building takeovers right in my own living room, but I believed it didn't concern me. It was happening in another world. The closest I had come to the war was listening to my older friends agonize about the draft lottery, their numbers, and cutoff points. Now I had to register for the draft. I knew I had a college deferment, but for the short time I was filling out the papers, I was somehow involved in it all. I also realized how lucky I was to be in school. Although it was hard sometimes, it was still a very safe and secure place to be. I felt that the coaches cared about me, and I had my friends.

That night Kenny and I got some beer and partied. We drove around campus; it was one of the few times we had a serious talk. I told him how I had registered for the draft that day, and we started talking about the war and protests. All we really knew about the war was that the United States was trying to stop the spread of communism to prevent a domino effect in Southeast Asia. The hippies and college students were protesting it, saying it wasn't our war. The mixture of beer, my draft registration, and political talk simmered and erupted into trouble. We ended up on the lawn of the Administration Building, shouting obscenities and throwing beer cans. We were having a two-man protest against the Vietnam War. We were lucky nobody caught us.

Our next game was against Wichita State. I didn't start but played the entire second half at defensive tackle. We won 36-7. Then we beat Iowa State 54-15. In that game, someone ran into Coach Ross on the sideline and broke his leg. We all felt bad for Coach, who was in his fifties. He limped around in a cast after that. I kept improving and eventually worked my way back into the starting lineup by our last game, against Kansas State. We beat them 44-0.

Once the season was over, I couldn't wait to get my freshman football jacket. It was red and had *NU Frosh* plastered across the chest in white lettering. It was a status symbol and it gave me some prestige, but there was a pecking order at the university, and freshmen were at the bottom. Above freshmen were the redshirts; above redshirts were the guys who played in the varsity games as third-teamers, followed by the second-teamers; above the second team were the starters, and above them were the All-Americans. People on campus seemed to react to football players according to their rank on the team. For example, if All-American Rich Glover was standing around in the Union, students would treat him with awe and respect. Put a redshirt or a freshman in the same situation and they'd get less attention. Overall, students did treat all players with deference. Being a player also helped in getting dates. Once I was sitting in the Union and tried talking to a cute girl next to me. She ignored me. Later a friend came by and asked me about one of our upcoming games. The girl looked over at me and said, "Oh, do you play on the football team?" We talked for a while and she then gave me her name and phone number.

The pecking order was most evident at the training table. One time I was standing in line and two starting varsity offensive linemen and All-American quarterback Jerry Tagge came walking in and went right by me to the front of the line. They didn't hesitate, never even stopped their conversation with one another. It was a common practice for the starters. But redshirt sophomores wouldn't do it, and second- and third-teamers wouldn't do it unless they were with a starter.

My relationship with the varsity was that of an observer. When the varsity was 10-0 and rated No. 1 in the country, set to play what was being billed as the Game of the Century against No. 2 Oklahoma, I read about the game in the newspaper just like all the other students. I was part of the program, but I was still a fan. I watched the game at my parents' house with nervous excitement. What a game it was going to be! The publicity surrounding it was tremendous. We were on a twenty-game win streak playing a team that was thought of as being offensively unstoppable. The game was being played at Owen Field in Norman, Oklahoma, in front of, at the time, the largest TV audience ever to watch a college game.

The game lived up to its billing. Johnny ("The Jet") Rodgers scored first for Nebraska on an electrifying, zigzagging 72-yard punt return. Rich Sanger kicked the first of five extra points and we were up 7-0. Oklahoma kicked a field goal and the first-quarter score was 7-3. Our I-back, Jeff Kinney, added to our lead with the first of his four touchdown runs early in the second quarter. But Oklahoma quarterback Jack Mildren had the Oklahoma wishbone offense moving and they scored twice to take a 17-14 lead at the half.

In the third quarter, Jeff Kinney scored twice and we took back the lead, 28-17. Persistent Oklahoma came right back and scored on a Jack Mildren run to make the score 28-24. By this time I was pacing the living-room floor of my parents' house. When Oklahoma took the lead 31-28 with 7:10 left in the game, I resorted to watching the game with my hand covering my eyes, intermittently peeking through my fingers and praying for a score. I thought it was over, that we had lost the game. But the team never gave up. Under the leadership of quarterback Jerry Tagge, the offensive line kept making holes and Jeff Kinney kept hammering away, twisting and turning for extra yards, until he scored with 1:35 left in the game. After that, our star-studded defense, led by All-Americans Rich Glover, Larry Jacobson, and Willie Harper and All–Big Eight Joe Blahak, stopped them to preserve the win.

Back at school there was a new excitement in the fall air. Everyone was talking about the game and about how we were gonna kill Alabama in the Orange Bowl. I passed all my classes, made some new friends, and moved into a new dormitory, Harper Hall, with my good friend Donny. What a great semester, I thought. The icing on the cake came one day when a member of the yearbook staff asked me to write an article about freshman football for the yearbook. This is how I felt and what I wrote:

Freshman Football

The freshman football team finished with a perfect record for the third straight year with four wins and no losses. One reason is the excellent coaching staff. Jim Ross is head coach. He is assisted by Jim Walden, who played for Bob Devaney at Wyoming. The other four assistant coaches are all former Nebraska football stars.

The players, from all parts of the country, were inspired to live up to the Nebraska football tradition and worked hard for perfection.

The first game against the Missouri frosh was far from perfect, however. The team gave up several fumbles and lost a 20-point lead. We won by only four points.

The last three games of the season were against Wichita State, Iowa State, and Kansas State. They were all fairly easy victories with the Little Big Red taking the lead early and working well as a football unit.

The last few weeks of practice I felt the intensity of this winning tradition, especially during the Iowa State game. After Ritch Bahe ran ninety-nine yards on a kick return Coach Walden exclaimed, "That's what Nebraska football is all about!"

Freshman football is intended to familiarize the new athletes with Nebraska's system and to prepare them for the Big Eight's tough competition. Besides learning techniques, we learn a variety of offensive and defensive plays and what it means to work as a team. The discipline required for any winning team is strictly enforced during practice.

The point is this: Nebraska football tradition is not just winning, but an accumulation of individual skills, team work, good coaches, and a strong sense of pride.

George Mills, Defensive Tackle

5

The Ax Handle

The trouncing of Alabama in the 1972 Orange Bowl game
capped a tremendous year for the varsity; it was proclaimed one of
the greatest football teams of all time. It was unbelievable to me
that I was a part of that same program. I had come a long way
from playing at Mason schoolgrounds. The excitement at being a
part of such a successful football program was not always with
me, though. I got excited for the games, yet was relieved when the
season was over. I was sick of football. I relaxed and concentrated
on being an ordinary college student concerned with grades, parties,
and girls. I walked around campus wearing my red frosh football
jacket but without thoughts of football, except when someone was
willing to acknowledge my membership on the team, because I
was now going to be a member of the varsity. In those cases I'd put
on my game face and play the role of a player, giving the impression that I did nothing but eat, drink, and sleep football. The truth
was, it was only a small part of my life. Playing the game was
hard, but accepting acknowledgment that I was a member of the
team was easy and rewarding. I hated practice and working out,
while I was gracious to the celebrity status that went with playing.
I know many of my teammates felt the same way. It was comforting
to know I wasn't the only guy with an inconsistent attitude about
playing.

It was January 1972 and I was feeling on top of the world. I had
passed my first-semester classes, not by much, but enough to stay
eligible, which was my only concern then. I didn't have to practice

football or work out, although many of the other freshmen and varsity members were lifting weights on an informal basis. I was treated by the other students on my dormitory floor with respect because I was a ball player, which made me feel important. Donny Moriarty, my roommate, and Kenny Knoblauch and I went out looking for girls every night. We'd hang out in dormitory lobbies, game rooms, or snack bars and strike up conversations with cute girls. I got lots of names and phone numbers. In between classes I'd hang out at the Union, read the sports page, and talk to friends and to girls I wanted to meet or I'd play the pinball machines or Foosball. Sometimes I'd skip class. This was definitely my speed. No pressures, no hardships, just enjoyable moments. But it was about to end. Next on the football calendar was winter conditioning. I had heard the older players talk negatively about it, but I really didn't give it much thought. However, when the first day came, I felt a little nervous, not knowing what to expect.

Actually, winter conditioning was a class for which football players received credit. I think everyone got *A*'s; at least I always did. Which was always a welcome sight on my dismal-looking grade report. The purpose of the class was to whip us into condition for spring ball; the coaches didn't want us to lounge around all winter.

The class was held in Schulte Field House underneath the north end of Memorial Stadium. The building housed our locker room and weight room. There were also racquetball courts. On the lower level was a wide-open space about one-third the size of a football field, covered with AstroTurf. Along the three-story-high walls were a dozen rectangular windows that provided natural lighting; the thick glass windows were covered with metal cages. It was here that we'd meet three times a week at 3:30 P.M. from late January until the beginning of spring football in April.

All the freshmen reported on a Monday to begin the rigorous conditioning program. We would go through it twice without the veteran players as part of an orientation program. They'd begin on Friday. During the class we'd wear Gibber Grays, a name given to our gray practice shorts and gray T-shirts in recognition of Gib Babcock, the equipment manager. After a workout we'd return a white towel, jockstrap, knee-high white sweatsocks, and the gray shorts and T-shirts and Gib would exchange them for a clean set, all rolled tight inside the towel. It was great always having clean workout gear. Guys were always trying to steal socks or shorts or T-shirts. They'd come to the counter window where the equipment room was located and say, "Hey, Gib, it's all here," and toss the sweaty clothes into a large laundry bin, leaving out whatever they'd be trying to steal. They'd expect Gib to give them a new roll, but Gib had been around a long time and was wise to tricks like that. He'd sort through the laundry pile to make sure that everything was there before he'd issue the new roll. Once in a while, if it was really busy, with four or five guys there at once, someone would get away with it, but in general Gib did a good job of keeping track of stuff.

On the first day as I walked out onto the turf, the scene was a familiar one. Terry Luck and the other quarterbacks were throwing passes to receivers, playing catch. A few guys were stretching out. The offensive linemen were sprawled out on the blocking bags, relaxing. I walked over to a group of four or five guys stretching out and began to wrestle around with Tony Davis, who by now had become a pretty good friend. We were always grappling. Tony was definitely strong for a running back. I felt at ease seeing all my old teammates. During the months that had passed since our football season ended, I had rarely seen them all together at one time. I'd see some of them at lunch or dinner or walking to class. Many times I didn't eat dinner or lunch at the training table, so sometimes I wouldn't see any of them for days. But we were again together. Being with my team gave me confidence, especially being with Tony; he was always so enthusiastic.

Gradually, as the time to begin drew near, we began to position ourselves in rows. We'd line up in the same fashion as we did before our practices in the fall. Team leaders like Terry Luck, Tony Davis, and Ritch Bahe lined up in the front row. By this time the coaches and trainers had shown up. Since this was the middle of recruiting season, many of the position coaches were away on recruiting trips. Consequently the graduate assistants helped out and in some cases ran the drills along with George Sullivan and Paul Schneider, who were the team trainers and were listed as the instructors.

Once the whistle blew, our lines became straight, the individual conversations stopped, and we prepared ourselves for the business of conditioning. Boyd Epley, who was then just developing as the strength coach, demonstrated the techniques for the various stretching exercises that we did first. The other graduate assistants would walk around between lines making sure everyone was doing what they were supposed to.

After about ten minutes of stretching, Boyd read off names to form eight groups of about six people each. There would be eight different exercise stations, and we'd spend five minutes at each one. When the whistle blew, we'd go to the next station. The drills varied. For example, at one station we learned to run correctly by practicing form running, which broke running down into its basic parts. First we'd stride out as far as we could for forty yards. Next we'd spring up, trying to get as much height as we could, for forty yards. Then we'd bound, combining height and distance, for forty yards. In each exercise we'd exaggerate the motion and pump our arms in unison with our stride. We did several of each and finished the drill by running ten or fifteen sprints. After that the next station might have been distance running, where you simply jogged for the entire five-minute period. There was an agility station where you performed a variety of drills, such as seat rolls, grass drills, and crabbing, all of which involved prone contact with the AstroTurf. At another station we put on a harness and a partner ran along behind us, holding the harness and providing resistance. At Boyd Epley's station we lifted weights. The weights were made of a steel rod or pipe connected to two large coffee cans filled with cement. We did thirty repetitions of several different lifts that were designed to work each major muscle group. We ended the session with thirty knee-ups (similar to sit-ups). Boyd would make us count out each repetition, and he'd give you a difficult time if you weren't working hard, as would the other coaches if they saw someone loafing. Boyd would say things like "Get your butt in gear" and stand right in front of you, staring. Basically, everyone tried to go as hard as they could through the whole routine. Coaches usually didn't have to single anyone out for criticism.

The one station that everyone dreaded was the ax-handle drill. It was conducted upstairs in one of the racquetball courts where a couple of wrestling mats had been laid out. The object of the drill was to take an ax handle, which was padded on both ends, from an opponent. To start, each man grabbed hold of the handle, the whistle blew, and you'd have thirty seconds to take it out of the other man's grasp. When the whistle blew to end the match, the two combatants were supposed to run and touch the entrance wall and return to the mat five times.

When the forty minutes of drills were up, we'd line up one more time and do some jumping jacks and spell out *Nebraska*. The first two days, we went through it at about half-speed because the coaches just wanted to teach us how it worked and what we were supposed to be doing.

On Friday all the coaches and the varsity players were there. The atmosphere was definitely different; it was more alive, more intense and upbeat. It was exciting, but it was also scary. Seeing the whole team of 120 or so players at once was intimidating. These guys weren't college boys; they were full-grown, enormously big men. Many were unshaven, which added to their ferocity. I was to be in a group of defensive linemen. That meant guys like Rich Glover, John Dutton, Monte Johnson, and Bill Janssen. All of them were so much bigger and stronger than I. I sized them up as we lined up, then gasped. The sophomore redshirts were equally big, equally old looking. In fact, at 215 pounds I was the lightest of the defensive linemen. My standing next to Glover was like a before-and-after picture. I was the guy who needed to lift weights and improve, and Glover was the end result of a massive weight-lifting campaign. In addition to their larger-than-life stature, the older guys were confident, very confident. And why shouldn't they have been? They were the national champs.

The whistle blew and we lined up, stretched, then got started. With all the varsity coaches there, everyone was hustling to the maximum. Everyone seemed to be working at a faster pace. After the first drill I was exhausted because of the stepped-up pace and the nervousness that always comes with competing. From that moment on for the next five years, I would be competing to be a starter. My intensity level would vary, but nevertheless my position coach would always be comparing me with other players. As time went on, eventually I would be consumed by competition.

Sprints, weights, ax handle—only three more to go, I thought, plodding to the next station. This was the most grueling exercise I had ever been through. My body did not respond to my commands. My legs felt like Jell-O. I looked around, and everyone else seemed to be handling it. Almost everyone. The offensive linemen looked like they were about ready to fall over. That was encouraging to me. I had now found someone in worse shape than I was.

At the weight station we had just finished the knee-ups when the whistle blew. "Hustle up! Get to the next station! Only one more to go!" Boyd yelled. We scrambled and ran up the stairs to the racquetball courts. As I walked onto the court, an eerie feeling set in. Although fatigued, I was alert, ready to face danger. Grappling over an ax handle with an animal was definitely dangerous. Once inside, I took my place as a spotter (we lined the mat so no one would fall off) alongside the mat and crouched low on my knees. The coach conducting this drill was Monte Kiffin, the defensive coordinator and line coach. "Let's line up," he barked as two combatants jumped onto the center of the mat and grabbed the ax handle. Each jockeyed to gain an advantageous position. "All right now, let's get after it! I want to see some hustle!" he screamed as his voice rose to high-pitched intensity. He blew the whistle, and in a spasmatic exchange the two guys twirled, pushed, and pulled. Watching them made my gut clutch as they struggled with all the aggressiveness of bitter enemies. In thirty seconds the whistle blew again and one guy had the other down, straddling him, his knees buried in the loser's underarms, on the verge of pulling the handle away. The two popped up, struggling to untangle, and sprinted between the spotters to the entrance wall and returned to touch the end of the mat, repeating the journey five times. Then they too became spotters. When they left the mat, two more combatants entered, the whistle blew, and there was the same burst of aggravated energy: pushing, shoving, twisting. The whistle blew, and they were off to the wall. For the first four matches I was mesmerized, frozen with fear. Then I began to review the ranks of gladiators who hadn't yet gone, trying to figure out who I'd like to be matched against. I scanned the mat and saw across from me a pair of eyes that were also scanning the mat. They belonged to fellow freshman Rod Norrie, a Shrine Bowl teammate. He was thinking the same thing I was. At the next opportunity, we jumped out onto the mat together. The whistle blew and we too exploded into a frenzy of movement, but it was a façade. Underneath it all was the instinctive bond of friends who choreographed a battle scene just like the previous ones. I got away with faking it, but before spring ball I'd have to go for real against some of the older guys, including Glover, who did not pretend.

At the time, I thought the older guys preferred going against the younger players since they were bigger and stronger. Older guys were expected to take the stick away from a younger guy. Or if they didn't, they were at least supposed to maul the younger guy. Most of the time, as I found out, and lucky for us freshmen, the older guys were content to go against players their own age or against friends. The general rule was that if Kiffin was there, it was full speed and people really tried to take the handle away. If he wasn't around and a graduate assistant conducted the drill, the combatants were not as intense. In other words, they put on a good show like Rod and me. I noticed that many guys would go against the same partners time after time, but there was still enough rivalry among teammates to see some real battles, and not everyone adhered to this informal buddy system. I remember one occasion when I went against Bob Nelson, a big linebacker who was in our group. He and I were both freshmen, but we really hadn't gotten to know each other that well yet. Kiffin was there. The competition was real. As we wrestled, he stood up and braced himself and I attempted to pull the handle, or so he thought. Instead I pushed. The ax handle struck him on the forehead, dazing him, yet I didn't get it away from him. After practice they discovered he had suffered a mild concussion. Injuries were commonplace. Guys were always wrenching their arms or twisting something; that's why most players disliked having to do it.

I knew the ax-handle drill was intended to make us more aggressive and therefore more competitive football players. Nevertheless, I grew to hate it because it forced me into a new, intense zone of awareness that was primeval. The feeling was similar to the way I felt just before I'd get into a fight in high school. My heart beat fast, and the adrenaline was flowing. Coiled, I was ready to take part in the purest form of competition: one-on-one, man-to-man fighting. The drill forced me to confront my limits, exposing both my strengths and my weaknesses in front of teammates and coaches. There was one simple rule: Be mean and aggressive and win, or be beaten and embarrassed.

The drill was a paradox. We were supposed to be teammates and all that signifies, yet the drill bred hostility and aggression.

How could I be friendly to some guy who kicked my butt and humiliated me three times a week in front of my teammates? How could some veteran like me if I happened to be fortunate enough to take the ax handle away from him? There were times when even Rod and I had to try our hardest because a screaming Kiffin would accept nothing less. When Kiffin was there, the outcome was much more important. I'd always feel more anxiety, which created stress and caused tension. I felt like a packed spring. I exploded at the whistle, anticipating the immediate gratification of Kiffin's praises or the obvious humiliation of being beaten. Most of the time there were draws, but the fear of having the ax handle ripped from your grip was real. After thirty seconds, I came back to civilization. In a way it was like being back at school when I was a kid and guys were fighting to see who was the toughest. Just as I did then, I respected winners and felt sorry for, and had less respect for, losers. And now, as then, I'd do anything not to be embarrassed in front of my friends.

After several weeks of winter conditioning I felt more confident, which made me more daring, not afraid to bend the rules. I remember one day heading up to the racquetball courts for ax-handle drill. I was the last one in my group going up the stairs, following two big sophomore linemen. To my surprise they ran by the racquetball room down the hall to the bathroom. I figured they were just going to gulp down some water from a bathroom sink. I was thirsty, so I followed them. At least if I got caught I'd be in company. We all gulped down some water and I assumed we'd head back to the drill, but they didn't. I didn't either. We just stayed in the bathroom the entire five minutes. All the while I heard the whistles and the shouting of Kiffin. I was petrified of being caught, but at the same time I was relieved that I didn't have to go through the drill. Every time Kiffin's voice rose, it pierced my spine: it seemed as if he were getting nearer. I imagined him coming into the bathroom and finding me. As the players who had just finished the drill ran by on their way to the next station, we jumped in line. I felt guilty about skipping the drill, but I later found out that other players were skipping the drill too. Despite the guilt, I skipped a couple more times, but I never felt good about it and eventually I returned to going through the drill. I hated the ax-handle drill, but I hated feeling like a coward even more. Maybe the drill was a rite of passage; maybe I'd emerge a man, ready for the rigors of major college football.

I found that in spite of the unpleasant nature of the drill, I felt good when it was over. I felt like I had accomplished something. After the last station the final whistle was always welcome. We'd get into our rows in the open area of the field house, our Gibber Grays soaked with sweat. Then we'd start clapping our hands. More than a hundred players would start screaming, yelling, and whooping it up. The coaches would be clapping, walking around saying, "Get it up." Kiffin especially would be exuberant, saying things like "All right, men, three in a row," referring to winning a third consecutive national championship. Then we'd start chanting in unison, "Three, three, three, three, three, three." The roar was deafening. The feeling was exhilarating. I stood in line, tall and proud, clapping and chanting. Chills ran up my spine. After a couple of minutes, we'd end with a few calisthenics and it was over. The funny thing is that the esprit de corps we felt would always be there when we finished. It was like a reward. Work hard, bust your butt for an hour, and be rewarded with an inner glow.

If you can believe it, after forty minutes of nonstop conditioning, three dozen or so players would go lift weights on their own. Every class had about ten or so guys who were dedicated enough to do it. Of those ten, some would lift hard, a few would lift moderately, and there would be some guys who'd just go in the weight room and make a token appearance, just to make sure a coach would see them lifting. At that time in my career, I think I played all three roles. In general I was apathetic to lifting, mainly because I was exhausted after conditioning. I used to wonder when it would all end. Seeing my fellow freshmen walking into the weight room as I walked away made me feel guilty. I was bitter because I didn't feel like lifting, yet I knew how important it was to become bigger and stronger, which is what I needed to be on a par with some of the older guys. Some days the guilt would be too much and I'd go in and lift. I'd concentrate on bench pressing. I'd get in line with a group of three or four other freshmen at one of the bench-pressing stations that had been set up.

Boyd Epley, who had experienced the benefits of weight training as a pole vaulter, sold the idea to the university football coaches and was given the OK to develop a program. In the west end of

Schulte Field House, Boyd planted the seeds for the future. Thus Nebraska became one of the first schools in the country to have a strength coach and actively promote weight lifting.

At that time there was one room, and much of the equipment was either built by Boyd or donated. Boyd was a very impressive specimen of what weight training could do for a person. He looked like Mr. America, yet he wasn't bulky; he looked like an athlete. He could bench-press more than 400 pounds. He weighed around 215. So he really was an example of what weight training could do. He'd come around to our little group of freshmen and demonstrate the correct technique. He'd say, "Keep your shoulders flat, butt flush on the bench, and arch your back," while he demonstrated. Then we'd all try to do it correctly. I was weak. I couldn't even bench-press my weight then, while some of the freshmen were well over 300 pounds. Bob Drinkwalter in fact could lift 335.

To increase interest in weight training, Boyd started the 300 Club. To be a member, you had to bench-press 300 pounds. You'd have to do it strictly; that is, you weren't allowed to lift your butt off the board (doing so would give you an advantage), and when you brought the weight down, you'd have to hold it on your chest until Boyd clapped once. When you felt ready to be tested, you'd ask Boyd to judge you. The successful lifter would be awarded a 300 Club T-shirt and his name would be put on the membership list. At that time there were only twenty or so members, so becoming a member of the 300 Club became a goal for me.

One of the by-products of winter conditioning and weight lifting was association with the older players. I had just turned eighteen a few months earlier and was still very impressed by everyone. Guys like Willie Harper, Rich Glover, Johnny Rodgers, and Bill Janssen were almost like idols to me. I was a part of the team, but I was more like a fan. To work out with them and talk to them was special. Johnny Rodgers wasn't around very much; he'd had surgery on his hand and wasn't required to go through winter conditioning. But he'd show up once in a while and talk to the coaches, usually Coach Osborne. Rodgers was a celebrity; on the other hand, Glover, Harper, Janssen, and the other starters were all just regular guys. Glover and Janssen, especially, were nice to me, offering me advice and words of encouragement. There was a kind of common bond among players of the same position, especially between the older and younger guys. In most cases the older guys didn't have anything to fear. I certainly wasn't going to beat any of them out for a starting position.

But competition was everywhere, and arguments sometimes developed. One day while waiting for winter conditioning to start, Willie Harper, a defensive end, and Ralph Powell, a fullback, both of whom had physiques that looked as if they had been chiseled from granite, got into a little shoving match. The next thing I knew they exchanged a volley of blows that were every bit as quick as a Muhammad Ali fight. The exchange lasted only a few seconds and was broken up by coaches and players, but it reinforced my earlier thoughts that none of these guys were people to mess with. They were all big, tough athletes who could handle themselves.

As the weeks passed, I got used to my routine of school and working out every Monday, Wednesday, and Friday, but I was still adjusting to the constant competitive spirit that existed in school and especially while working out. As a result, many Tuesdays and Thursdays I wouldn't even go near the field house or training table. I'd eat my meals at my dorm cafeteria, where I enjoyed seeing all the pretty young coeds. In fact, one day in line I met a pretty coed named Janie. She was tall and had red hair. We struck up a friendship, and she became my first college girlfriend. Gradually I began to spend more and more time with her. When it came time to report to conditioning class, it was always hard to leave her. One particular day we were having such a good time that I called in sick. I called George Sullivan, the trainer, and said in a sick voice, "George, I think I've got the flu." He instructed me to report to the Student Health Center for an examination. "Fooled you, George," I thought as I sat around talking to Janie. At first I felt great, but I felt increasingly ashamed for missing the workout and lying to George. Actually, I felt terrible. Conditioning was hard, but skipping it made me feel worse.

Right before spring ball started, the pro scouts came and timed us in the forty-yard dash. This is important because a fast forty translates into more money at draft time. Juniors just wanted to get noticed for next year. The freshmen were just excited to be there, but we too wanted to impress, if not the scouts, at least our own coaches. As freshmen we were still unknowns, and the whole point of winter conditioning was to get us ready for spring football so we could show the coaches what we had to offer. This was just an opportunity to show what kind of speed we had.

We started off by lining up and stretching out as usual. We went through an abbreviated workout of three stations, with only a couple of minutes at each. Then the pros measured off forty yards and congregated into three groups of about five each. They came in all sizes, shapes, and ages, many of them with insignia on their jackets to indicate the teams they were from: Bears, Lions, Cowboys, Jets. Most of the pro teams were represented. The scouts would line up, stopwatch in hand, eyes fixed on the tape that marked the forty yards. As the seniors began to take their turn, I watched. It was really something to see. As each runner crossed the forty-yard spot, the scouts would, in unison, stop their watches in a bobbing motion. Then they'd compare their times to see if they were accurate. Most of the interest was, of course, directed toward the seniors, especially the name players: Rich Glover, Willie Harper, Joe Blahak. The scene reminded me of some kind of horse-buying affair; we were the horses and the scouts were the stockmen.

We'd get three chances and then we were free to leave. By the time it was my turn, the place was almost cleared out. I was nervous as I lined up, but nevertheless I exploded off the line and sprinted toward the scouts, pumping my arms all the way. As I passed them, I heard the watches click and saw the bobbing motion of the scouts out of the corner of my eye. When I trotted back past them to do it again, I looked over the shoulder of the student manager, who was recording our times. To my amazement he wrote down a 4.7. I felt damn good about that. Heck, Glover didn't run it that fast. When I got back, all the other freshmen asked, "What was your time?" I couldn't wait to answer, "Four-seven." "Wow," they said, "no shit?" I almost felt embarrassed to answer because many of the other linemen were 5.2 or 5.3; some even ran 5.4. It might have been a fluke, I thought. I ran it again at 4.7 and again at 4.7. Each time the other guys asked and were amazed. I was one of the fastest freshman linemen. That didn't mean I was a good football player, but it did make me feel a little special. And at that time I needed it.

As the weather warmed up, a new feeling came over us: the anticipation of spring football. In our thoughts we all dreaded its coming but realized its importance. It was proving time. As a freshman, I had a lot to prove.

6

Read the Head

Spring ball is generally a proving time when coaches evaluate each player extensively and try to decide who among the 120 or so will be the top 44 in the coming season. Coaches usually have a good idea who the starters will be from returning starters of the previous year, but if those people don't perform up to expectations, they will be replaced. This kind of competition is what makes good football teams. I found out early on that it's hard to move up on the depth chart but easy to move down or, at best, stand still.

The coaches have thirty days to hold twenty practices. From a player's point of view, it's probably one of the most grueling times of the football year because all you do is hit, hit, and hit. Every day there is some kind of live contact drill. During the season, contact work is minimal, except for the games, of course. The coaches like spring ball because they have lots of time to work on improving players' techniques and abilities. The coaches can also take time to work with the younger guys; during the season, they don't have that luxury because all of their attention is directed toward preparing the starters for the next opponent. There simply is not enough time to work with the younger players.

I was also about to find out the meaning of repetition. Over and over again the defensive line would practice reading the head, the technique used by Nebraska's defensive linemen. In reading the head, you'd key the offensive lineman's head as he faced you and try to determine instantly what kind of block he was going to make. Keying the offensive lineman's head meant watching it for any movement. His head movement would tell you in which direction he was moving and what type of block he would try to make. For each type of block an offensive lineman would use, we had a corresponding defensive action or technique which, if performed correctly, would neutralize and defeat the block. When lining up across from the offensive tackle, all of my attention was directed at reading his head, its direction and movement, and responding with a step and forearm which, as Coach Kiffin would say, should stand him up, breaking his forward or lateral motion. As I said, we practiced it again and again to make it instinctive. The goal was to have the entire defense react without thinking in a coordinated effort to thwart any offensive movement.

Spring ball was also a mental game. I was always wondering how I was doing compared to other players. Every scrimmage was filmed, so judgment was always forthcoming. The films didn't lie, and seeing myself on film either proved or disproved earlier thoughts about my performance. The object for me was to move up on the depth chart. I started out on the fifth team. To move up, I had to outplay the people listed ahead of me. We usually scrimmaged on Wednesday and Saturday. During the scrimmage the same old thoughts would go through my head: How am I doing? Will I move up? Sometimes I'd make a play and immediately think, That was a good play. I'd say to myself, I can't wait to see that play on film. When I'd make a bad play, I'd think, Oh crap, I'll get criticized for that. You'd pay double for bad plays. I'd agonize over scrimmages well into the night and into the next day, playing it over and over in my mind. If I were standing on the sidelines waiting for my turn during a scrimmage, I would evaluate the guy I was competing against, being happy when he goofed up or if Kiffin yelled at him.

As a younger player, I really didn't pay much attention to what was going on with the team as a whole. All I knew was that on April 3, 1972, we'd start spring practice and it would be hard. As usual, I was nervous. On the first day, I lined up with the rest of the varsity players for stretching. We did our calisthenics. The whistle blew, and everyone sprinted in different directions on the huge grass field to their position coach. I heard Coach Kiffin yell, "Defensive line with me," and I joined the fifteen other nose guards and defensive tackles.

Describing Coach Kiffin as high strung and animated is an understatement. He was one of the most intense men I had ever met. He was demanding and tough. He commanded respect. He was also the defensive coordinator.

One of the first drills we worked on was pass rushing. One of the defensive linemen in our group would serve as the offensive blocker and the others would take turns pass rushing against him. While standing in line, John Dutton and Bill Janssen warned me not to make excuses if I goofed up. "Whatever you do, don't make an excuse," Dutton said. "Kiffin hates excuses." I listened intently and nodded. It was nice that the older guys would take the time to warn me.

Kiffin watched the other guys go before me, either complimenting them or criticizing them. Sometimes he demonstrated the technique, saying, "Do it like this." Standing there watching him relaxed me. He seemed OK. He was like any other coach, I thought, so by the time it was my turn, I was confident. The whistle blew and I shot toward the blocker and put on a quick move to get around him, but I slipped and landed on my knees. "Horseshit," Kiffin said. "That's horseshit, Mills." Nervous, I got up with a dumb smile. "I slipped," I said. No sooner had the words slipped from my tongue than Kiffin was in my face. "You think that's funny?" he snapped. "Well, we won two national championships without you, and I don't want to hear your excuses. And if you don't like it, you can get your ass out of here." Quickly my smile was gone. I looked down and headed back toward the end of the line. Later, Dutton and Janssen told me to forget it. They said if I could pass rush well, Kiffin would forget what had happened.

One day after practice, Tony Davis and I were walking to the training table, talking about our status on the team. I was still on fifth team, just concerned about not getting yelled at and hoping maybe to move up to fourth team. Tony, on the other hand, was angry. He was determined not to be redshirted and felt he wasn't being given a fair chance. He described to me, quite objectively I thought, the strengths and weaknesses of each of the running backs. He felt he was better than any of them. Tony threatened that if he was redshirted he was going to transfer. "I'm going to Tennessee," he said. Tennessee had also recruited him and had offered him a scholarship. I don't think he meant it, but he went on and on about it. He was really upset. He even went so far as to compare his speed, size, and muscles to those of the other I-backs. At the same time, I was comparing my attitude with his. Why wasn't I as confident? I thought. The answer obviously was my lack of commitment. I felt inadequate. Eventually, our conversation drifted to school, girls, and parties, although not necessarily in that order.

One of the worst features of spring football is that it comes during one of the most beautiful times of the year. Nebraska is so pretty in the spring. The first week the weather was Marchlike, cool and blustery. By the second week, it was warm and breezy. Everything was blooming. The scent of lilac bushes was in the air, and spring colors were everywhere. During the winter, Nebraska girls seem to hibernate, but when the temperature hits seventy, they are outside or on the roofs of sorority houses, sunbathing. It seemed like everyone was having parties, throwing Frisbees or just lying around. For those reasons, more than anything else, spring ball was unbearable. I had never played football in spring before; it didn't seem natural.

When the time started rolling toward 1:30 P.M., I hated going to the field house to get suited up. The thought of practice made me sick. It was always the same. All we did was read the head, go one on one with offensive tackles, and scrimmage. During the read-the-head drills, Kiffin would stand behind me so I couldn't see him. He'd motion with one hand to the blocker facing me what kind of block he was supposed to make. Kiffin would signal him to hook block (in which case the blocker would shoot his head to my outside hip), dive block (he'd fire out straight), down block (he'd shoot to the gap on my inside), or pass block (he'd pop up backpedaling, simulating pass protection.) As I said, for each of these blocks we had a corresponding move designed to neutralize the block.

For example, when I'd read dive block, from my three-point stance I was to deliver a forearm blow with my down hand. My blow was supposed to neutralize my opponent's forward movement or, better yet, knock him backward and clog up the running hole. On a hook block, I was to do the same thing, except I was to do it while moving laterally to keep the blocker from walling me off to his inside. When he'd down block, I was to jam him, knocking him off stride, so that he couldn't reach the linebacker in time to block him. On a pass block, I was to rush toward his inside shoulders, getting my hands on his shoulder pads and pulling him toward me before he could get back and set up to deliver a blow on me. Once I had his shoulder pads, I was to slip my inside arm over his head and maneuver my body past him and then tackle the quarterback.

"Their head won't lie," Kiffin said. "Key it and you'll know where they're going." Over and over he'd say, "Key the head." To play defense for Monte Kiffin, you had to master reading the head. For me it was the hardest thing to do. Not only was I supposed to read the blocker's head and respond to his movement correctly, I was supposed to step with the proper footwork while delivering a ferocious blow with the forearm, which was supposed to drive the blocker into the backfield and, hopefully, screw up the play. In 1971, Larry Jacobson mastered the technique and won the Outland Trophy, which is awarded to the best collegiate lineman. Dutton, Janssen, and Monte Johnson also did it well. The middle guards keyed the ball and responded to movement in a similar fashion, delivering a blow to the center. Nose guards Rich Glover and John Bell were excellent. It amazed me how well they used their techniques.

Knowing beforehand which block was to be used was an advantage, but Kiffin stood behind you. There was no way to know what block he'd signal for, so you had to read that head. If you read wrong, Kiffin would yell at you. If you read right, you'd get praise. The praise, of course, was wonderful. Sometimes Kiffin inadvertently used identifiable patterns in commanding the blocker. One time I noticed the pattern and began to guess. I guessed right and made a great play; praise came. I guessed right again. "Good play," he said. But with the next block, I guessed wrong. Obviously so. I stepped the wrong way. "Dammit, Mills, you're guessing," Kiffin yelled. "Read the damn head and do it right." After that episode, I returned to reading the head.

I didn't give up hope, though. I continually tried to improve my head-reading ability, but whenever the opportunity presented itself, I'd cheat. Like the time when Coach Kiffin stood with his back to the west. The sun was low and Kiffin cast a long shadow that I could see. It was heavenly to be able to see the shadow of his arms waving and pointing out the blocks. Everyone that day had a great day reading the head. At other times, I'd use peripheral vision to sneak a peek and cheat. All this hurt my chances of improving, but I couldn't help it. Like Pavlov's dogs, I was being conditioned to praise.

When we weren't reading the head with Kiffin, we'd do it on our own with each other, sometimes for as much as forty minutes while he was off working with first- and second-teamers. He took turns, working one day with us lower-unit guys and the next day working with the top units. On those occasions we were supposed to take turns blocking one another. Rod Norrie and I would always team up. Whenever Kiffin glanced in our direction, we'd always crack into each other at full speed. When he turned away, we'd hit at half-speed. Sometimes graduate assistant Dave Walline, a former defensive tackle, would come out to assist Kiffin by working with the lower units. Dave was a good player who had graduated a couple of years before. He was a kind of legend to us because, for one reason or another, he never had to go through spring ball. I dreamed of being so lucky.

I'll never forget the day I blocked against All-American Rich Glover. It was a read-the-head drill and I played offensive center. When Glover moved to the middle-guard position over me, I thought, This is it. I'll see what I'm made of. After a couple of weeks of spring ball, much of the awe that I had for the older guys was gone. Oh, I respected them all right. They could, for example, read the head better and they were stronger, but I just wasn't intimidated anymore. I really wanted to make a good block on Glover. Kiffin gave me my signal, and I fired out as hard as I could drive my legs. Glover stood me straight up before I could even get going, then tossed me aside. I tried it three more times with the same results. It was reaffirmed: Glover was big and strong and his technique was perfect. I didn't feel so bad, though, because he had demoralized many a center.

About every other day, the defensive line would go one on one with the offensive line. Just before we'd jog over to the offensive line's section of the field, Coach Kiffin would get us together and start insulting the offensive linemen. "Let's go down there and show those big fat-ass offensive linemen how we pass rush," he'd say. "Let's knock the shit out of them." He'd get us all fired up and then he'd yell, "Hey, Coach Fischer, you ready?" And Fischer would answer, "Bring 'em down." Then we'd jog behind Kiffin over to the offensive linemen. The line coaches loved this; it was a chance to show off their players.

It was a battle, them versus us, with them standing on one side and us on the other. Coach Fischer would call a play and the offense would break loudly from their huddle and run up to where we'd be lined up. We'd have three lines: one for the left defensive tackle, one for the middle guard, and one for the right tackle. There was about eight yards or so between our three lines so that we wouldn't run into each other and so the coaches could have a clear view to evaluate us. Coach Fischer would stand about seven yards behind his offensive linemen and pretend to be the quarterback. He'd have his familiar red baseball cap on, and his whistle would be dangling down on his chest. He'd laugh a lot. He and Coach Kiffin would say things like, "We're going to find out who the hitters are today." Then, in his rough, scratchy voice, Fischer would bark out the signals and, one by one, each of the three pairs would go one on one. Sometimes, when the coaches were short of time, all three groups would go at once. I preferred it that way because it was harder for Kiffin to watch three guys at the same time. If I goofed up, he might not see it. But when we took turns, he'd see everything. He'd stand up right next to me with his hands on his knees, watching intently.

Being a freshman, I was always near the end of the line during these drills. It gave me a chance to see the older guys pound each other and figure out what I was supposed to do. And worry about it. Was I going to get yelled at, or was I going to get praise? My insides would start knotting up. My old familiar friend, Mr. Butterfly, would start fluttering his wings. My mouth would go dry; my legs would feel weak. I feared making a mistake, looking bad. I hated the thought of the other players' thinking that I wasn't a good player. Their respect was as important as Kiffin's, if not more so, but after so many practices, the players' mental evaluations of each other were usually in sync with that of the coaches. After being evaluated by coaches over and over, we began to think like them. Their point of view became our point of view, so I knew whatever evaluation Kiffin would yell out immediately after my performance would also be the one the players would have.

I lined up, and out of the offensive huddle came a big sophomore tackle, Marvin Crenshaw. Quickly I went over all of the
blocks he could possibly try—hook, down, dive, or pass—and
tried to imagine what I'd do for each one. I kept telling myself to
read the head, read the head as I lined up across from him. Fischer
called the signals; intently I concentrated, my body coiled, anticipating the slightest movement. Then his head shot at my outside
hip, hook block, and I delivered a blow with my forearm, at the
same time trying to stay outside his block. We moved laterally as
the battle raged on, pads popping, him grunting, all along the line.
Then the whistle blew and we stopped, and I heard Kiffin belt out,
"That's not good enough, right tackle!" I cringed at his voice, then
felt relieved, realizing I was playing left tackle. I had escaped
criticism. I had escaped evaluation. Elation turned to despair,
however. "Same group, go again," he ordered. Now he'd watch
me. We lined up, the tackle fired straight out at me, a dive block.
Stand him up, I thought as I delivered a forearm into the heavy
projectile that was boring into me, but my feet buckled and I was
driven back a step or two. I heard Kiffin. "Not good enough, left
tackle. Deliver a blow," he said sharply. It was over. I jogged back
to the end of the line.

This went on for fifteen minutes or so. As days passed, I got
used to it and the criticism I usually received. I always tried hard in
these drills. Once in a while I got praise, usually when the blocker
would set up in a pass block. Most of the offensive tackles were big
and I was always quicker, so most times I'd beat them in a
pass-rushing drill and reach Coach Fischer quickly. But as Coach
Kiffin reminded me, I needed to improve my strength and deliver
stronger blows on running plays.

I found out that in addition to not making excuses to Coach
Kiffin, you didn't get hooked; you weren't ever supposed to get
hooked. If an offensive tackle hooked you, that meant the offensive play had a chance to go outside. In Kiffin's defensive scheme,
the defense was to prevent the offense from getting outside. By
getting hooked, I was in effect ruining a whole defensive scheme. If
one man didn't play his assignment against a team like Oklahoma,
it could cost our team a touchdown. This is what went through
Kiffin's mind. Seeing me get hooked in practice was like seeing
Oklahoma score. So whenever a defensive tackle got hooked,

Kiffin screamed, "You don't get hooked!" It was probably his most common criticism of younger players.

In all honesty, no one escaped Kiffin's wrath. I remember that after one scrimmage when we were in a film session he sat on the edge of his chair, leaning forward, intently watching the film. In one hand he had the control piece, which allowed him to replay the plays over and over. Streams of smoke from his cigarette would rise up through the projector light in the otherwise dark room. Sixteen of us defensive linemen sat there quietly listening to his evaluations. Rich Glover apparently had had a lackluster scrimmage because all of Coach Kiffin's comments were directed at Rich's performance. Time and time again, Kiffin stopped the film to point out Glover's mistakes. The coach was working himself up to a fever pitch. Then he exploded. "Dammit, Glover, you're supposed to be the All-American around here! Horseshit!" he yelled. "Look at yourself. If you don't start improving, we'll get somebody else in there who can do the job." The room couldn't have gotten quieter, but it did. Everyone was stunned, I think. Rich Glover was the most instant-replayed player on TV the previous year. He was the defensive standout during the Game of the Century against Oklahoma. I couldn't believe my ears. Coach Kiffin had expectations of each player; either you lived up to them or else. It didn't make any difference who you were. No exceptions. Including Rich Glover.

Another big surprise came off the field. Johnny Rodgers, on probation for a gas-station robbery his freshman year, was arrested April 22 on suspicion of possession of marijuana. A marijuana seed was found in his car when he was stopped by a state patrolman. Nothing came of it; no charges were filed. It was just a shock to hear his name mentioned again in connection with the police. The players wanted a third national title and any thought of losing him was scary. None of the players really knew what was going on except what they'd read in the newspapers. I think everyone breathed a little easier when he wasn't charged.

The monotony of spring ball continued. It seemed to last forever: endless drills and evaluations. The biggest evaluations were reserved for Saturday scrimmages, because only on Monday would the new depth charts be posted. Players' strategies were simple. Play well, whip the other man, get praise, and move up on the depth chart or hold onto your position if you're a starter. The intensity level of the scrimmages on Saturdays was ferocious. Everyone knew that a good tackle or a good block would be used by the position coaches during the film sessions as examples of how to play the game. I know I always felt good if Kiffin said, "Nice job," and showed the play over a couple of times. On exceptionally ferocious tackles, Kiffin would scream, "That's the way to hit! Them ball carriers don't run as hard after you tackle them like that. Good job."

Before each scrimmage, Kiffin would gather the defensive linemen together and pull out a little three-by-five-inch index card and tell us how much each of us would play during the scrimmage. For example, he'd say, "Left tackles. Janssen, you play for the first seven and a half minutes, Monte Johnson you play the next seven and a half minutes, Dan Lynch you play the next four minutes." And so on down the line. With only so much time available for each scrimmage, we were all limited as to how long we could play. Most of the work went to the top units or to positions where the starter hadn't been established. I didn't play much those first few scrimmages, maybe ten or twelve plays. There were six left tackles. During the first two scrimmages, I didn't do anything that met with either praise or criticism. I suppose I was kind of holding my own.

My fondest memory of spring ball my freshman year came from an injury. During the scrimmage before the spring game, I was in a pileup. Somebody drove into my knee and the blow stretched some ligaments. It wasn't a serious injury, but the knee swelled up so much I couldn't run. The trainer, George Sullivan, told me not to practice and said I wouldn't be playing in the spring game. It was great getting out of practice all week. I just limped around the practice field in my sweat clothes. Friday before the spring game it was absolutely a beautiful day, with a warm, gusting south breeze. I was musing that spring ball was over for me. School would be finished in another week, and I was just enjoying it all.

As I stood there and watched the defensive line go through drills, Coach Devaney walked by and said, "Hey, Mills, how's the knee?" "It will be OK, Coach," I said. "Get it healed," he said. "We might need you." And he kept on walking. Wow, I thought, Coach Devaney talked to me! He even knew my name! I was ecstatic. I mean, think of it. Here you had a coach who had just won two national titles in a row calling a lowly defensive left tackle by his name. For the first time, I felt like a varsity player. Then the newspapers listed me as a player who couldn't play in the spring game because of an injury. People back home would read that and think I was a big shot. What a way to end the year, I thought, my name in the newspaper and Coach Devaney spoke to me.

7

Redshirting

After my freshman year, I came home to a hero's welcome. For the first two weeks, everyone I talked to asked me about Nebraska football. "How's Dave Humm?" "Can you guys win three?" "What's Johnny Rodgers like?" Some people wanted to know if I was going to be redshirted. Knowing how far down I was on the depth chart, I said, "Probably." Being asked whether I was going to be redshirted had some status associated with it. In 1971, David Humm, a highly recruited quarterback from Las Vegas, had received a lot of publicity as a redshirt. He had been tabbed as a future star. The team already had two good, experienced quarterbacks in Jerry Tagge and Van Brownson, so the coaches did not want to waste a year of Humm's eligibility on some token appearance in a game. In the case of his redshirt year, it was a strategic move; the coaches were saving him. So as far as the public was concerned, to be a redshirt meant you were a special player. In my case, though, if I were redshirted, I doubt that the coaches would have given it a second thought. I wasn't good enough, and there was nothing else to do with me but redshirt me. Most of the people asking me questions simply did not know much about redshirting. To them, my redshirting meant the same thing as Humm's redshirt season: I was a valuable member and the coaches were making a strategic move. I didn't discourage that thinking.

Most of my close friends could not have cared less about my playing football. It rarely entered our conversations. For one friend, however, Cousin John Grandinetti, it was different. He was a tremendous sports buff and had a good sense of sports history. One summer day when we were joyriding in Omaha in his MG convertible, he said, "Do you realize you have a chance to play on a team that may win its third national championship in a row? Do you know what that means? It's never been done before. You could write a book about it if it happens." Up to that point, the only time I had thought about another championship was during winter conditioning when the guys would start chanting, "Three, three, three." My talk with John gave me a sense of history. It gave more meaning to playing.

Not everyone I met was amiable about my being a member of the team, though. That summer a friend and I walked into a bar. It was a popular bar and it was crowded, noisy with drunk people and loud music. I was standing near the bar checking the place out when some guy pointed me out to his two friends. They were close enough for me to hear their conversation. "He's a Nebraska football player," said the man who had pointed. "Shit, he don't look so tough," responded one of the guys in the group. After all the adulation I had been receiving, the negative comment was a letdown. I learned that while most people treated me with respect because I was a Husker, there were some, usually other athletes or tough guys, who would have liked to test me, or test themselves. They wanted to know if they were as tough as a Nebraska football player. Several times I came close to fighting testy individuals who wanted to prove something; fortunately, I never did. Most of the time I was introduced as "George Mills, he's a Nebraska football player" and was then given the utmost respect. It was my calling card.

Shortly after school ended, grades from the spring semester were sent home. I got two *C*'s, a *B*, a *D*+, and an *A*. The *B* came in English composition, and the *D*+ was in history—European civilization since the French Revolution. The two *C*'s were in speech and introduction to sociology. The *A* was for winter conditioning, for which I received one credit hour. I figured I deserved an *A* just for surviving it.

I settled into a summer routine which included construction work, lifting weights, running, and trying to gain weight. Coach Fischer had a contact who got me a job as a laborer with the Peter Kiewit construction company. Despite the good pay, I hated it.

Every morning I'd wake up for work hoping it would rain. In the evenings I'd go lift weights at Patterson's Health Spa. Boyd Epley, the strength coach, had sent all the players a booklet with a detailed summer workout routine that included lifting weights, stretching, and running. Had I followed it as I was supposed to, I'd have been working out until midnight. Working construction all day and lifting weights afterward was a difficult proposition; lifting weights was both boring and tiring, but I did it because I knew the other players were doing it. It was the only way to get stronger. After lifting I'd run a mile or so and do some agility drills. Dusk, the smell of cut grass, sticky humidity, and the shrill sound of cicadas were my constant companions as I plodded along during my runs. The solitude provided me with an opportunity to think. I dreamed of glory but strained while I did. My dreams were my medicine to get me through. It was much more fun to go out at night and play the role of big-time college football player, drink beer, and socialize. There were many mornings that summer when the bright sunlight hurt my head. On those days I struggled through work and definitely didn't work out.

When summer ended, I wasn't in great football-playing shape, although I was a little stronger from the weight lifting. On Thursday, August 18, 1972, nervous at the thought of what I would have to go through in two days, I packed all my belongings and headed for Lincoln. I reported to Harper Hall, which would be the team's home for the next one and a half weeks. As I walked into the building, a student manager gave me a key, a schedule, and a set of rules. Everything was organized. I was relieved to learn my roommate would be Rod Norrie. Rod was a great guy, down to earth and always willing to help someone out. Since the Shrine Bowl we had become pretty good friends, even though we were competing for the same position. I quickly put my stuff around the room and headed over to the stadium, where there would be a photo session later in the day. I was curious about the jersey number I would be assigned and where I was going to locker.

Photo day for the defending national champions was a big event. Reporters and fans were everywhere. Once we were all dressed and out on the field, the coaches arranged us for the photographer. There would be two team pictures. In the first one, we sat in the stadium seats with all the coaches sitting in front. I

found a place three rows behind them and in the middle so
everyone could see me. It was interesting to see where everybody
sat. David Humm and the rest of the quarterbacks sat in the last
row at the top, as did Johnny Rodgers. Starting offensive and
defensive linemen, such as Bill Janssen, Doug Dumler, Monte
Johnson, and John Dutton, were right in the middle behind the
coaches. I guess they wanted to make sure everyone saw them
since they didn't get as much publicity as the quarterbacks and
receivers. All-American Rich Glover was off to the side in the
back.

For the next team picture, we lined up in a giant circle around a
revolving camera. When we were all ready and in place, standing
motionless, the camera was started and revolved for one big
picture. I'd always wondered how they took those long team
photos I used to see in the barbershop; now I knew. It was
interesting to think that now I'd be hanging on a wall somewhere. I
was big time.

Afterward I walked over to the shaded area under the goalposts
and watched the reporters flock around the stars: Rich Glover,
Willie Harper, Johnny Rodgers, David Humm, and Joe Blahak.
Little kids with cameras would take pictures and ask for autographs.
Women would seek out players and pose with them. It was exciting,
but I felt left out since no one was asking for my photograph. As I
watched, I thought that someday it would be my turn for all that. I
don't think I really believed it, though.

Everyone, including me, was wondering what kind of team
Nebraska would have. Was a third consecutive national title really
possible? There was a clue during the spring game when the
Whites (made up of second- and fourth-teamers) beat the Reds
(made up of first- and third-teamers) 21-19. In the 1971 championship year, the Reds had routed the Whites by thirty points or so.

Going into fall camp, some positions were still up for grabs:
running back, linebacker, the defensive backfield, and the offensive line. As I said, my chances of playing much were slim. The
defensive line was probably the strongest part of the team. With
that in mind, I was totally surprised when I read the depth chart; I
had been moved to right defensive tackle and promoted to third
team. Part of the promotion was due to attrition. Several people
listed ahead of me in the spring were not in the fall camp. This isn't

unusual and it rarely gets much publicity, but a player on the lower units might drop out to concentrate on school or get married or just quit because he was sick of football. The promotion surprised me, but I didn't ask any questions. I rationalized and figured that part of the promotion was the result of my being a good pass rusher, which earned several compliments from Coach Kiffin during spring ball.

The first night in our room, Rod and I talked about what was to come. We'd practice twice a day, once in the morning and again in the afternoon, for nine days to prepare for UCLA. We were hoping to make the traveling squad so we could see Los Angeles. All of these plans were made in the comfort of our room; the real proving ground would be on the field. We would soon find out that reaching our goal would be much tougher than we had anticipated. We talked into the night before falling asleep.

From far off I could hear a faint noise which sounded like it was getting closer. Louder and louder it got. After a moment of listening, it was obvious that the noise was someone pounding on doors, but what maniac would be hammering doors at this hour? I thought. For a few seconds I was convinced that I was dreaming, but reality settled in like the Grim Reaper. Three quick pounds rattled our door and penetrated the warm comfort of my bed. I looked at the alarm clock and groaned: 6:45 A.M. So began the first day of practice for the University of Nebraska third-team defensive right tackle. I wanted to sleep some more. I wasn't ready to meet my goal of making the traveling squad.

I perked up as I walked over to Schulte Field House. It was clear and sunny, but the air was humid and there was almost no breeze. Some guys would eat breakfast, but I was too nervous to eat. I checked in, donned my Gibber Grays, and waited in line to get my ankles taped, since I was prone to spraining them. The night before, I had shaved the hair off each ankle to the calf. It looked funny seeing all the shaved ankles and knees.

The medical room was a busy place. George Sullivan, the team's physical therapist; Paul Schneider, the head trainer; and a host of student assistants were busy preparing yawning athletes for practice. Schneider, or Schnitzy, as we affectionately called him, had a lighted cigarette hanging over the edge of the table next to him. The table had stacks of tape, scissors, prewrap, and spray cans of a substance that enhanced the bonding of the tape to the ankle. There were guys joking around with Schnitzy, who I later learned always loved to tell jokes and keep things alive. But he was all business now, helping in the nonstop taping of one hundred or so players.

When it was my turn, I hopped onto a small medical table that was one of a row of five, all of which were occupied by players getting taped. I extended my ankle, and Schnitzy's magic hands quickly began enclosing it with a firm white cast of tape. With a slap of Schnitzy's hand on the last strip of tape, it was done. Then he taped the other one. He yelled, "Next!" and I hopped off. Schnitzy quickly retrieved his cigarette and took a deep drag. He exhaled and went on to the next pair of ankles. It amazed me how the trainers were able to get more than a hundred athletes ready for practice so quickly. Once you left the small room, the smell of Tufskin adhesive spray, creamajesic, and smoke stayed with you for a while.

I finished dressing and headed out to our grass practice field. Since the game with UCLA was going to be played in the Los Angeles Coliseum, which has a grass field, all of our preparations would take place on the grass field near the stadium. It was soon filled with red- and white-jerseyed players. The offensive players wore red, the defensive players white. The defensive players were given colored nylon-mesh pullovers. The first-teamers got the coveted black ones. The second-teamers wore gold, third-teamers green. Fourth- and fifth-teamers were given nothing; they just wore their white practice jerseys. When Kiffin tossed me a green shirt, I felt pride explode in me. I had practiced the entire spring in just my white jersey. Now I was promoted; it was a special moment, even though the guys who wore green were called Green Weenies. Of all of my freshman teammates, now sophomores, only George Kyros, a five-foot-nine safety from Grand Island, wore a black shirt. Whether the players admitted it or not, everyone noticed what team everyone else was on; there was very definitely a pecking order.

The coaches came out and joined the players, the whistle blew, and we got into lines and started stretching. This would be the most relaxing moment I'd have for the next two hours as the hot sun beat down from a clear August sky. With the humidity rising, the second whistle blew and players broke in every direction, jogging behind their position coaches. I followed the other defensive linemen who trotted behind Kiffin to a spot he had claimed on the huge green expanse.

For the next two weeks, Coach Kiffin concentrated on conditioning us and refining our reading-the-head technique. He was also going to pick his top six defensive linemen: the two middle guards and four tackles who would play the most during the season. Once practice started, I was as enthusiastic and as confident as anyone, but I didn't realize what was in store for me. If spring ball is characterized by repetition and contact, fall ball is characterized by conditioning and polish. There would be contact, but it was intended only to reacquaint us with that part of the game; it would allow those people fighting for undeclared positions to battle it out. But the closer we got to playing, the less we hit.

The morning practices were unbearable. Each group of athletes rotated around the field to various conditioning stations manned by a position coach. It was similar to winter conditioning and went on for thirty minutes. Then we went with our position coaches for thirty minutes to concentrate on technique. Defensive linemen worked on reading the head and other specific drills that were somehow related to the defensive scheme we would use against UCLA. After that was over, Kiffin had us do grass drills, which I hated passionately. We'd run in place, and then, on Kiffin's whistle, we'd hit the ground belly first, pop up quickly, and continue to run in place. The entire defense did the drill as a group. Coaches Kiffin and Warren Powers, the secondary coach, told us that to be a great defense we had to pay the price, and doing grass drills was part of the price. The drills also simulated a player's getting knocked to the ground. Getting up quickly was the mark of a great defensive player, but it was hard not to think of grass drills as some diabolical conditioning that bordered on punishment. Coaches Kiffin and Powers said our goal would be one hundred grass drills, to be performed on the final day of fall camp. They said they would do them with us, which brought a smile to all our faces.

The first practice we did twenty-five, and I was dead tired after fifteen. Getting up for the next ten was hard. Kiffin walked among us shouting, "We're going to have a great defense again! We're going to be in shape and get some shutouts! We're going to pay the price!" His enthusiasm was contagious, and in spite of being winded I was one of the first to pop up after the twenty-fifth grass drill. Kiffin didn't like overweight players, and during the drill he'd yell at any defensive player who had a big gut. "Get rid of that damn belly," he'd yell. "We don't have people like that on our defense." As we did grass drills, the offensive players, especially the offensive linemen, looked over and were probably relieved that they didn't have to do them too.

When the grass drills were over, we'd head for the country club, which is what we called our water break. There would be rows of tables and golf carts stocked with cups of water and orange slices at the edge of the practice field. Everyone would sprint over to the country club and drink as much as they could. We were like thirsty cattle stampeding toward a water hole. With my helmet in one hand, I squeezed sideways between several big bodies and plucked out four small cups. I backed up from the mass of bodies and chugged. Then I went back again for a refill. A group of offensive linemen got one of the coolers that were used to refill our cups and took turns hoisting it above their heads and gulping. After the mad frenzy, players sat in the grass or stood in small groups, enjoying the momentary calm before the next whistle.

During the last hour of practice, the first and second teams ran plays against the third and fourth units, or scout teams, as they were called by the coaches. The lower units would play UCLA's defenses and offenses for the top units. I simulated the positioning of a UCLA defensive lineman while using an arm dummy, which covered my forearm. Although the next hour was particularly boring, I liked it anyway because I was able to take it easy. Holding a dummy was not very strenuous, and with the temperature and humidity so high, I was drained of energy. All of the enthusiasm I had had at the start of practice was gone. Finally, the practice ended with ten forty-yard sprints. Even if a man was in shape, running forties always hurt. It was a matter of counting down: five more to go, then four, then three, two, and finally the last one. After breathing hard for a few minutes, my breathing returned to normal.

I showered slowly, walked over to the training table, and then headed back to the room for air conditioning and sleep. No sooner was I asleep than the alarm went off and I begrudgingly walked back over to the field house. The entire process was repeated in the afternoon: the walk over, taping, stretching, conditioning, technique, and teamwork. All the same. The only difference was that the afternoon practice was a little shorter because it was so much hotter. Also, instead of grass drills, Kiffin had us do monkey rolls. Three guys would line up as a group. At his whistle and starting from a crawl position in rotating fashion, we'd hop over and then seat-roll under one another until the whistle blew again. After a minute of it, the guys would get tired and start falling all over each other. Sometimes Kiffin would let us roll for two or three minutes. The objective of the drill was to build endurance and develop agility. It was a toss-up as to which I hated more, grass drills or monkey rolls. Both took me to the brink of exhaustion. They made me gasp for air until it hurt. The first day of fall camp was not a good one.

That night Rod and I had another talk about our future prospects of playing at Nebraska, but we weren't nearly as enthusiastic. The heat and hard work had sobered us on the realities of college football. The next day, our afternoon practice was moved back an hour because of the Shrine Bowl game, which was to be played at Memorial Stadium. The morning practice was just like opening day except Kiffin had us do thirty grass drills as we moved slowly toward our goal of one hundred.

Before the afternoon practice began, a couple of teammates and I stopped by the stadium to watch the Shrine Bowl game. We were all amazed by how big Bob Lingenfelter was. He was six-eight, 285 pounds. I knew he had been given a scholarship to NU, and I couldn't help but wonder whether he'd challenge me for a position someday. It seemed like there was no escaping competition. It was in front of me, beside me, and behind me; it was depressing.

After the Saturday afternoon practice, I didn't go directly to the training table. The campus was so peaceful and calm that I wanted to be left alone. It was getting close to 7:00 P.M. and obscure muscles in my body hurt, reminding me that they hadn't been used since spring ball. The soreness would leave in a few days, once my body got used to the rigors of football again, but for now I was sore and I needed to unwind mentally.

I just wandered, walking along Tenth Street. I found a soft patch of grass and sat with my back resting against the side of a building. As I looked to the west, I watched the sun drop to the horizon and change into a big orange ball. The sky exploded into a prism of colors. It was a beautiful sunset. How wonderful it was to sit, relax, and think. As always when football had me down, I began rationalizing about why I was playing and briefly thought of quitting. The practices were so hard, physically and mentally, that I think I would have quit and given up vague goals of glory if I had had an alternative plan. But I didn't have a plan, and besides, if I quit, I'd be letting people down, hurting people who believed in me—my parents, my friends, Coach Fischer. I couldn't do it to them. In the past, things got better; why wouldn't it happen again? Darkness fell, and I headed for one of the fast-food places that line the campus. The training table was closed by now, and I was hungry.

Sunday was our day of rest, at least in theory. The coaches scheduled only one practice. While at Mass at Newman Center, a Catholic chapel on campus, I prayed that I'd make it through fall camp. The 2:00 P.M. practice was our last in sweat clothes. Monday we'd put on all our equipment and pads and start hitting each other. Contact!

The first time each season that a football player puts on pads, he is struck by a sense of weirdness. The equipment feels bulky and strange. It also reminds him about the game, why he is wearing pads in the first place. I mean, King Arthur's knights didn't wear that armor because it was fashionable. Wearing pads reminds you that you're a football player, and that means you're on that field to hit and be hit. Your personality must respond accordingly. It usually took me a couple of practices to get used to being my other self again.

The format on the first day of contact was the same as in the spring; first the defensive linemen hit each other, and then we spent time going one on one with the offensive linemen. After that we did forty grass drills, which was twice as hard as before because of the weight and bulkiness of the pads and because the heat from my body was trapped inside my practice uniform. I felt like I was baking. When we finished, we were allowed to take our helmets off. I turned to the south, finding a breeze that cooled my face. I spent most of the practice in agony. The water break was lifesaving; at least that's how I felt.

As always, Johnny Rodgers was in the news. In addition to being on probation for his part in the 1970 gas-station robbery, he was appealing a thirty-day jail sentence for driving on a suspended license. It was up in the air when he'd serve the thirty days. The coaches and players were hoping it would be settled after the football season. That's what happened, because he played the whole season. During practices he showed why he was an All-American, hustling all the time and encouraging others. I always watched him during practice whenever he was at my station. I'd be holding the dummy, then I'd glance downfield to see him make some incredible acrobatic catch. He'd bounce off the ground and hustle back to the huddle. Sometimes he was late to practice, but once he was on the field he was something to see.

After our first scrimmage, we were in a film session with Coach Kiffin and I thought, How boring. Practice all day, then watch films and have meetings at night. It was especially boring for me because I really didn't get into many plays during the first scrimmage. I just wanted to be outside enjoying the few precious hours before the next practice. I don't think anybody really enjoyed the film sessions except maybe one senior, whom I won't name. He went out of his way to help Kiffin, scurrying around, setting up the projector, stringing the film. He eagerly did whatever the coach needed. He made the players, especially the veterans, irritable. He had the reputation of being a brownnoser, which everyone did to a degree at times. The way to move up on the depth chart was to please the coach who was making the evaluations. It couldn't hurt your chances if he happened to like you. Most of the older guys joked with Kiffin once we were off the field. My strategy was to stay out of his way and do the best I could during scrimmages so I wouldn't get yelled at.

Toward the end of two-a-day practices, the team voted on captains. We gathered in the old NU Coliseum basement and elected lineman Doug Dumler, an offensive center, and Bill Janssen, a defensive tackle. I was angry because, even though both were good choices, I thought Johnny Rodgers and Rich Glover, both black players, should have been voted in. Dumler and Janssen were nice guys and deserving, but I felt bad for the other two,

Glover and Rodgers, because they deserved to be captains too. They had been instrumental in helping the team win last year's national championship. Why couldn't NU, I thought, have four co-captains? But the players voted and that's how it came out. Perhaps Rich was too quiet, Rodgers too controversial. I don't know. But I was angry about it; I felt it wasn't fair. Maybe I hadn't been familiar enough with the varsity players to make a fair judgment about who should be captain. There was no discussion of it, no campaigning or anything like that. I don't know how John and Rich felt about not being named captains. If I were either of them, I would have been mad. I don't think race was a factor. From my limited perspective, race was not an issue on the team. The election results probably were due to popularity. Dumler and Janssen were extremely well liked by the other players, and guys voted for friends just as they did in high school. I thought it would be different in college.

The last day of two-a-days is the happiest day for anyone who has ever played football. Spirits rejoice because the agony is ending. But this time the last day was even more significant because we were about to do one hundred grass drills. Normally the players dread that, but we were happy because defensive coaches Kiffin and Powers were going to do them too. We delighted in the images of the coaches struggling along with us. Both were former Husker players, not overweight, and still in their thirties, and we felt it would be healthy for the coaches to reexperience what football practice was like.

As we lined up, the players were all smiles. I had some worries, though. Although we were supposed to work up to 100, we had never got beyond 75. I was concerned I might not be able to finish, but I felt much better when Kiffin, just before we started, said we could take off our shoulder pads. The whistle blew, and we started running in place; another whistle, then we hit the ground. In the beginning Kiffin and Powers were joking around and guys were laughing. Coach Powers, I thought, had been a reluctant participant all along. I think the coaches' joining us had been Kiffin's idea. At 25, 26, 27, all of the players were popping up at once. The coaches were holding their own. At 50, 51, 52, the players were popping up in unison. The coaches were slowing down. By 75, the players began getting ragged. Some players could hardly get up, while others, who were in shape, were popping up like grass drill No. 1. I was somewhere in between. The coaches looked beat, as if they had just finished on the short end of a donnybrook. They barely had the strength to call out the next number. The last 25 dragged on forever. The laughter and joking had disappeared around 30. There was a lot of grunting and groaning and gasping for air. The pistonlike knee action had given way to staggering. Most heads were looking down. At 90, someone yelled, "Suck it up, let's get it up, only ten more to go," and like a recharged battery, the group, except for a few players and the coaches, kicked into gear and popped up in unison. Then 91, 92, 93, and on to 99. Then someone yelled, "Last one! One hundred." A struggling Kiffin said, "Take a knee," but by then most of the players were already on one knee, breathing hard. It was over. We took a break, the longest of the year. Later when Powers and Kiffin were huddled together, smarting, I heard Powers tell Kiffin he wouldn't be doing grass drills next year.

The next day, both coaches seemed to be walking somewhat gingerly. Coach Kiffin told us he was real sore. I don't know why Kiffin wanted to do grass drills with us. I mean, he had to know how much it would hurt, and he had to know that it would humble him. He already had our respect. Did he want more? Or maybe he too had some need to prove himself. Whatever his reason, it didn't hurt his goal of having us become a close defensive unit.

There is another tradition at fall camp: the hazing of rookies. At the training table we'd have to carry the trays of food for the older players, which didn't bother me. But I wasn't wild about standing on my chair, as rookies are supposed to do, and singing. It was particularly embarrassing because we didn't know all of the veterans yet. At dinner a veteran would simply call your name and say, "I want to hear a song," and you'd have to sing. One day a bunch of the older linemen were sitting together and I was hiding among the other rookies across the room, hoping they wouldn't single me out for a song. Somebody yelled out, "We want to hear Mills." There was a pause, "Get up, Mills, sing." I was frozen, and then they took up a chant: "Sing, sing, sing." I tried to ignore them, but they wouldn't let up and a loud demanding voice rose up, "Mills, get your ass up and sing." Then the rookies at my table

turned on me and started yelling at me to sing. I gave them a dirty
look, stood on my chair, and looked out at all of those laughing
faces. The blood rushed to my head, I was embarrassed, but I
began to sing:

> Let me tell you about my baby—
> you know she comes around here about 5-feet-4
> from her head to the ground.
> And her name is G-l-o-r-iiiii-a,
> G-l-o-r-i-a,
> Gloria!
> I want you to shout it out:
> Gloria.
> Ya ya ya ya.

I turned from a reluctant participant into a show-off ham. Once I
started singing, I gained confidence and began gyrating my hips
and pretending I was singing into a microphone. The players loved
it. It was much more entertaining than the two previous guys, who
whimpered through "My Country 'Tis of Thee" and "God Bless
America." The guys went wild. I sang the whole song and received
an ovation. The next day they had me sing it again, and this time I
must have enjoyed myself too much because they booed me and
told me to sit down. So much for my singing career.

The rookies were also supposed to put on a skit for the veterans
and the coaches. A week before showtime, some of the guys
started putting ideas together. Players suggested songs or skits of
locker-room or training-room scenes. It didn't take me too long to
decide what to do. I would imitate Coach Kiffin. I had imitated
him before when I told other players about how he yelled at me. It
was natural; I had his mannerisms down pat. I had seen him praise
people, and, unfortunately, I had seen him get mad. He was always
chewing me out for something, and his words would keep ringing
in my ears, even after practice. We both had similar features: dark
and about six-four, except he was fifteen or twenty pounds heavier.
I was pretty sure I could do the ultimate Monte Kiffin impression.

On the night of the show, I was nervous. I wasn't sure how
Kiffin was going to take it. What if he got mad? I started thinking
about my Cornhusker career, but it was too late. When it was my
turn, I walked out in front of the players and coaches. I was

dressed just like Kiffin dressed for practice: white turf shoes, gray sweats, and red nylon jacket. I started pacing back and forth, head down, as he did preceding every practice just before he told us what we'd work on that day. In my imitation of Kiffin, I appeared to be thinking intently, not quite looking at the audience. The crowd started laughing. After pacing a few moments, I looked up at the crowd while imitating how Kiffin looked when he was thinking intently: eyes squinting and lips pulled back in a grimace. It must have been good, because the room filled with a roar of laughter. But I didn't stop. I whipped out a cigarette and let it hang from my lip. I pulled out some three-by-five-inch note cards, just as he did every day before practice, and pretended to read them. Then I started yelling at the defensive linemen, using his choicest language. By this time, the laughter was uncontrollable. I especially heard Coach Fischer's distinct machine-gun laugh. Everyone was clapping. As I walked off, I wondered how Coach Kiffin would take it. He never said anything about it.

I guess that night reinforced some of the reasons why I played: friendship, togetherness, belonging to something which I felt and those around me felt was important. It was a great time, a great time. Everyone did his skit, and we all had a good laugh. We ended it by singing together a song that one of the guys had made up. It summarized the feeling we had for Coach Devaney and our hope of winning our third national championship in a row. The song was supposed to be sung to the melody of "Take Me Out to the Ball Game"

> One was a joyful experience that we all know,
> Two was the happiest moment since the No. 1,
> But three will be the gladdest experience that
>   we'll ever know,
> So it's 1, 2, let's make it 3,
> For good ol' Bobby D.V.

Our harmony was awful. The words didn't fit the melody, but that didn't matter. It was still a crazy, wonderful moment. We were all pulling for one thing: winning a third national championship for Bob Devaney. The spirit and togetherness were genuine. We were a team with a cause.

The Saturday before the UCLA game, the top two units squared off against the lower units in the team's final scrimmage. The lower units formed the scout team, which ran UCLA's offensive and defensive formations. It was the ultimate mismatch: the defending national champs versus us. Kiffin huddled us and told us to give it our best shot and make it tough on the varsity. We did give it our best, but we lost 39-7.

Since I didn't get moved up to the second team, I knew that I'd be redshirted, which wasn't so bad, considering that most of the players from my class were redshirted. There were some guys who made the traveling squad, but only George Kyros, who'd start at safety, Ritch Bahe, a wingback, and linebackers Ruud and Nelson figured in the game plan. Rod Norrie made the traveling squad, which made me jealous. I tried to be objective about it. I hadn't played that well. I'd have a good play, then reel off several bad plays. The coaches were looking for consistency. I was a good pass rusher, but at 215 pounds I still wasn't strong enough to stuff running plays as Glover or Dutton could do. In short, I wasn't good enough to play on a national-championship team.

As expected, when the polls came out, Nebraska was rated No. 1. Bookies and prognosticators were favoring us to beat UCLA by several touchdowns, mainly because of our veteran defensive players. Offensively, despite having Johnny Rodgers, there was considerable uncertainty. Quarterback David Humm was talented, but he lacked playing time.

UCLA, despite being a three-touchdown underdog, also had talented players. Quarterback Mark Harmon, son of Michigan All-American Tom Harmon, was a passing-running threat. He had some good runners to hand off to in halfbacks Kermit Johnson and James McAlister. Pepper Rodgers, a former Kansas University coach, said he felt his team had a chance.

Since I didn't travel with the team, I went home to my parents' house. The game began at 8:05 P.M. in Los Angeles, 10:05 Omaha time. I lay on my bed, looking out the window and listening to the radio. I had listened to many games this way in high school, but this was different because I was a part of the team. I knew those guys. My heart was with them.

When UCLA scored first on a 25-yard field goal by Efren Herrera, I figured it was a fluke. Our losing never entered my mind. Nebraska was the No. 1 team in the nation. We had twenty-three straight victories, thirty-two games without a loss. In fact, the last time Nebraska lost was 17-7 to Missouri in 1970.

I started feeling sick when UCLA went up front 10-0 on a 46-yard pass from Harmon to Brad Lyman. I couldn't believe it. Then we clawed back. First, Rich Sanger kicked a 28-yard field goal to start the second quarter. Next, Johnny Rodgers scored on an 11-yard run; Sanger's kick tied the score. All right, I thought, here we come. But UCLA intercepted a Humm pass, and Harmon later scored on a 2-yard run. With 14:01 left in the game, Humm hit Jerry List on a quick pass over the middle for a 44-yard touchdown. Sanger's kick was good, and we were tied. The last six minutes were agonizing. Methodically, UCLA moved the ball up the field, eating up the clock. Several times, just as we appeared to have them stopped, they'd make a third-down conversion. Then, I remember, there were 28 seconds left, and the KFAB announcer, Lyell Bremser, said, "This is the ball game. There's the snap. It's up, [pause] it's good." My heart sank. I wanted to help, to do something, but in the confines of my room I was helpless. It was a nightmare. We got the ball back with 22 seconds left, moved it down to their 40 yard line, and the game ended. So ended the dynasty; so ended "Three, three, three." The postgame what-ifs centered on the fumbles, interceptions, and miscues we made. Mighty Nebraska had fallen. We were now mortal.

As it always does, the sun rose again, and life went on as usual. The following Monday, the coaches and starters got on with the task of improving and I settled into my role as a redshirted third-team defensive tackle, which meant I'd be held out of competition to save three years of eligibility. Academically, the extra year would help me. I was taking only twelve or thirteen hours a semester, and I needed the extra year to accumulate enough hours to graduate. On the practice field I'd have to go through the same drills as the starters, but during the last half of practice I'd assume the role of a defensive lineman from Texas A&M or Army or Missouri, whoever happened to be that week's opponent. Then, like everybody else, I'd run the forty-yard sprints at the end of practice.

During the varsity–scout team portion of practice, I always lined up against Daryl White, an All-American offensive tackle. He was six-four, 245 pounds, and very strong. I hated dive plays because he'd fire out straight at me. There was no avoiding the hard collision. One thing I liked about Daryl, though, he wasn't gung ho in practice. Some offensive linemen took joy in clobbering us. They'd knock us on our butts, go back to the huddle, and laugh about it. There was an unwritten rule that offensive players were supposed to tell us when they'd be blocking us from a direction that we weren't looking. It gave you a chance to protect yourself. Daryl always let you know if it was a blind-side block. He was good that way.

But sometimes I'd make him mad. The whole purpose of the scout team was to give the offense a realistic picture of the upcoming defensive team. To do that, we'd have to go full speed. That meant that after we'd get blocked we'd try to shed the block and hustle to the ball. I was quick, and sometimes I'd get to the hole after Daryl's block. One time, Carl Selmer, the offensive line coach, saw me fend off White and get to the hole. "White, get your butt in gear," he yelled. Daryl got hot, and he started firing out every time at full speed, trying to drive me into the ground, pushing me so that I couldn't escape to get to the hole. I couldn't wait until that practice was over.

Sometimes Daryl would warn me beforehand. "Man, take it easy or I'm gonna go hard." I wasn't trying to be a dummy hero, a name given to overzealous dummy holders. But defensive coaches would be yelling for us to go hard, to give the offense a good picture, so maintaining an equilibrium was hard. Often Daryl and I would have to mix it up. Usually I got the short end of the battle. Most of the time, however, our efforts coincided, so I guess you could say we had a good working relationship.

As scout-teamers, we wore an oversize yellow pad on the forearm to protect ourselves. This was great because my arms would have taken a beating otherwise from the blocks coming every which way. Once in a while, the coaches would say throw the bags away and we'd go live for a few plays. The offense would rip through us for eight or nine yards at a crack. Once in a while we'd stop them for no gain, but usually the holes were wide enough to drive trucks through. There was never any doubt about which was the first team and which was the scout team.

The redshirt season is supposed to be a time when young players can develop and get bigger, stronger, better, and concentrate on grades in the classroom. That's the idea behind it. But many guys, including me, looked upon it as a vacation, a time to relax, take it easy, and party. Some redshirts did lift weights and got noticeably bigger. My trips to the weight room were split between token appearances and some serious bench pressing to make the 300 Club.

Football slipped lower on my list of priorities. Oh, I'd get psyched up about football games—who wouldn't get excited about running out in front of 76,000 screaming fans? I'd get excited about fun things, such as football ratings and bowl talk, but that was it. My No. 1 priority was to have a good time. I went out at night every chance I could, chasing after wine, women, and song. I found out that being a Nebraska football player was a great conversation piece. Nonchalantly I'd happen to say something that would tip off some young lady that I was a football player. Some weren't impressed but many others were, and as a result I had plenty of dates. For me, there were just too many distractions to keep me from concentrating on football and school.

I associated more with friends from the Neighborhood who had moved to Lincoln than with members of the football team, but on occasion I'd go out with my redshirt teammates. One Friday night Tony Davis, Jimmy Burrow, and I went to Peru, Nebraska, to watch Tony's alma mater, Tecumseh, play football. I got a chance to see the football atmosphere in a small town, and I liked it. The three of us drank some beer and got nostalgic about old times. We were all nineteen.

One of my biggest thrills was the first time I ran out onto the field at Memorial Stadium suited up with the team. The band was playing "There Is No Place Like Nebraska" and 76,000 red-clad fans were chanting "Go Big Red!" With raised neck hair and goose bumps, I literally flew out onto the field. Once the game against Texas A&M started, I stood watching like the other players, but I wasn't sure how I was supposed to act. Was I supposed to cheer, or watch my position and learn? It was hard to accept the fact that I was a member of the University of Nebraska team. I was always a fan, but now I had to get used to the reality of actually being suited up and standing on the sideline as a member of the team.

The game was boring; we butchered Texas A&M 37-7. I think the players were taking out their frustrations after the disappointing loss to UCLA. During the second half, I found a nice spot at the end of the bench, watched the cheerleaders, and waved to friends. Actually I was hungry and wanted a hot dog but was too afraid to eat one that a friend had offered me. Kiffin would have hit the ceiling if he had caught me. As the season wore on, the novelty and excitement of suiting up for the home games wore off. I passed the time by moving from one corner of the bench to the other, following the game and daydreaming of what I'd do after the game.

The team got better. On national television we beat Army 77-7 and routed four more teams, all shutouts: Minnesota, Missouri, Kansas, and Oklahoma State. We beat Colorado 33-10. We soared to No. 2 in the Associated Press and United Press International polls. People began talking No. 1 again. Then, on a soggy field at Iowa State, we were tied 23-23; more dreams were shattered. But even after the Iowa State game it was still obvious that at 7-1-1 we'd be invited to a bowl game. We had a high-scoring team with an Outland Trophy candidate in Rich Glover and a Heisman Trophy candidate in Johnny Rodgers.

The season seemed to last forever. As freshmen, we had five games, so things were getting monotonous for us scout-team players. Consequently, we began to drag in practice. I remember Coach Mike Corgan getting mad at us one day. He told the defensive position coaches that we weren't hustling, that we weren't giving his offensive team a realistic picture of the defense. The week before the Kansas State game, Kiffin reminded us that not everyone would get to go to the bowl game. He said only those scout-team players who hustled would be allowed to go. "I'll tell you right now," he said, "only about seven or eight redshirt linemen are going, and I'll tell you that it's a lot of fun in Miami, swimming and lying on the beach." He added that at bowl games, "we practice for a couple of hours and then go have fun. So if you wanna go, get your ass in gear."

The next day, Coaches Corgan and Selmer reminded us of the same thing. "We're gonna have to leave some of you guys at home," Corgan said. The mere thought of staying home while the team was at the beach was enough to get us going again. From the very first day I had been at Nebraska I had heard stories from the older guys about how great the bowl games were. They talked about the beaches, girls, and partying that had gone on in Miami the last two years. I imagined being there. Others must have been thinking the same thing because some guys who had been absolutely loafing all season began to hustle. I had days where I didn't work as hard, but I didn't get singled out as someone who was loafing. Nevertheless, I was still worried, so the last three weeks of the season I stepped up my pace. Daryl White didn't like it much, but I was not to be denied the Orange Bowl or the Cotton Bowl or wherever we were going.

The week before our tenth game, against Kansas State, the newspaper reporters and broadcasters were speculating where we'd be going. By consensus, the players wanted to meet Alabama, not only because the 1972 Orange Bowl made the Crimson Tide a big rival but also because Alabama was the highest-rated team we could play. We had slipped to No. 5 after the tie at Iowa State, and Alabama was rated No. 2. Southern California, the No. 1 team, and Michigan, the No. 3 team, were scheduled to play in the Rose Bowl. Oklahoma, which was rated No. 4, was scheduled to meet us on Thanksgiving.

According to newspaper accounts, Alabama was not interested in playing us and was supposed to be leaning toward the Cotton Bowl and Texas. If we couldn't play Alabama, our next choice was the Orange Bowl. Notre Dame, which had ended its no-bowl policy, was another possible opponent. I loved going to the Nebraska Union and reading about all the bowl speculation. I tried to be confident that I would be taken to the bowl game, so I was reading this stuff with more than a passing interest. To be quite frank, I didn't care who we played as long as we went to Miami. I wanted to see the beach.

The team went out and got Bob Devaney his one-hundredth NU win, against Kansas State. After the game, Coach Devaney was presented with the game ball. In the locker room it was announced that we were going to the Orange Bowl to play Notre Dame. The coaches said it wouldn't be official until 6:00 P.M., but that didn't keep the guys from screaming and yelling. I looked around at the happy players and said to myself, "Please, please let me go."

Monday it was back to business. There was still a Big Eight championship to win. Everyone knew what the Oklahoma game meant. In addition to the Big Eight championship and pride in defeating our biggest rival, it would be Devaney's last home game. It would be the last home game for seventeen seniors, including Johnny Rodgers and Rich Glover. In three years their only loss had been to UCLA. They deserved to go out as winners.

During Oklahoma week, everybody gave 100 percent. Everybody, including those of us who wouldn't play, wanted it. No one needed to be coaxed to hustle in practice. We were playing the Sooners.

Just before the game, the team assembled in the lower level of Schulte Field House. Dressed in our uniforms, some of us sat in folding chairs facing a chalkboard which was just to the side of the entrance. Others sat on the AstroTurf, stretching. Some guys just lay there, using their helmets as pillows; still others paced, nervously pulling up on their thigh pads as they walked. The chatter among players was quiet. Never in my brief experience as a Husker had I seen such intensity. These were the game faces of college gladiators who had been to the top and knew the price of winning. I didn't see a smile, just the serious look of warriors about to do battle.

In came the general, dressed in his familiar red ball cap and Nebraska letterman jacket. The big white *N* on his chest was a symbol of pride. Coach Devaney told us to gather up and listen. As he paced back and forth, going over last-minute instructions, I couldn't help but feel that I was witnessing a legend. It wasn't so much what he said, it was the feeling he evoked with his presence. "You're going to go out there and knock the crap out of them guys," he said. "You're not going to turn the ball over." He turned back for another pass in front of the troops. He went on for a few more minutes. We had heard it all before, but somehow this was special. The fiery little man had transformed a mediocre program into a national power. He had taken the seniors to the top, and now they and all the players wanted to repay him. He left the room so the captains could speak, as they do before every game. Dumler and Janssen gave us their message: "Let's go kick their ass and win this one for Coach Devaney." Then Johnny Rodgers stood up and said, his voice high pitched and hurried, "Let's just do it." We all rushed up the ramp, headed for the playing field. I helped fill in the mass of bodies and energy that was ready to explode. We waited impatiently at the door leading out to the stadium.

Then came the OK, and we walked through the crowd of fans to the chain-link fence that surrounded the field. Again we gathered; once assembled, we burst onto the field. The roar of the crowd was deafening, and it was all goose bumps for me. Then they chanted, "Go Big Red!" On the far sideline, we jumped and piled on one another. We're going to win, I thought. We're going to annihilate this team.

We took the early lead. Our fullback, Bill Olds, scored on a 14-yard draw play in the first quarter. Just before the half, Rodgers caught a pass deep and scored, but the play was called back when the officials ruled that he had stepped out of bounds while running his pattern. We kept the pressure on, and running back Dave Goeller got us a 14-0 lead early in the third quarter when he scored from a yard out. I thought to myself on that sunny day: We've got the game won. But Oklahoma teams don't quit.

As clouds started darkening in the sky, the Sooners began to make a comeback and tied us at 14-14 in the fourth quarter. As I watched Oklahoma, I couldn't help but admire them. They were different from the other teams that I had seen from the sidelines. They were poised, confident. Their comeback was methodical. Finally, with eight minutes left in the game, they kicked a field goal: Oklahoma 17, Nebraska 14. Just like last year, we'll make a comeback, I thought. But Oklahoma intercepted two passes, the last with thirty-nine seconds remaining. It was over. Listening to a loss on the radio is one kind of agony, but experiencing it on the sidelines is horrible. I felt bad for Coach Devaney and the seniors, yet they would all have a chance to end the season on a winning note with an Orange Bowl victory. But I didn't know for sure whether I'd be with them.

We were given two weeks off. No practice. We were told that a traveling squad would be posted on the bulletin board and only those players listed would report for practice. All the way up to the day the bowl list was posted, the other scout-teamers speculated on who and how many of us would get to go. I made a case for myself and hoped I was right.

The day the list was posted, I couldn't wait to get out of class so I could go to the field house and see whether my name was on the list. As I walked in, I saw a bunch of guys crowded in front of the list. There's my future, I thought. I stood behind five or six guys and couldn't see anything, so I went to the side, worked my way over to the list, and began scanning the names. Where is it? It's got to be there! Then I saw it near the bottom: George Mills. I yelled at the top of my lungs, "Miami!"

We won the Omaha Class B CYO championship game in 1967. I'm third from the right in the last row. In the Neighborhood, sport was king. Courtesy *Omaha World-Herald.*

Before signing my Big Eight letter of intent, I had dinner with NU Assistant Coach Cletus Fischer. Standing behind us are two other Nebraska recruits, Tim McGuire (left) and Jerry Lloyd. Courtesy *Omaha World-Herald.*

At the Shrine Bowl camp in August 1971. Courtesy *Omaha World-Herald.*

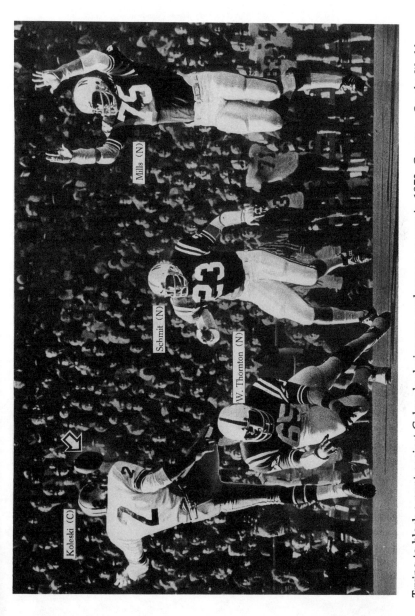

Trying to block a punt against Colorado during my sophomore season in 1973. Courtesy *Omaha World-Herald*.

John Dutton (90) sprints to clean up on a ball carrier John Bell has wrapped up in our 1973 game against Kansas. My wish was to be as intense as Bell and as dominating as Dutton. Courtesy *Omaha World-Herald*.

Bob Devaney (right) humoring his successor as head coach, thirty-six-year-old Tom Osborne, in 1973. They were two of the winningest college football coaches of all time, and I was fortunate enough to play for both. As different as night and day, they had one thing in common: winning. Courtesy *Omaha World-Herald*.

This 1973 photo shows two of NU's greatest players: Rich Glover (left) is holding the Lombardi Award (he also won the Outland Trophy), and Johnny Rodgers is holding the Heisman Trophy. Courtesy *Omaha World-Herald.*

Monte Kiffin synchronizes his watch with the other coaches before a spring ball practice session in 1975. He was the dominating force in my life while I was at NU. He commanded respect. Courtesy *Omaha World-Herald.*

Being helped off the field after sustaining a serious injury in 1974. The injury kept me out most of that season. Courtesy *Omaha World-Herald.*

Pass rushing against Colorado in 1975. Courtesy *Omaha World-Herald.*

My fellow seniors and me after a 1975 Fiesta Bowl practice. We never beat Oklahoma or won a national championship, but from 1973 through 1975 we were 28-7-1, attended three bowl games, and were Big Eight co-champions in 1975. Not bad. I'm sitting second from the right in the second row. Courtesy *Omaha World-Herald*.

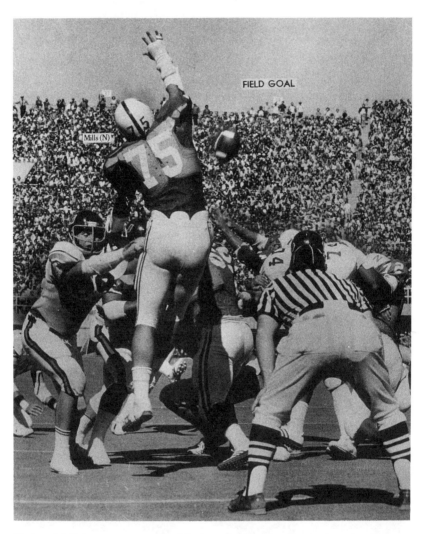

Skying high in an attempt to block a field goal against the University of Miami (Florida) in 1975. Courtesy *Omaha World-Herald*.

8

Miami

"All right, Miami Beach!" somebody yelled. Then everyone began scrambling to look out the windows, leaning over one another. It got quiet for a moment except for the sounds of Santana's "Black Magic Woman" blaring from Rich Glover's cassette. Everyone seemed absorbed in his own thoughts at the sight of Miami Beach.

On the plane ride down to Miami, I had been sitting next to Rich Glover, who had won the Outland Trophy a couple of weeks earlier for being the nation's best college lineman, and all the way we talked football, Miami, and music. I had a million questions for Rich about what the bowl was like and what we'd do in Miami. He had been there the two previous years, so he knew the ropes. He patiently answered all my questions, giving me the ins and outs of bowl life. I knew I was lucky to make the trip, since only twenty-one of the forty or more redshirts were going. A lot of players were left behind in the cold of Lincoln.

As the plane completed its turn and leveled off to land, I got one last glimpse of the sparkling blue ocean; the excitement was overwhelming. I felt like I was in a movie. I was living a dream. What a way to start off my nineteenth year: sitting next to the Outland Trophy winner, listening to Santana, and about to land in Miami Beach to play Notre Dame, which was at one time my favorite team. I was devastated when Southern California beat them in 1964 and ruined their undefeated season.

A warm blast of tropical air greeted me as I stepped off the plane. There were all kinds of people to welcome us to Miami: Orange Bowl Officials, pageant girls, Nebraska fans, and reporters. Not bad for a guy from the Neighborhood. My friends couldn't imagine, nor could I accurately describe, how exciting and fun it all was.

I was handed a sack of oranges as I boarded a bus and we were led by a police escort, nonstop, to the Ivanhoe Hotel. The Ivanhoe was a stately looking building erected in the 1930s. Its landscaped lawns were dotted with colorful flowers and palm trees. While I waited at the front desk for my room assignment, I became antsy. I set down my luggage and made a beeline through the lobby to the dining room. The sunshine poured through the picture windows and turned every glass and piece of silverware into sparking reflections of the bright sunlight. I looked out and there it was. I stepped through the glass doors and walked across the patio and beyond the pool area to a retaining wall. Looking out over the small beach, I saw and felt the spray and smelled the Atlantic Ocean. It filled my senses, and I guess I could have stood there forever, captive. But reality set in. We were on a tight schedule and had a practice that afternoon, so I had to get back to business. The team buses would leave at 3:00 P.M., which didn't give me much time to check in and unpack.

I didn't know who my roommates were to be and was happy to find out they were a couple of Omaha boys. Bob Wolfe, or Wolfy as I called him, was from Omaha South, and Bob Schmidt, Schmitty, was from Boys Town. Wolfy was a massive lineman at six feet, five inches tall and 250 pounds. He had been a starter until he hurt his knee, but now he was recovering from his injury. Bob Schmidt was a backup linebacker. Those two were already good friends. We made a good group and got along great. Our only disagreement was over who would get the two beds and who would have to sleep on the cot. The fact that Wolfy and I were both over six-four and Schmidty a mere six feet settled the discussion.

By 3:00 P.M. we had boarded the bus and were headed for Dade Junior College, where we'd practice. It was a short and enjoyable trip. Anything we did the next eleven days would turn out to be fun, including looking out the windows of the bus as we rode to practice. Dade's grass football field seemed to stretch endlessly. Our locker room was a small block structure on the edge of the field. We collected our travel bags, which had been piled up outside the bus, and headed for the lockers. We were greeted by armies of ants; they were everywhere. The room was an empty white shell with no partitions, and we hung our clothes on hooks sticking out from the wall.

I learned quickly that while the Miami sun was terrific for sunbathing, it was murder to practice under. We had left subfreezing temperatures in Lincoln, where I had a hard time working up a sweat during practice. In Miami I was perspiring shortly after warming up. The humidity was high, as high as it is in Nebraska in August. Under the warm sun, we went through our drills, and all the while I was anxious to get it over with. Coach Kiffin was especially enthusiastic, but then he didn't have to work the way we defensive linemen did. By the time practice ended, I was eager to get back to the hotel and hit the beach, so I showered quickly and caught the lead bus back. Tony Davis and I sat together on the ride back, and it became a routine for us. We'd talk about how great it was to be in Miami and what we were planning to do that evening. We hardly ever talked football.

We had a late meal at 5:30 P.M. in a grand dining room with elaborate place settings presided over by friendly waiters. I gobbled down my food and headed for the beach. As I stepped out onto the sand I thought, Finally, I'm on the beach. I waded out into the ocean with a couple of other players and let small waves crash off my waist. In between waves, the warm water gently swelled up and down my thighs. Up and down the beach, hotels dominated the view as far as I could see. Each hotel beach area was partitioned by railroad ties. Looking ahead, I saw an endless blue-green sea that melted into a soft blue horizon. One white cloud stood alone overhead. This panoramic view made all the months of practice worth it. And it was just beginning. Impulsively, I dived into a wave and swam. When I stood up, the water was up to my neck. It burned my eyes, and the taste of salt was a shock. Now I knew why it was called saltwater; for me, just out of Nebraska, this was a profound discovery.

Next on the agenda was collecting my allowance. Each player was given $160. I lined up behind the other guys thinking how incredible this all was. Spending money! I signed the ledger and stuffed the crisp bills into my pocket. I thanked Mr. Fischer, the business manager, and was off to stash it away.

Since it was Christmas Eve, the Orange Bowl people put on a Christmas party for all the players, coaches, and wives. It was the first Christmas I had ever spent away from home. Christmas at Grandma's house with all the relatives had been such a big part of my life, but with all the excitement of the Orange Bowl I barely thought about it. After eating some great food, I buzzed around from table to table, talking and laughing. It seemed that the only topic on everyone's mind was what they were going to do with their free time.

Before sacking out, I had to see the ocean again. The closer I got to the ocean, the louder it got. I imagined it to be a beast ready to devour me if I got too near. I crossed the pool area and cautiously took my station on the wall that separated the beach from the pool. I looked out into the darkness and listened. My heart beat fast. I sat there for an hour, just thinking, with the breeze blowing in my face. This became my place, a ritual to do every night while I was in Miami.

The Christmas Day agenda included a 10:00 A.M. brunch, afternoon practice, and dinner at a fancy restaurant, the Luau. The brunch was outside and outstanding. I sat with three teammates, who were equally as thrilled with the experience, looking out at the ocean. I wanted to go out to the beach before practice, so I ate in a hurry. The ocean had me in its power. I sat on my wall as long as I could. When everyone began disappearing, I knew it was time for the bus and work.

The coaches gave us a scrimmage for a Christmas present. Scout team versus the first and second units. We ran Notre Dame's offense and defense. We were short a redshirt linebacker, so I assumed the position. We were a makeshift team, with many guys not playing their normal positions. It had been a long time since we had gone full speed in a scrimmage. During the season we would throw the bags away and go live for five or six plays, but this was full scale. For the first time in a long while, I was nervous again. Part of the uneasy feeling came from the inactivity, but it was mostly due to the fact that I was playing an unfamiliar position and going against the top units. I had not really changed physically. I still weighed about 215 and felt skinny, but I had improved my strength and could now bench-press 270 pounds.

During the scrimmage, the varsity ripped through us with ease. After all, they were one of the top ten teams in the country. It was just like spring or fall ball in that it was warm and the hitting was intense. One play made a big impression on me. Dave Humm dropped back as if to pass. Instead of backpedaling and getting back into the pass protection zone the way linebackers are supposed to do when the quarterback sets up to pass, I stood still, slow to react. With my eyes fixed on Humm, I watched him hand the ball off to Bill Olds. It was a draw play. I immediately rushed in and made what I thought was a vicious hit on Olds shortly after he received the ball. He took the hit and switched directions, shaking me off, then ran downfield for about ten yards. As I scrambled off the ground in pursuit, I realized just how powerful he was at six-foot-two and 230 pounds. I had given him my best shot and had bounced off him like I was nothing, as if I were a Ping-Pong ball. It was a long scrimmage. When it finally ended, I think I was the happiest guy on the team.

At the hotel I spent the rest of the day lounging either on the beach or beside the pool. That evening, everyone got dressed up and boarded buses for a dinner at the Luau. The restaurant's tropical decor was a perfect complement to the festive atmosphere. We ate and listened to speeches by bowl officials, and then we received gifts. I wasn't expecting any gifts, so I was really surprised when we were all handed an assortment of small packages. I stripped the wrapping paper off the biggest and found a white knit pullover with the red Nebraska emblem on the chest. Another package included shaving gear and cologne, while another had Orange Bowl cuff links and a matching tie clasp, Orange Bowl emblems and pins, and a bottle of Aramis cologne.

I couldn't wait for the next day because the coaches had scheduled a morning practice in the Orange Bowl stadium. I had always dreamed of playing there, but I thought it would never happen. At Mason School when we were kids, we used to do play-by-plays of Nebraska against Alabama. But instead of losing 39-29 as Nebraska did in 1966, Nebraska would win. "Ladies and gentlemen, this is the Orange Bowl game," we'd say. "Nebraska is trailing 21-17 in the fourth quarter with three minutes to go." And sure enough, we always came through and beat the Crimson Tide.

Walking out onto that field was living a childhood dream. I was so full of energy as I looked around. The seats were painted orange, which somehow surprised me. I was also shocked by how old the stadium was, but I guess that added to the mystique of it. I thought of how many great pro and college games had been played there. It was the home of the Miami Dolphins, 15-0 at that time and headed for a Super Bowl win and an undefeated season. In back of one end zone, I saw palm trees. Unbelievable. It was a wonderful feeling. In the realm of football, this was sacred ground.

Before practice began, a couple of linemen and I took a football into an end zone and started playing catch. Then we started pretending it was a real game. I was the quarterback and radio announcer, just as I was at Mason School. I'd say, "Last play, score tied with two seconds left on the clock." I would yell the snap count, "Hut one, hut two," and take an imaginary snap from an imaginary center. "He rolls out, the pass is off. Touchdown!" The other linemen went along with the charade, and after catching the easy pass, they would fall to the ground pretending to have made an acrobatic catch. For a brief moment we were heroes. Then the coaches came out and practice started. The whole practice was fun. I hustled all over. I wasn't a hero or even a starter; I was a lowly redshirt sophomore who was grateful to be there. For the first time ever, I was disappointed when practice was over.

Back at the hotel, things were great too. Brunch, beach, lunch, beach. Plus, I met Janet, a pretty girl from Chicago. She was seventeen, tall with long black hair. She was staying at a nearby hotel with her family. She told me they came here every winter. That night the team was scheduled to go see jai alai, but I wanted to go see Janet, so I paid one of the student managers five dollars to count me present on the bus. I spent the evening walking and talking with her on the beach. I suppose it was risky, sneaking out of a scheduled event. It was probably stupid too, but I was out of control. The beach, sun, and breeze had cast a spell over me.

By the next day, Wednesday, December 27, things were hopping around the hotel. The guys were getting comfortable with Miami. Miami seemed like a million miles from the nasty cold of Nebraska. At our morning breakfast we swapped stories. I'm sure, in trying to outdo their teammates, players were giving slightly inflated reports of their activities. But one thing was for sure: all the planning that had gone on during the bus rides to and from practice was starting to bear fruit. Guys were reporting on what they had done, neat gifts they had brought, where to meet girls, and where to go scuba diving. We also found out that the hotel was providing us with limousine service. A couple of guys had used it to go to a shopping mall. Another guy told us how his cousin, who was a resident of Miami, had a key to the Playboy Club. He also said his cousin knew about some great bars that were good places to meet girls. It didn't take long to put that all together and make plans. That night was a free night, which meant there weren't any scheduled activities except a 1:00 A.M. curfew. So Chad Leonardi, Bob Schmidt, a couple of other guys, and I planned to go bar-hopping via the limousine. We had thought our plan to use the limo was a secret one.

By the time we got out to the car at about 7 P.M., the sidewalk was filled with Cornhuskers. It seemed like everyone on the team had made similar plans. As a result, the limo driver turned cabby. He took us out in shifts of five or six players. Each group would have to wait an agonizing twenty minutes or so for the limo to return. Some guys got impatient and called taxis, but we held out and forced our way into the limo. As I pushed my way in, I said to the driver, "The Playboy Club, James." The other guys piled in laughing, and we were off. We pulled up and met our contact, who showed his key to the doorman. The club was dimly lit and plush. There was a super buffet and I tried one of everything, but the food took a distant second to all the beautiful girls in the skimpy Bunny outfits. Before long the manager asked us who we were; apparently we didn't look like businessmen from New York. We told the manager that we were Huskers, and he got all excited about it.

The manager bought us drinks and introduced us to a couple of beautiful Bunnies. We didn't know how to act at first, but after a short time we relaxed and began talking to them. We didn't say anything inappropriate, at least not to their faces, but we all eventually asked them out for a date. We were politely rebuffed or ignored. We then turned our attention to the jazz band that was playing; it had us tapping our forks. After about an hour we decided the drinks were too expensive and, aside from the Bunnies, who were out of our league, there really weren't any eligible women there, so we decided to leave. We called the hotel and requested the limo. A half-hour later it showed up.

The limo took us to another bar that was supposed to be a hot spot. We were surprised when we walked in and saw twenty other teammates on one side of the room and Notre Dame players on the other. It was a shock. We walked over to our side. It reminded me of a confrontation between street gangs; each group discreetly sized up the other. A few of the opposing players did mingle, but mostly we stayed on either side of the bar. It was as if battle lines had been drawn. It was weird seeing our opponents unexpectedly like this. They were just like us—out having a good time. Seeing each other simply was a reminder of what we were there for.

I was having a great time, but it was getting late. Players had been filtering out for a while, and I was getting nervous. I didn't want to be punished for missing curfew. At 12:30 the limo left with another full load. There wasn't any room for Chad, Bob, and me. The driver promised us he would hurry and come back to get us, though. We told him we would have to run extra wind sprints if we were late. We waited anxiously outside the bar. We were just ready to call a cab when he finally showed up at 12:50 A.M.

Every guy has special moments in his life, and the ride back to the hotel was one of mine. As we cruised back to the hotel, I felt like a millionaire. As we crossed the canal leading to the beach, the windows were down, and a warm breeze steadily rushed in. I was sprawled comfortably in the backseat. The moon was low, and the light cascaded off the canal and ocean in a long sparkling stream. It was like a storybook tale: we were Cinderfellas heading home before we'd turn into normal people again. I thought of the night, what we had seen and done, and I didn't want it to end.

Thursday was cool compared to the previous days. Practice was bearable except I wanted to talk to the guys about all the fun we'd had the night before. The coaches were in a good mood and were enjoying themselves, but they were very businesslike. They had one thing on their minds: beating Notre Dame.

Kiffin surprised us when he called the redshirt running backs over to participate in a drill with us. "We're going to find out who the hitters are," he declared. "We're going to find out who's ready to play." He told the first- and second-team offensive linemen to line up in single file, and then he told the redshirt running backs to move back seven yards and get into a single line and face the linemen. "When we go out there Monday night, we're not going to be outhit," he yelled. "We're going to take it to them." He grabbed a football and tossed it to Tony Davis, who was at the head of the line. "All right backs," he said, "run tough."

Kiffin called the snap count, "Set, hut," and Tony bolted full speed at Bill Janssen, the first lineman. As they got close to each other, both lowered their torsos and prepared for the collision. Tony was intent on running through Janssen, and the defensive team captain was preparing to slam Tony down. Helmets cracked and pads popped loudly as Tony kept pumping his legs, but Janssen recoiled again, this time taking Tony down. "Dammit! That's the way to hit!" Kiffin screamed. "Ole Tom Clements is going to be sorry he came out on the field." Tom Clements was the Notre Dame quarterback.

Kiffin jogged over to Tony and grabbed the ball. Backing up, he flipped it to Burton Burns, who, on the count, sprinted and collided with Monte Johnson. Over and over, collision after collision, it went on. Each time the coach was shouting and cheering and screaming, firing up the contestants. Whenever the tackle wasn't hard enough for him, Kiffin snorted, "That's not good enough. Do it again." Kiffin had worked himself into a frenzy, and it was infectious. The watching players were shouting and cheering and the combatants were attacking each other like battering rams. I stood off to the side with the other redshirts. This drill was only for the guys scheduled to play Monday night. I felt relieved that I didn't have to do it. I had never seen hitting so intense. My eyes were focused on Tony. He never hesitated, never paused at impact, and after each blow, he popped up quickly to get back in line. I had respected Tony before, but after this exhibition he soared in my mind. He bulled into and over the likes of Dutton, Janssen, and Glover with a lot of guts and aggression. I didn't know it before, but I sure knew it now that he would have a great career, be one of the all-timers at Nebraska. Kiffin saw what I had seen, and I think he knew it too. He made sure every one of his defensive linemen would get one crack at Tony.

It was still cool later in the day when I went swimming. My body puckered up with goose bumps. I wasn't the only idiot, though, as there were other players splashing about and braving the sixty-degree temperature. That night we were scheduled to walk over to the American Hotel nearby and watch a stage show, but as a result of my swimming in a cold ocean and being run down, I caught a cold and decided to skip the show. I wasn't sick enough to stay in bed, though, so I went to see my friend Janet. I called and met her at the beach, where we walked and talked until 11:00 P.M., when I took her home. By the time Wolfy and Schmitty came back to our room, I was there.

Most of the players were also run down by practice and all the activities. Everybody was tired, and a few of the guys even had the flu. Despite being tired and run down, I had this nagging feeling that I was missing something. I got out of bed and went wandering out into the hall and ran into Tony. He told me that he and a couple of other guys had sneaked out after curfew the previous night and had gone up to the roof of the building and they were going to do it again. Well, I now had something to do.

I went back to my room and waited until after bedcheck, then crept out and made my way to the top of the building to find my friends. I climbed the metal rigging that housed a billboard and roosted there with them. High over the ocean in the darkness, I reminisced about my past and what had brought me to Miami. When I exhausted that, I pondered my future. I had spent a year and a half reaping the benefits of my scholarship. I had become a minor celebrity on campus, a major celebrity back home, and I had gotten three free semesters of school. I was now enjoying the best vacation of my life. Next year, could I make the transition to starter or top reserve? Could I face the pressure of having to perform before seventy-six thousand people? Could I be depended upon by my teammates? Could I someday replace Glover or Janssen? Did I want to? I had seen at practice that afternoon what it took to be a good football player. I had seen Tony running full blast into people, pads popping and heads snapping back. What would my family and friends think if I really didn't want to do that? Whose life was I living? Oh well, I told myself, that was a long way off. I was safe for now. I was a redshirt with no expectations placed on me except to be a good dummy holder, and I could do that.

The next day marked the beginning of the countdown to the game. Our practice reflected that by becoming easier. The coaches wanted us to get our leg strength back. It also marked the last night we would be staying out late before the game. We had the option that night to go to the Newport Hotel and see the Four Tops, a popular rhythm-and-blues band, or go to the Diplomat Hotel and hear the Fifth Dimension, another popular group. I went to see the Fifth Dimension, and it was a riot. The singers introduced us as a team, and the audience clapped for us. We sang along with them; being a celebrity was fun.

That same night, John Bell went out after curfew to get his wife a pizza and got caught. The next day he was the topic of conversation; players and coaches kidded him about getting caught. After practice he had to do some extra running as punishment. When he came into the shower, he looked beat, and somebody jokingly yelled, "Hey, Bell, I hope your wife enjoyed the pizza!"

Saturday, December 30, was a free day because practice wasn't until that night at seven o'clock in the Orange Bowl. Everyone hung around the hotel. I spent the day with Janet, watching guys like Tony Davis do flips off the diving board. Rich Glover stayed at poolside, listening to music and taking it easy. Abe Gibron, then coach of the Chicago Bears, was there; he and Tony had struck up a friendship. All day long Janet and I just took it easy. We swam in the pool or walked along the beach, just talking and enjoying the moment. Some guys in rowboats came paddling by and said they would set us up with scuba gear and take us on a short underwater excursion for twenty-five dollars. Many guys took the plunge. I was tempted to, but I wanted to save some money for gifts; plus, I wanted to go to the horse races at Calder Tropical Race Track on Tuesday, the day after the football game, so I passed on the scuba diving. Besides, I was enjoying myself too much, sunning next to Janet by the pool.

Sunday was also an easy day. It began with a short trip to a nearby chapel for Mass. Practice was in shorts. It was the day before the game, so we just ran through a few drills and made sure everybody knew what they were supposed to do during the game. Real easy. After practice Janet and I boarded a bus and headed for a shopping mall down the coast. As we moved down the beach, the hotels got older and older, and the people boarding the bus changed too. We were obviously moving toward a less glamorous part of Miami, but seeing all the different kinds of people interested me. I think we were seeing the part of Miami where people lived and worked and not the Miami that Miami shows to the world. I loved it. At the mall Janet and I saw a movie, *The Poseidon Adventure*. Because we were near the ocean, it had more impact than if I had seen the movie in Lincoln or Omaha. I got back to the hotel just in time to make the team dinner. It was steak, and I didn't waste any time eating it.

That night, as a part of the pregame ritual, the coaches showed a movie to the team. It was the usual blood-and-guts action movie that coaches felt would appeal to the team. I didn't go. Instead I spent time with Janet and talked about life, the universe, and existentialism. Being in Miami had made me quite philosophical, or so I thought. We eventually made our way to the lobby and watched the Sugar Bowl on TV, Oklahoma versus Penn State.

When I woke up it was Monday, New Year's Day, game day. Since I wasn't scheduled to play, I didn't feel any butterflies. I was just a fan who had a chance to watch the game from field level. No pressure. No worries. Just fun. There were two light meals at 10:00 A.M. and 2:30 P.M. The rest of the day followed the usual pregame routine: team meetings, lying around, then taping up. George Sullivan and Paul Schneider, the trainers, had converted one of the hotel conference rooms into a medical room where the players could get taped. Many players spent their time watching the other bowl games on television or playing cards.

The buses were scheduled to leave for the stadium at 5:30 P.M. I was up in my room getting ready. Since we were going to be on national TV, I took extra care getting ready, just in case a TV camera happened to show me on the sidelines. I buzzed around the room, shaving, combing my hair once or twice, talking to Schmidty and Wolfy all the while. Before I left, I made one last inspection in the mirror. I'm ready, I thought with satisfaction. I noticed that Schmidty and Wolfy were already gone. They had probably taken off early to get a window seat or something. I strolled down the hall to the elevator and through the lobby, figuring I really looked like a champ. There wasn't a player in sight. Wondering where everybody was, I began to panic. What if I had missed the bus? Sprinting toward the street, I heard the bus engines rumbling. As I approached, I could see a man pacing back and forth, puffing intently on a cigarette. I recognized him instantly. It was Coach Kiffin. Terror struck. I'm dead, I thought. As I got near him, he stopped, straightened up, and tossed his cigarette. "Dammit, Mills," he snapped, "get here on time! Next time we're leaving you home." I hopped on board, and while most of the guys were busy talking, a few guys chimed: "Mills, get here on time, you jerk, or we're leaving you home next time." Kiffin boarded after me, gave the signal, and we were off.

The entire time we were in Miami, the press tried to create some interest in our game. We were second fiddle in Miami because the Dolphins were on their way to a perfect National Football League season and a Super Bowl win. Our game wasn't for the national championship, but it was to be a contest between two teams rich in tradition with two famous coaches, Bob Devaney for us and Ara Parseghian for them. They had some great players in quarterback Tom Clements, linebacker Greg Marx, split end Willie Townsend, and tight end Dave Casper. We, of course, had the Heisman Trophy winner, Johnny Rodgers, and Rich Glover, the Outland Trophy winner. We also had All-American defensive end Willie Harper and a great passer in Dave Humm.

The entire week our practices had been shrouded in secrecy, and it didn't take long for the fans to see why. Johnny Rodgers lined up at I-back for the first time in his varsity career. The coaches had put in new plays that would get him the ball. Coach Devaney never told us why he made the change, but I think his confidence in the team was shaken after the Oklahoma game, where we simply couldn't move the ball on the ground. So he moved Rodgers, his star, from his normal position of wingback to I-back. I also think Coach Devaney wanted the fans to see Johnny Rodgers demonstrate his enormous talents and versatility as a football player. He wanted to put on a show.

Although Nebraska fans claimed Coach Devaney could walk on water, he was only human. Our 8-2-1 season was probably a big disappointment for him after winning the national championship the two previous years. He certainly wanted to win his last college game as a coach. I felt the players wanted to win the game for him for that reason too. On paper we looked like the better team, but Notre Dame had a good coach, good players, and tradition. We certainly weren't a lock.

The pregame intensity was as strong as it was before the Oklahoma game. We began on offense, with Johnny Rodgers running for 13 yards. We continued moving the ball on a 76-yard, 11-play scoring drive. Rodgers carried the ball the last 8 yards for the touchdown. When he scored, Coach Devaney turned to the sidelines, clenched fist flying through the air, and yelled, "We got pride, that's what we got!" Coach Devaney is the kind of man who would play hard, give 100 percent, no matter what the situation was, no matter what the game was. His kind of spirit was contagious, and we caught it. By halftime we were leading 20-0 and eventually won 40-6. Notre Dame hadn't been beaten that badly since Doc Blanchard's Army squad whipped them 48-0 in 1945.

The Orange Bowl turned out to be a tremendous game for Rodgers, who ran for three touchdowns, caught a 50-yard pass for another, and even threw a 52-yard touchdown pass to Frosty Anderson. He showed his Heisman Trophy skills and proved on the field that his selection was no fluke.

During the game I was determined to be seen on TV. I figured that since this was Coach Devaney's last game, the TV people would get plenty of shots of him on the sideline. My plan was simple: follow Coach Devaney around. I also knew which camera to face: the one with the little red light shining. For the viewers it must have been unusual seeing the same lineman, No. 69, with helmet off, standing around near the coach. I followed him everywhere and constantly kept track of the camera with the red light on. At the final gun I was one of the first to grab a leg and hoist the coach up, hoping that my family and friends back home would see me. But during the ensuing melee I was pushed aside by a couple of offensive lineman. Everyone wanted a piece of Coach.

After Coach Devaney quieted us down in the locker room, we took a knee and said a prayer. Coach thanked us for the going-away victory. The celebration lasted all night long, and it started with the bus ride home. Sirens blaring, we followed a police escort back to the hotel. We did not stop once, weaving in and out of Orange Bowl traffic that normally would have gotten us a ticket. The players were yelling and screaming, chanting and singing. At one stoplight, traffic was backed up and the police took us into the opposite lane. Oncoming cars pulled over, and several times we barely missed crashes with parked cars as we wheeled around tight corners. Whenever the bus driver appeared to slow down or gave the indication that he was being cautious, the players booed. He'd respond by speeding up, and we cheered. The entire trip reminded me of a ride I took on the Scrambler at the Nebraska State Fair.

To show his appreciation for the team's efforts, especially those of the outgoing seniors, Coach Devaney had arranged for a couple of party rooms. Pop, kegs of beer, and mounds of sandwiches covered the tables. I don't know whether the beer was meant for our consumption, but we drank it anyway. Our New Year's Eve celebration came on New Year's Day. I gave up and tried to get to sleep about 2:00 A.M., but the party raged on. The next morning, I heard all the stories. Some guys supposedly threw lawn furniture from a balcony into the pool. I also heard that a player had taken off his clothes and put on flippers and a diving mask and walked around the halls, imitating the Creature from the Black Lagoon. Some guys didn't go to sleep; they just stayed up all night partying. I did hear Coach Tom Osborne, referring to the postgame celebration, say, "Next year, things will be different." Nothing bad had really happened, just a bunch of happy football players being silly and mischievous. They had just beaten Notre Dame in the Orange Bowl.

On January 2 we were given the option of going fishing, attending the horse races, or doing whatever we wanted. I chose the horse races, but before I boarded the bus to Calder Tropical Race Track at 11:30 A.M., I called Janet and said good-bye. She was leaving that night. We exchanged addresses and promised to write. Back on the bus, Coach Fischer, who loves horse racing, was the chaperon for about ten of us. I had $75 left out of my $160 allowance and lost it all. I blew the last $10 on a 15-1 long shot.

That evening the entire team and staff went to Indian Creek Community Country Club for an awards banquet. After all the excitement of the previous days, I wasn't too enthusiastic about going because I thought it would be dull. It wasn't dull by a long shot. The club was one of the most exclusive in Miami. It was built in Spanish-style architecture and was on an island in Biscayne Bay. The Notre Dame players were there, too. Johnny Bench, the Cincinnati Reds' star baseball catcher, was master of ceremonies. Busloads of modeling students were brought in. They had a curfew, of course. The food was exquisite: giant bowls of crabmeat, shrimp, and oysters and every kind of hors d'oeuvres imaginable. I remember standing out by the pool with a teammate, Dave Redding, and a couple of models, looking out beyond the palm trees at the moonlit ocean and thinking how much I was going to miss Miami. At the banquet we each went up and shook hands with Johnny Bench and were given a digital Orange Bowl watch.

On Wednesday, January 3, I had planned to get up early and take a 6:30 A.M. bus ride out to Disney World, but when 7:30 came I was still in bed, tired and run down from eleven days of nonstop action. I got out of bed about ten o'clock and borrowed ten dollars to go with a few guys who were taking a taxi out to a fish marina. After we returned, I headed down to the beach for one last swim. That night I sat on my wall, peacefully enjoying my last night in Miami.

The next day we arrived in Lincoln shortly after noon. I stepped off the plane and was welcomed by a windchill index of ten below zero. I had returned to the real world. I preferred Miami.

9

I Quit

After the Orange Bowl game, we ended up being rated No. 4 in the nation by Associated Press. The feeling among coaches and players was that even though we had not won the third straight national championship, we had had a successful season. But now it was back to business. Second semester was the beginning of a new football cycle of winter conditioning, spring ball, summer workouts, and then fall ball again.

There was a lull on campus after the football season ended. The campus turned gray and cold. We had two weeks off before winter conditioning started, so it was the perfect time to concentrate on school and start the new year on a positive note. But it was tough to get motivated for class. All I thought about when my alarm went off at 7:30 A.M. was how cold it was going to be walking into that north wind that ripped across the campus. I'd peek outside from my warm little room in Harper Hall. The parking lot and trees beyond looked like a barren, frosty wilderness, and I'd hear the wind howling. Then I'd begin to rationalize why I shouldn't go to class. I'd think, I can get the notes from Pete or Mary; or, Mid-term tests are a month away and I have time to catch up. In the end, though, I usually went. I'd put on the old World War II pilot hat and long overcoat I'd bought at the Salvation Army store and head out, complaining all the way.

Motivating me was the thought that I'd be a laborer for some construction company my whole life. No offense to laborers, but it's hard work. I was lazy and I didn't like hard work, which is what football was, so I also knew I wouldn't be a professional football player. During the last season before practice, Rod Norrie, Dean Gissler, and I would lie in the grass and talk philosophically about life and football. We'd talk endlessly about why we were playing. My reasons varied, but in the end I decided that it was the only way I would get through school. They felt the same way. Some players loved playing, and that's why they played; but for me football had become a means to an end. My means-to-an-end attitude was the wrong kind of attitude to have at Nebraska. From day one the good players had the attitude that they wanted to be great. Tony Davis was a good example; he wanted it more than the other guy. His attitude made him a good football player more than his actual physical ability. I also think I was too rational—I thought too much. I always questioned why I was playing. It's only a game, I'd tell myself. Why should I torture and destroy my body? As a sophomore, that's how I felt.

Once in class, I'd pay attention and take a few notes. After three semesters, I had established a C average. I was slipping and sliding my way through school, doing just enough to get by.

With my first class out of the way, the day would get easier. I especially enjoyed the social part of campus life. And when the north wind wasn't blowing, walking to class was actually fun. I'd look at the faces of people walking in the opposite direction. I was always on the lookout for pretty girls or friends. "Hey, what's going on," I'd say to a passing teammate. "Not much. I gotta go to class," he'd say. Or around lunchtime I might say, "What's for lunch?" "Garbage" might be the response, but almost always the food would be quite good.

Scholarship athletes ate at the training table at Selleck Quadrangle, a series of dormitories with grass courtyards, located in the middle of campus. Our cafeteria was separated by a wall from the larger cafeteria the residents of Selleck used. Our food line opened at 11:00 A.M. Sometimes I'd get there early and wait with the other athletes in a small TV room that served as a foyer for the dining room. Some guys would lounge and watch TV game shows or soap operas, while others would read the *Daily Nebraskan*, the school newspaper, also known as *The Rag*. When it got near eleven o'clock, there'd be a ruckus to see who'd be first in line.

Once the line had formed at the door, the players would become impatient if it didn't pop open at exactly eleven. Someone would start pounding on it. Doris, a middle-aged woman with a large mound of coal black hair, ran the kitchen. She was a sweet, sensitive woman whose feelings were easily hurt. Doris never appreciated the pounding. When the door popped open, whoever was doing the pounding would hop out of the way so as not to appear to be first in line. If someone from behind did the pounding, the first guy through would say, "It wasn't me, Doris." Doris was like our mom. She had the unenviable task of feeding us, or, I should say, beefing us up.

The long smorgasbord line had a variety of food for a balanced meal, but it was also supposed to help guys like me gain weight. There were juices, gelatins, salads, vegetables, sandwiches, hamburgers, and sometimes (my favorite) a large selection of cold cuts and cheeses that allowed us to make our own sandwiches. We were allowed to take only one dessert, but usually I tried to sneak a second. At the end of the line there'd be glasses filled with a powdered protein supplement that we mixed with milk. The concoction was supposed to help us gain weight. The flavors were chocolate and vanilla. After eating I'd always gulp down a couple of glasses of it. The stuff never mixed very well and usually left me with a white-powder mustache.

The dinners were much larger and usually featured lots of potatoes. We had T-bone steaks Mondays and Thursdays. On Fridays before Saturday games, we'd eat porterhouses that filled up the plates.

Coaches ate at the training table too. They'd sit together in the back next to where the black players sat. The room wasn't segregated: friends just sat with friends; the seating pattern had developed that way. Every guy had his own special place to sit, but on occasion blacks would sit with whites and whites with blacks. I don't feel there was any division or tension between black and white players. The nature of a winning team is such that cooperation and teamwork are essential for victory, and any form of team dissension would be damaging to that goal. Racial tension would be totally unacceptable. I think at Nebraska the coaches set the tone by treating all the players as individuals and with respect. In general, most of the players, black or white, got along. I think my attitude was reflective of the team's when I say there were some blacks as

well as whites whom I didn't care for as individuals, just as I'm
sure there were players who didn't like me. If I didn't like somebody,
it was usually because I thought he was a jerk or I didn't like his
personality. My reaction might have been to be less than friendly
or just avoid talking to him. When groups of white players got
together, they didn't refer to black players with racial slurs. I'm not
saying whites never called blacks vulgar names in private; that
would be like saying racism and prejudice don't exist. What I'm
saying is that as a general rule black and white players respected
each other and acted accordingly. In essence, the success of the
team was supreme; any racial prejudices individuals may have
brought with them to Nebraska became subordinate to that goal.
Negative feelings were at the least suppressed while in the company of the team. And to a large extent the camaraderie we felt
was genuine and a powerful enough force for individuals to forget
temporarily any biases they may have had. Simply put, the team
was bigger than any of us.

When the coaches weren't around, the players sometimes acted
goofy. For example, if a pretty girl walked by, you could always
count on five or six guys running up to the large picture windows
facing the courtyard, making catcalls and acting obnoxious. There'd
be more roughhousing and cussing too.

The time between the beginning of second semester and winter
conditioning was nice. I'd go to the Union after morning classes,
see a friend, maybe Tony Davis, and he might say, "Wanna play
some Foos?" Foosball was the craze then, and I'd play every chance
I could get. If I didn't play Foos, I'd sit at the Union, talk with
friends, read the paper, or girl-watch. Just a regular student.

The dormitory I lived in, Harper Hall, had its own kind of social
life. Late at night there was a regular group of people who hung
out in the lobby. I'd visit with them after a night out. I'd join them
in a game of chess or pretend to play the piano while they talked.
I'd always make a stop at the snack bar for a sandwich and pop.
Then I'd play the pinball machine; I was great at pinball.

School was never more fun than just before winter conditioning.
The thought of it starting again was appalling. I kept thinking
about the ax-handle drill and gasping for air. Plus, we had a new
head coach, Tom Osborne, who had been the receivers coach. I
thought about what I knew of Coach Osborne, which wasn't

much, and I wondered whether things would be different. I just hoped things wouldn't be any harder.

I had a talk with Coach Osborne in the fall. I asked him about switching positions, moving to tight end. I wasn't happy about being a defensive lineman, so I approached him hoping he'd give me the OK to switch. He was very serious and direct as he said, "Maybe you should give it more time at defensive tackle." He seemed really sincere. After the Orange Bowl game I had heard him say, "Things will be different next year," referring to the postgame party, so I knew he'd take a more serious approach to the team and the way the players conducted themselves than did Coach Devaney. I was impressed by the fact that he was always jogging after practice. I thought, "Man, this guy's in shape." He was young and athletic, clean cut, kind of bookish, and very serious. Joking didn't come easy for him like it did for some coaches, but he was friendly and smiled a lot.

When Devaney announced his retirement, I had thought Coach Carl Selmer would succeed him. Coach Selmer was very intelligent, and he was serious. He had an air of authority about him. At his station during practice, I always hustled because he had a keen eye and would point out loafers. He was a part of Coach Devaney's original staff from Wyoming. I was surprised when I heard he was leaving Nebraska for a job at the University of Miami. I guess every assistant coach dreams of being a head coach, and he probably felt his chances at Miami were better, since Coach Osborne was only thirty-five.

When winter conditioning began, I expected a lot of changes, but there were none. Everything stayed exactly the same, except now I was expected to earn a position on one of the top two units. That's an expectation all sophomores have after their redshirt year, but now I'd have competition from the freshman players. During the first day of winter conditioning I checked out the freshman defensive linemen. I knew who was ahead of me, but I didn't know who was behind me. Throughout the first week of winter conditioning I paid particular attention to the new faces and sized them up. I recognized Bob Lingenfelter, the giant lineman I had seen at the Shrine Bowl game, and Jim Sledge, my former opponent from Omaha Creighton Prep.

Winter conditioning is always winter conditioning. I found it was as difficult as the year before, but I carried a certain amount of satisfaction in knowing I had survived it the year before. I was no longer low man on the totem pole, and I found myself closer to the front of our lines. The freshmen were behind me.

Going into the ax-handle drill against freshmen made me realize how the sophomore guys in the previous year must have felt. I didn't want to get beat by a freshman. They were my competition. I noticed one freshman right off, Rik Bonness from Bellevue. He brought a new level of intensity to the ax-handle drill: he was a maniac. He pushed and he shoved; he twisted harder than anybody else despite being only six-four and 210 pounds. Rik was like a Tasmanian devil. At one point I decided to go against him in the ax-handle drill. I wanted to test him. Actually I went against him several times, with neither of us ever taking it away. It was always a good battle. As I watched others go, I noticed that some players were acting and some went hard. Some resented those guys who went hard because it forced them to do the same. There were also those who wanted to maintain the status quo and not get beat or beat anyone. Looking back, I played all those parts. But I learned something about competing from Rik. His competitive drive inspired me and made me want to try. Unfortunately, gaining inspiration from other people is only a temporary thing. The permanent kind of motivation, like that of Rik Bonness and Tony Davis, had to come from within. I didn't have that yet.

The end of an era had come. Harper, Johnson, Janssen, Glover, and Rodgers had used up their eligibility. I'd see them working out, lifting weights and preparing for the NFL draft and pro careers. Glover and Janssen were still giving me advice. "You've got to have a strong upper body and strong legs," Rich would say. "Do bench presses and run the stadium steps." His nickname was befitting: Breeze. He was cool and laid back, unassuming, and that's why I liked him. He treated me with respect. Janssen, more outgoing and talkative, had the same down-to-earth qualities as Rich. Janssen told me I needed to work on playing the run better. He said if I improved I could be a starter because I could pass rush.

Among the returning players new leaders would have to emerge. I wasn't surprised that it was John Dutton and Daryl White. The school was pushing them as All-Americans, and I couldn't argue much with that. I had battled both in practice, and they got my vote. Dutton was from South Dakota, and White was from New Jersey. Both carried themselves with the aura of leaders. You respected them. They stood in the front row when we did our stretching exercises. They looked like they belonged there.

We also got some new coaches as Coach Osborne put the finishing touches on his staff. He hired Rick Duval, a linebacker coach from Colorado. An overtly religious man, Rick was very enthusiastic, a rah-rah type of coach on the field. George Darlington had an M.S. from Stanford. He was a lot like Coach Osborne and was a member of the Fellowship of Christian Athletes. Jerry Moore had a similar temperament, plus a Texas drawl. They all seemed like capable coaches, although my contact with them was limited. Players were quick to do imitations of them and crack jokes about their mannerisms. Even Coach Osborne wasn't spared; we referred to him as Ozzy. Osborne's big cuss word was dadgummit, which we got a lot of mileage out of.

Near the middle of March I went home one Friday after winter conditioning. I usually went home on weekends during the spring semester to see my family and friends. I went out that night with some of the guys. We had been to a couple of parties and were heading home when Dave Jensen, the driver, decided to stop at one more party. We went in and checked it out. I was mingling in a small living room when I suddenly noticed the most beautiful pair of eyes staring at me. I stared back for a long time. Gradually we worked our way near each other and began to talk. We hit it off immediately. I got her name and phone number before we left the party and called her the next day. We went to a movie and fell in love. Her name was Kathy. She was all I could think about that week at school. I wrote her a letter every day. All I wanted to do was be with her. Each weekend thereafter, we went out on dates. Nothing like this had ever happened to me before.

It was Friday afternoon, April 6, 1972. It was springtime, it was beautiful outside, and I was in love. I was in my room agonizing over the start of spring football practice on Saturday. My attitude was terrible. I didn't want to play football. My new love complicated things because I wanted to go back to Omaha so I could see her every day. A battle raged in my mind. One moment I would say, Quit. Who are you playing for anyway? It's certainly not you; you hate it. Quit kidding yourself. Quit. The next moment I said,

Think of all the people you'll disappoint. How will you be able to look them in the eye? How would I ever graduate? This went on for a couple of hours, and finally I said, To heck with it. I'm quitting. I've got to live my own life. I made a plan: get a part-time job and finish school at the University of Nebraska at Omaha. After all, school is the most important thing, and as long as I graduated, who could fault me? I quickly packed and began to carry my things out to the car of a friend who was going back to Omaha. As I carried out a bunch of shirts, I heard Terry Luck yell out of the dorm window, "Hey, Mills, where you going?" I yelled defiantly, "I'm going home. I quit this frickin' game." The ride home seemed to last forever as I anticipated what my parents and friends would say.

When I got home, I was glad my dad wasn't home from work yet. I'd tell my mother first. Her reaction was immediate disappointment. She turned quiet. I didn't know what to say, so I left. Then I told my friends. They said I was a dumb ass for quitting. By this time it was about 5:30 P.M. and my true love was home from work. I expected sympathy and understanding from her, and that's what I got. She said she didn't care what I did as long as I was happy.

But I still didn't feel good about my decision. It wasn't over yet. At home on Saturday we didn't talk about it. I knew people would be disappointed with me, but seeing it on their faces was too much. It was a lot worse than the little daydream I'd had on the way back from Lincoln, where everyone was at first disappointed but ended by saying, "That's OK. Whatever you want to do is fine." Reality was depressingly different. I couldn't believe that not playing football was such a big deal, but it was. Nebraska football was the biggest thing in the state and I was part of it. It was a black hole that sucked you up emotionally and physically. Once within the Cornhusker vacuum, you had to compete or get swallowed up. I was basically a noncompetitive person, and competing all the time was hard to get used to. Everything about my life in Lincoln was competitive. You competed in the weight room. You competed on the practice field. You competed for your position. You competed for grades. There were times when I'd be with players in a social setting and we'd compete to see who was the coolest, toughest, and baddest. We'd compete to see who had the most girls and drank the most beer. I had reached a point where I was really tired of competing. I wanted to graze—I was tired of the meat-eating world of football. But the outside forces had said, "No you can't quit, we won't let you." At least that's how I felt.

The guilt feelings were alive during the ride back to Lincoln. They were strong feelings. I thought about all the disappointed people, especially my mother. I had decided that I would go back and play. I didn't know how to explain to the coaches why I missed practice. I wasn't about to tell them I was sick of football. I'd lie and say I was sick or something.

Coach Kiffin called me that night at the dorm. He wanted to know what was up. Basically, he wanted to know whether I'd be at practice on Monday. I said yes, and it was over. I must have sounded confused over the phone, but he was nice and made it easy for me to return. I guess coaches were used to dealing with young people who sometimes get confused and aren't sure about what they want.

When I showed up at practice Monday, I was just as confused as before. I wanted one thing, and others wanted another. Very dysfunctional. Boiled down, I didn't have the guts to quit or the incentive to try hard. That is not the attitude to have at Nebraska, especially during spring ball, when even the most motivated players at times question the sanity of the constant contact work. I was even more confused when I noticed that I was listed at No. 2 defensive tackle behind John Dutton. I was not deserving of it.

It was obvious from the way I was playing that my head wasn't in it. I just wanted spring ball to end, but practice seemed to last forever. I hated the entire time I was on the field.

At first Coach Kiffin was patient with me, but gradually his patience gave way and the yelling started. Every day he'd ride my butt. I think he felt I had some potential. His goal was to have a great defense, and that meant getting the most out of all his players. There was definitely a conflict of interests.

The situation reminded me of a movie I once saw in which an army deserter returned to his squad and the sergeant was intent on making him regret that he had quit. I wasn't shot for desertion, but Coach Kiffin's constant criticism made me wish I had been. The other players knew my heart and mind weren't in it; they could tell I didn't want to be there. Rod Norrie used to console me and say,

"Don't talk back to him. Just don't say anything or you'll just get Kiffin more angry." But on some days I'd be steaming. He'd yell, and I'd glare back at him. I'd look him straight in the eye. On more than one occasion I was ready to fight. He didn't scare me anymore because I didn't care whether I played or not, so pleasing him wasn't a concern. I just wanted him off my back. Eventually he realized I was hopeless and let up. I was dropped down to the lower units, which was somewhat embarrassing. Nevertheless, I was glad he had given up on me.

Most of Coach Kiffin's energies were directed at finding a replacement for Bill Janssen, the left tackle. Every week he'd have a new face there, trying to find the right player. He tried Doug Johnson and Dean Gissler, the six-nine transfer from the Air Force Academy. The guy who looked the best was Ron Pruitt from Compton, California. He was six-three, 258 pounds, a true freshman. Ron wasn't that quick or even that strong, but he did the job better than anyone else. He didn't make mistakes. He could read the head. He surprised a lot of people when Kiffin told him one day to put on the black contrast shirt. He wasn't a surprise to the other black players on the team. I sat next to them at lunch one day during the winter and overheard their conversation. They were discussing the positions that were opening because of graduation. When they got to defensive tackle, my ears pricked up. They said Pruitt would claim left defensive tackle. I remember the moment well because I thought to myself, No way, I'll be the man. Then I tried to figure out who Pruitt was. If anything characterized me during that point in my career at Nebraska, it was this: I didn't like practice and working out, but when imagining myself reaping the glories of a Nebraska career, I was great. I had made a halfhearted mental claim to starting at left tackle even though I hated practice. Unrealistic, I admit.

Before Pruitt declared himself at left tackle, Coach Kiffin, despite his displeasure at my performance and my attitude, gave me a shot at the left side. During one scrimmage I went against Rich Costanzo, who was listed on the third team. Since he was part of the same recruiting class, my competitive spirit came alive. I didn't want him thinking he could whip me, so I really went at him hard. On one pass play I put a tremendous move on him and was around him and in an instant was bearing down on the quarterback for a sack. I was two steps past Rich when I felt contact and then an incredible pain in my ankle. I went down clutching my ankle and moaning. Somebody apparently had clipped me, hit me from behind. As the trainer helped me off the field, I turned and yelled, "Cheap shot! Cheap shot!" so that whoever did it would hear.

At the next film session, I hobbled in on crutches with a severely sprained ankle. I couldn't wait to see the part where I was injured and see who had clipped me. As the play unfolded, Coach Kiffin spoke, "Mills, this is the play you got hurt on." He waited a moment then played it over. "Mills, this was no cheap shot. This was a tackle who was beat, who was scrambling to recover to protect his quarterback." He played the film at least three more times. "Shoot, Mills, this is just a man doing his job," he said, his voice rising. "Where do you get off calling someone a cheap shot?" My anger flamed, but I didn't say anything. I was also embarrassed because when I yelled, "Cheap shot!" I did it without thinking. I was in pain and I was angry. I had yelled it without knowing what had happened, which was a mistake. Now I felt that Rich, as Kiffin had pointed out, was just trying to scramble back to protect his quarterback. When I left the film session, I was really angry with Coach Kiffin because he had embarrassed me. What a jerk, I thought. I'd get over that, but what didn't go away was the pain in my ankle. I didn't know which was worse, the pain in my ankle or the rehabilitation process.

There is an unwritten rule of spring ball that you practice with cuts, bruises, muscles strains, and colds. It didn't matter whether you had five sprained fingers, a couple of AstroTurf burns on your leg, or a bruised shoulder; you practiced. The only exception was a severe sprained ankle or knee, and then you were excused until the swelling went down. At that point the trainers could tape it for you as tight as a cast. They'd make sure you couldn't twist it again. So it was always important to get the swelling down on an injury.

Immediately after I was hurt, ice bags were placed on my ankle. Then it was taped to prevent further injury, and I was told to elevate it and ice it more that night. From then on, each day I'd go through what is known as hot-and-cold treatments. I'd put my ankle in an ice-cold whirlpool five minutes; then I'd put it in the hot whirlpool for five minutes. I'd do that three times. Each time I'd switch tubs, I'd have to adjust to the temperature and there'd be a lot of pain. After a couple of minutes, my ankle would get used to the heat or cold and the pain would go away. I could then move my ankle back and forth to loosen it up.

By this time I had come to the conclusion that in addition to having a bad attitude, I also had bad ankles. I had sprained my ankles several times since coming to Nebraska (in addition to all the times I sprained them in grade school and high school). The supportive tissue around the ankle had been stretched, and I had a condition known as loose ankles. This meant it was critical that my ankles be taped securely, even for the easiest workouts.

When I went home that weekend to see Kathy, I showed her my taped ankle and unknowingly turned my weakness into a sign of valor. She thought I was tough and said, "You play a nasty, mean game don't you? It takes courage to play, doesn't it?" It was so ironic. At school I was the disenchanted, misunderstood football player, but back home, to my girlfriend, her parents, and people who didn't really know, I was still a football hero. The fact that I was in Coach Kiffin's doghouse and hadn't played a down of college varsity football didn't matter. I was a Cornhusker, a member of the team, and that was good enough.

On Sunday I labored back to Lincoln, even though my heart was back in Omaha. During the ride I daydreamed of summer, no school, and, especially, no football. Only a couple more weeks, I kept telling myself. I quickly calculated the remaining practices: eight plus the spring game. I would make it. To make it through the remaining two weeks, I did only what I had to do to get by. I tried not thinking of practice. I kept busy concentrating on finishing up my classes, which was hard because I'd left so much to do until the end. I wrote letters to Kathy in Omaha and listened to a Crosby, Stills, and Nash album every chance I could. I'd read the sports page, filled with stories about recruits, spring practice, and graduating seniors. Despite my displeasure with spring practice, I was still a Husker fan. I was excited to read how many seniors had been drafted by the pros. Rodgers was drafted by San Diego. I was especially happy to see Glover drafted by the Giants and Janssen by Pittsburgh. In all, nine Huskers were drafted.

The Friday practice before the spring game, I was in ecstasy. I had made it through all of the hitting, conditioning, and injuries that are so much a part of spring ball. During the last week, I thought I had played a little more respectably. I had tried harder, but my attitude was still far from great.

On Saturday the teams were divided up into the customary Red (first- and fourth-teamers) and White (second- and third-teamers) squads. I was a member of the White team. It was cold and rainy the day of the game. My parents were there, and it was a good time—a great opportunity—to wake up, change my attitude, and make amends for a poor spring. But I didn't. My heart wasn't in it. The Reds won 35-25. Coach Kiffin pretty much summed up my performance as I was walking off the field in the fourth quarter. "At least you could hustle off and look like a football player," he said.

10

Playing Time

When I went home for the summer, I had expected to see Kathy every day. Instead, I found she had changed. She had bought a new motorcycle and said she wanted to be free. She said she didn't want to be tied down to a heavy romance. I felt hurt and cheated. The romance that had aided and abetted my poor showing during spring ball was over. I had put a tremendous effort into the relationship, and now I had nothing to show for it—except I was at the bottom of the depth chart. With her out of my life, my attention returned to football. I started working out, running, playing pickup basketball, and lifting weights. I was also working construction again.

The big event of the summer for me was when my cousin Tim Lalley decided to give college a try. I had been trying to talk him into it ever since he graduated from Rummel High in 1972. It meant we'd rent a house together, a party house, along with Donny Moriarity. Living with Tim and Donny was going to be great. I was fired up for the new semester to start.

Before I could move off campus, I had to make arrangements with the athletic business office. I would be paid the equivalent of my university room expense and apply it toward my share of the rent. The houses in Lincoln were expensive. Landlords asked and received outrageous rents for marginal places. We gave up on trying to find something close to campus because those houses were the most expensive. Frustrated and tired of looking, we decided on a house quite a distance from campus, and even it was more than we wanted to pay. It was an older, yellow, two-story house with four bedrooms and a big porch. It was located on South Street, so we called it the South Street Palace.

When fall ball started, my attitude about playing had improved, in part because I was a little older, but in a large way I was fired up because my cousin Tim was going to be with me. He had always psyched me up when we were little kids in the Neighborhood. Tim always tried hard whenever we'd race, wrestle, or fight. It made me try harder because I didn't want him to beat me. He was my inspiration that fall.

On photo day, we checked into the new locker rooms that had just been built under the south end of the stadium. With my new attitude, I went to the equipment manager to check out my uniform, No. 69, the number I'd had the year before, and the rest of my gear. To my astonishment, they had assigned my jersey number to somebody else. "You're kidding," I said to Gib. "No," he said sympathetically, "they don't have a number yet for you." About a half-hour later he gave me No. 99. As I walked out onto the field, I was fuming. Why did they give my jersey to someone else? Sixty-nine was my number. With nothing else to brag about, it was the only thing I had. My number was like my name, and now they had taken it away. It was embarrassing, but not as embarrassing as finding out that someone else also had No. 99.

Whatever confidence and enthusiasm I had developed over the summer was lost. I didn't feel part of the team. When we situated ourselves on the bleachers for the team pictures, I purposely sat in the second row in back of Coach Kiffin. I couldn't show my anger to him because I knew what he'd say. He would have reminded me of my crummy spring. Each time the photographer snapped the picture, I'd look at Kiffin's back and snarl.

After the pictures had been taken, I couldn't wait to get out of there. I got on my ten-speed and pedaled across town to the South Street Palace. My roommates were still in Omaha, so I sat in an empty house, thinking. Even though I didn't deserve to have my old number back, I still felt dejected and inadequate. Coach Kiffin had given up on me in the spring, and it had carried over. I knew that not assigning me a number meant he didn't figure me into his plans. I knew I wasn't worthy, but the realization was still a shock. After feeling sorry for myself for a couple of hours, I decided to do something about the situation. I felt I was as good an athlete as many of the other defensive tackles listed ahead of me on the depth chart. I felt that if I tried—I mean really hustled—I could beat them out. When practice started, I was going to hustle all the time. All the time.

During the first three days of two-a-days, we wore sweats. Even so, players were still losing massive amounts of weight because the temperatures that August hovered in the 90s. One day we were told that the temperature on the AstroTurf surface was 125 degrees. The heat rose up and baked us. I lost 8 pounds that day and dropped to 213. Some guys lost as much as 10 pounds or more. I regained about 3 to 4 pounds by drinking quarts of water and juice after practice.

The Sunday practice was the first in pads. I was a little nervous but still very intent. I continued to hustle, even after seeing myself listed on the fourth-team depth chart. Kiffin told us from the beginning that he was going to put his top six defensive linemen on the field and that he didn't care who they were. The first and second teams made up the traveling squad. I figured neither John Dutton nor John Bell would get beat out. That meant there would be one middle-guard slot and three defensive-tackle positions open. Counting Dutton, there were nine defensive tackles in fall camp. That meant there were eight defensive tackles competing to fill three open spots. I would have to beat out five other guys to win a spot on the traveling squad.

We practiced every day at 9 A.M. and 3:30 P.M., and every day I rose to the occasion. After each practice and particularly after each scrimmage, I evaluated my performance and that of my competitors. That fall the coaches had the lower units doing an unusual amount of contact work. Many of us were close in ability, and Coach Osborne and the rest of the staff needed the contact work to evaluate who would be part of the traveling squad.

As in the spring, Pruitt looked like the best defensive left tackle. For a time, Dean Gissler looked like he was in the picture, but Gissler hurt his knee and missed some practice. Letterman Doug Johnson, a converted defensive end, was given a try. Then big John Lee was given a good look. At six-four and 240 pounds, John ran a 4.6-second forty. He was from New Jersey, and he had sat out the previous year while he worked on improving his grades to meet

the NCAA requirements and be eligible for a scholarship. I first
noticed him during winter conditioning, standing off to the side,
watching us go through drills. He was immense. He looked like a
ten-year National Football League veteran. He had received publicity without playing a down. He had huge legs and a big barrel
chest. I died a little when Kiffin shifted him from middle guard to
defensive tackle. Another guy to beat out. Kiffin gave Jerry Wied,
a redshirt sophomore from my class, a good look along with a
six-four, 240-pound freshman from New Jersey, Stan Waldemore. I
didn't let it discourage me. I just kept hustling, plugging away.

Coach Kiffin moved about the practice field with, I thought,
even more intensity than the year before. There was uncertainty
about our defensive team. Gone were Glover, Willie Harper, Monte
Johnson, and Janssen, all fairly high draft choices. Our opening
game against UCLA was to be nationally televised. UCLA ran the
wishbone offense, and it would be hard to stop them. Several
UCLA players who had contributed to our loss against them the
previous year were back, including quarterback Mark Harmon
and runners James McAlister and Kermit Johnson. Most of our
pregame preparation was concentrated on stopping option plays.

My responsibility as defensive tackle started with jamming the
offensive tackle with a strong forearm shiver as he tried to block
the linebacker. The shiver was supposed to knock him off stride
enough to allow the linebacker to get outside cleanly to cover
either the quarterback or help on the pitch man. Then I was
supposed to play off the fullback's block, if there was one, and get
outside to help on the quarterback. Specifically, I had to tackle him
before he pitched the ball or turned upfield to run. Reading and
reacting to the option play was very hard. It took strength, quickness,
and agility. During practice I could usually get outside quick
enough, but my forearm shivers to the offensive tackle still weren't
particularly effective. I'd usually go against either Mark Doak,
270 pounds, or Daryl White, 245, and it was frustrating. I just
wasn't strong enough. Sometimes the quarterback, simulating
Harmon, would run belly plays, handing the ball straight ahead to
the fullback, and all the offensive linemen would fire straight
ahead at us. On that kind of play I'd usually get pushed back.

But occasionally they'd pass and I'd be happy because I could
maneuver past Doak, who wasn't as quick. The ease with which I

beat him on passes and the ease with which he knocked me around on belly plays made Kiffin suspicious. He accused us of collaboration. During one film session, he yelled, "What the hell, Mills, do you and Doak have some kind of buddy system going?" Kiffin was hot. "How come he blows you out on one play, and you beat him on a pass rush on another?" he snapped. I tried to tell him that things were on the square, but I don't think he believed me. In any case I ignored his accusations and concentrated on the occasional praise I received. It kept me going.

Fall practice ended and classes started. On Monday, August 27, 1973, I headed over to the locker room to see the final depth chart that was posted. The last few practices, I had worked with the second team, but that didn't mean a whole lot because people were constantly being shifted around. The final depth chart was the one that would be basis of the traveling squad. I looked up at the list and let out a yell. "Yahoo!" There it was: George Mills, second team, backup to John Dutton. I would wear a gold mesh pullover shirt for practice. I was so proud of myself. I had started fall camp in a white shirt, a fourth-teamer, and had moved up to second team. I had accomplished my goal. Maybe, I thought, someday I'd wear a black shirt like Dutton.

Second team had many advantages. For one, I'd now get a regular number instead of old No. 99. I was given No. 75, which was worn by All-American and Outland Trophy winner Larry Jacobson two years before. I'd get a locker in the new locker room instead of Schulte Field House. I'd travel to away games and most likely earn a letter. I'd also get six free tickets to home games. But, unexpectedly, I found the most important reward was respect from my peers. I remember going over to Dave Redding's room after practice that day, and a bunch of players from my class were there. Redding came up to me and said, "Congratulations, George Mills, for earning the gold shirt." I was surprised. My battle to earn the gold shirt had been a private one. The rewards I contemplated were also private. But I had never expected admiration from my teammates. I didn't think anyone else thought it was a big deal.

For the next few days, I was in a dream world. The magnitude of my accomplishment began to set in. If John Dutton, All-American, were injured, I would take his place. If we were beating a team badly, I would play. It was hard to comprehend. I was truly a part of the team. Only a handful of players from my freshman class were on the top two units. I felt lucky. Each day after practice, I sojourned my way across campus to the training table. Sometimes I'd go to my favorite spot across from the 501 Building, watch the sun set, and think; other times I'd stop by the fountain at the Union. Every day after each practice, I thought about how lucky I was. I also wondered how I'd respond once I got into a game.

Coach Kiffin and I were now on somewhat better terms. He still yelled at me when I goofed up and he kept saying that I had to play the run tougher, but more often than not he spoke to me in a more congenial tone. Once, I remember, the defensive linemen were in a group when he said jokingly to the other guys, "Old Mills is probably going to crap his pants when he gets out there before those 76,000 people. How about it Millsy? You won't have to worry about getting up for the game. Your old heart'll be a pumpin' and you'll be ready."

Coach Osborne seemed very relaxed the week before the game. After each practice he'd call us to the middle of the field for a short team meeting. He was extremely businesslike. He'd tell us how he felt the practice went. He told us that we would play a game like we practiced and that if we practiced hard and didn't make mental mistakes, then the same usually would be true during the game. "You play like you practice," he said. Then he reminded us about NCAA rules regarding the selling of game tickets. He talked about the importance of going to class and keeping our grades up. He warned us against the use of drugs and marijuana. And in the end, he reminded us what was at stake. Sometimes he'd crack a joke, and we'd all laughed, but the meeting was a neat scene, almost solemn. It was the coming together of 120 athletes around a lone figure, a tall, lean, red-headed man clad in sweat clothes and a ball cap, in an empty, shadow-covered stadium. Most of us listened intently to his words, except a few guys on the fringe of the huddle would be joking or struggling to unsnap shoulder pads. The scene was repeated after every practice. The man cared. We cared. For a brief moment, we were a family.

Then came the wind sprints. We lined up at the 40 yard line, backs first, then ends and linemen. The whistle blew, and I'd labor the forty yards to the goal line. Pumping elbows and kicking heels, we sprinted painfully toward Kiffin, who was facing us. "All right," he'd yell. "It's the fourth quarter. Let's suck it up." The whistle would blow once more and Kiffin would backpedal as we ran past him, cheering us on to hustle, to go hard, and to pretend it was the fourth quarter. Other position coaches would offer words of encouragement to their players. With the conclusion of the tenth forty-yard sprint, the human motors stopped, many with their upper torsos collapsed forward, hands on knees, gasping for air. Others walked slowly, eyes squinting in pain, hands folded behind their heads, sucking hard at the precious oxygen. The thoroughbreds, the running backs or ends, were tired and gasping, but amazingly they recovered very quickly. They would line up for extra pass-catching drills.

Then Coach Kiffin would call the first and second defensive units over to the southwest corner of the stadium for some extra work, what we called Alpines. "Now, we're gonna have the best damn defense in the country this year, and we're gonna pay the price," he said. While some of the guys were still peeling off shoulder pads, others were already ascending to the top. I scrambled to follow the man in front of me, pumping my arms and legs in pistonlike fashion all the way to the top of the stadium. Kiffin followed us, doing his slow-motion version of the drill. We had a brief rest going down, and then we climbed back up. Three times.

When it was over, student managers handed us each a cold can of Pepsi from a cooler. Sometimes, impatient players would plunge a hand into the cooler and come up with one can, sometimes two. Those who dared to take two cans would get yelled at by the trainers and student managers. I'd take my reward and make the short trip under the stadium through the tunnel that led to the locker room. The carpet was red, the walls white, and at the end of the tunnel was a bench with tape-cutting instruments. There I'd take off my shoes and frantically try to slice the tape off my fingers and ankles. I kept dislocating the little finger on my right hand. To protect it, I always taped it to the finger next to it. I pulled down a pair of scissors that hung on the wall. When they were sharp, the tape came off easily, but when they were dull, removing the tape was a major project. With all of the players vying for the same scissors or slicers, it got congested. Within a few minutes the place was littered with piles of sweat-soaked tape and tape wrap. There were also canisters of ice water, which guys would hold up and chug. The slightly salty taste discouraged me from drinking any. Getting through the logjam in the tunnel was always an experience.

The new locker room was fantastic. The lockers and carpet were bright red, and the lockers were huge. I had plenty of room for all my equipment, clothes, and books. The room was spacious, with a half-dozen or so bays, each lined by lockers. The area in the middle of the room was wide open. We were lumped together in bays according to position. I was with all the defensive linemen at the far end near the exit. Outside the locker room was a long corridor. To the right was the equipment room, manned by Gib Babcock. Beyond that was an elevator that serviced the athletic offices upstairs. At the far end was the state-of-the-art training room, with all its fancy equipment. There were ultrasound machines, an enclosed whirlpool room with several tubs, several taping and therapy tables, and an office for George Sullivan and Paul Schneider. There was even a sauna. The last room at the end of the hall was for weight lifting. The old field house had free weights and was still the main lifting place, but this room had weight machines and two benches that were designed for maintenance work. After practice, a couple of times a week, we were supposed to do a specific number of lifts for each muscle group so that we wouldn't lose any strength during the season. It was Boyd Epley's doing. He had now become an assistant. He was the strength coach. Most of the guys didn't like the idea of having to lift weights after a two-hour practice. The workout only lasted ten or fifteen minutes, but I hated it. Sometimes I'd skip it or just not lift very hard. Bad habits are hard to break.

I'd take my time showering and dressing while others hurried to get to the training table. The stragglers usually did a lot of joking around. Before leaving, I'd always stop by the medical room to use some alcohol to clean my face. The area where the helmet rubbed my forehead and cheeks broke out in pimples, and the constant sweating and rubbing irritated my skin. There'd be three or four guys doing the same thing, taking a towel, squirting a little alcohol on it, and rubbing their faces. Some guys would have the student trainer do it to their backs. I really enjoyed George and Paul, so I joked around with them for a while, and then I'd make my way up the elevator and out the front door of the offices. Each time I'd pan the lobby and glance over at the big trophy cases that housed the bowl awards.

That week's Monday, Tuesday, and Wednesday practices were hard. On Thursday we practiced with sweat clothes and helmets. Thursday and Friday practices before the games, we basically went over our assignments. The Friday practice was really short, forty-five minutes at most, and we'd just go over the entire kicking game. It reminded me of high school, where the days before our games were also easy. The spirit was light, with lots of joking and kidding around.

On Friday evening at training table, we had a team meal: porterhouse steaks that covered the plates, with baked potatoes and sour cream, salad, green beans, and dessert. The steaks dwarfed those we ate on Mondays and Thursdays and were much tastier. I felt like a gladiator going to do battle, and the meal was befitting.

That night, players from the top units attended a movie. My roomies dropped me off in front of the theater. I proudly walked up to the entrance wearing my maroon blazer. All of the traveling-squad members were issued the maroon blazers and were supposed to wear them. Since I rarely wore anything but Levi's and T-shirts, I had to go out and buy a pair of dress slacks and what I thought was a neat shirt. I bought a silky thing with maroon-and-white paisley designs, a large, open collar, and a big, black elastic waistband. My flared slacks were tan. I really felt cool. Before going to the movie, I stood on the corner so that I could be noticed. I was the first player to arrive. As the other guys arrived, we just stood around talking and watching all the daters go into the theater. Then Coach Kiffin rounded us up, and we went in.

After the movie we exited to a waiting bus that took us to Kellogg Center on East Campus, where the top two units spent Friday nights before home games. I took the time on the bus to check out what everyone else was wearing. This was my first overnight with the team, and I didn't want to look out of place. Many of the guys wore shirts that were similar to mine, so I felt OK.

At Kellogg Center we were given a room number and a key. My roommate was John Dutton. Before attending a meeting with our position coaches, we were to stop by a table set up by the trainers to get a hoagie sandwich, an apple, and a bag of potato chips. It was a kind of midnight snack. We were only supposed to grab one sandwich, but I stuffed one in each inside pocket of my blazer, plus an extra bag of potato chips. I also got a red sleeping pill, then went to the meeting with Kiffin.

There I was with John Dutton, John Bell, Ron Pruitt, Willie Thornton, and John Lee, the big boys. Except for Bell and Dutton, all were either redshirts or true sophomores. Kiffin came in. He seemed happy and eager. He made a couple of jokes, and then it was like school as he quizzed us on our assignments.

In Kiffin's system, defensive tackles had to remember a few basic assignments. On pass plays, we either have containment or take an inside pass rush, which meant charging to the inside of the tackle's shoulder. On running plays, we had to read and react to each particular block and especially never get hooked, that is, never let the offensive tackle wall us off to his inside. Then we had two basic slants that we had to remember. On an Okie Fire, we slanted to the offense's power (the strong side of the formation), and on a Bingo Fire, we slanted away from the offense's power (the weak side). In each case the maneuver was designed to get someone to the hole the coaches believed the ball carrier was going to hit. Before the game, the coaches created a chart, outlining the play tendencies of the opposing team from viewing its past game films. For example, say it's second down and the offense needs three yards for a first down. Our coaches have anticipated that, based on past tendencies, the play to be called will be an inside run to the other team's weak side. The defensive captain gets a signal from the coach on the sideline and calls "Okie" in the defensive huddle. At the line of the scrimmage, the linebacker notes that the split end and slotback line up on the offense's left side, so the offense becomes strong left. The linebacker yells "Right" to alert everyone. Since we're reacting to their alignment, we shift our strength to our right. The defensive backs and linebackers adjust accordingly. For the defensive line, this means that our right defensive tackle (me), reads the head and our left defensive tackle slants hard to the inside to occupy the block of the offensive tackle and guard on that side. The weak-side linebacker in our 5-2 alignment then scrapes off the butt of the slanting tackle and fills the hole. All this, of course, is designed to confuse the offensive linemen. Supposedly, we'd then have an unblocked linebacker ready to make the tackle.

"Thornton," Kiffin would say, "what do you do in a Bingo?"

Willie made the proper response. I was panicking. I knew my assignment but was always nervous when Kiffin questioned. I'd hesitate or freeze up as blood rushed to my head. Then he said, "Mills, what would you do in an Okie and it's strong left?" I tried not to sound nervous and said, "Slant." Kiffin fired, "What if the tackle shows dropback pass?" "I'd come out of the slant and take an inside pass rush." I answered correctly again, and around the room he went. The questions lasted only ten minutes. Once he was satisfied we knew our assignments, Kiffin began to reassure the younger players that the nervousness would leave quickly once the game began.

After the meeting, I headed for my room with Big John. Because of his enormous size, six-seven and 265 pounds, because he was a senior co-captain, and also because I was his understudy, I couldn't help but think of him as a big brother. John had been nice to me. He took over the role of Glover and Janssen as he tried to teach me the ropes. Often during practices he would say something helpful to me. That night we talked about a number of different subjects, including the usual football, coaches, and girls. He told me about the floods in his native Rapid City, South Dakota, where several people had died. As the season went on, I got to know John fairly well. We didn't run around together, but we became good friends.

One bad thing about spending the night in Kellogg Center was that the beds were about six feet long and I was six-four. Sleeping in a strange bed was hard for me. That night, in spite of the sleeping pill, I didn't sleep well. I could hear the outside noises: squealing, horns blowing, engines roaring, and occasional loud screams. It was Friday night, and people were partying. I wanted to be a part of it. I wondered what all my friends were doing.

After a wake-up phone call, we headed for the lobby to wait for the pregame breakfast to begin. Some guys watched cartoons, others read the sports page or played cards, and a few just stayed in bed waiting until the last minute to get up. We filed into the cafeteria for a light meal: a roll, a piece of ham, and half a peach.

Next came a team meeting with Coach Osborne. I was impressed with his authoritative style as he meticulously covered each aspect of the game—offense, defense, the kicking game—and reminded us of our responsibilities and general assignments. He cautioned us about mental mistakes, penalties, and fumbles and how they could kill drives and eventually beat us. Members of the specialty teams were read off. I was on the kickoff team. He reminded us of our goals: win every game, win the Big Eight championship, and go to a major bowl. Then he closed the meeting with a speech that he would repeat over and over for the balance of my career. With unblinking calm, he said: "Don't worry about the other team. All we want you to do is go out and give 100 percent. That's all we can ask. If we practice hard and play hard and don't make mistakes, then if we're the better team, in most cases, we'll win. Just go out there and play hard and do the best you can do."

With that, we piled into buses for the short ride to the stadium. All along the way I saw red-and-white-attired fans making their way to the stadium, which by kickoff would be the third-largest city in the state. Fall Saturdays in Nebraska are equivalent to national holidays. Everyone is focused on the football team, which is claimed as its own by the entire state. The support is frenzied and raucous, and it's the same from Ogallala to Omaha. Wherever you are, whether it be at a restaurant, in a department store, or just visiting a friend who is working on his car in the driveway, the radio volume will be up and the game will be turned on. Weddings are scheduled around games so that the ceremonies are certain to be over by the 1:30 P.M. kickoff, with the reception beginning after the game. The state also turns red in its support, with people wearing red T-shirts, sweatshirts, hats, pants, and even underwear, and that's true for the people who don't even go to the games. Banners, flags, and signs of support are everywhere. Game tickets are prized possessions, enough so that it's not uncommon for people to battle over them in divorce court. Even after their owners die, season tickets are rarely turned back to the university; they are bequeathed to a specific heir. Coverage of the games, players, and coaches dominates local newspapers and TV stations. Players' names are more recognizable than those of politicians, especially with the young kids. They would know the name of the Nebraska quarterback long before they'd know the name of their mayor or governor. Former Huskers are never forgotten. Two reasons for all the support are that there is no other competing Division I university or professional team in the state and everybody loves a winner, which is what Nebraska teams have been since the arrival of Bob Devaney in 1962. When you consider the fact that merchants sell Big Red toilet paper and toilet seats that play "There Is No Place Like Nebraska" and that fifteen thousand fans consistently show up for away games against teams like Kansas and Kansas State or as far away as Hawaii, it's easy to say there are probably no other fans in the country who support their team like Nebraskans do.

We entered the stadium through the west service entrance. There was a small crowd of fans gathered there, and kids were trying to talk their way past the guards as we walked in. Some begged us to get them in, while others shook hands with us or patted us on the back as we passed the caged gate. The pillared underside of the stadium was dark and cool. Concessionaires were busy getting ready for the arrival of a city of hungry and thirsty people.

Once we were inside the red-and-white locker room, the stereo music was turned up. In a personalized ritual, each player began to dress in his game uniform. I undressed and hurried to the training room to be taped by Schnitzy, who on game days wore only a white T-shirt tucked into white underwear, thin black nylon socks held up by supporters, and black wingtips. On this day he was in rare form, cussing and cracking jokes nonstop. "Get your ass up here, we ain't got all day," he barked at an offensive lineman. Beads of sweat were already forming on his bald pate. Schnitzy was an institution at Nebraska, and he was performing his game-day ritual. We all loved him. While waiting, I prepared my ankles by placing square pieces of gauze smeared with a lubricant on the bridges and heels of my feet and then stuffed a handful of gum sticks into my mouth. "Make it tight, Schnitzy," I said, chomping away. When he had finished, I hopped down from the table and he said as I walked away, "Mills, don't shit your pants out there today." Still laughing, I began putting my pads in my game pants, knee pads first and then the thicker thigh pads. I strung my cloth belt through the hip pads and into the tight slits of the pants. Game pants fit extremely tight. The material was elastic, but there was little give as I shimmied into them. They made me feel like I was wearing another layer of skin one size too small.

Next I pulled my game socks up to my calf. I took particular care in lacing my shoes, tightening them up after each lace. My massive shoulder pads slid on easily. I locked the elastic underarm straps into place on the fiberglass chest piece, tightened and tied the strings up the front. I needed help to pull the tight red jersey over my shoulder pads. I tucked in my shirt, tied the strings, and secured the belt on the front of my white pants. In the restroom I examined myself in the mirror. I liked seeing myself all suited up.

Kiffin came in and huddled the defensive players together for a few words as specialty players were called out to the field. While we waited, I had one of the student trainers tape my end two fingers together on my right hand. Ten minutes later, I was out on the field and lined up for calisthenics. We stretched first, then performed a series of quick drills and ended by spelling out *Nebraska* to a set of jumping jacks. I always felt pride when we did that. "Nebraska! Nebraska!" we roared, and then the 110 or so of us broke away into every direction, joining our position coaches for our pregame workout.

The workout consisted of the same drills we did in practice, except they were shorter and much more intense. When it came time for the form-tackling drill, Coach Kiffin yelled, "OK! We start right now! Let's see some hitting! Face in the numbers and wrap up the arms!" And we then took turns form tackling each other. The difference between form tackling and real tackling is that in form tackling you don't take the man to the ground. Everyone's adrenaline was flowing, and the initial hits were as hard as live ones. Hitting someone face first flush in the numbers always reminded me of running into a wall, but it made me feel good when Kiffin said, "Good hit." The loud cracks and pops let the people in the seats above us know that a game was about to be played. When we finished, we merged with the rest of the team and headed back to the locker room.

The press and public may have wondered about Coach Osborne's competency, but we didn't. Nothing had changed about the way we practiced or prepared for a game, except we were in better shape than the previous year. We had practiced hard and were well prepared mentally and physically. I had the utmost confidence in Coach Osborne. What we didn't know was how good UCLA was. They still had Mark Harmon, Kermit Johnson, and James McAlister. We didn't have Johnny ("The Jet") Rodgers, Rich Glover, or Willie Harper, but we had Dutton and Daryl White, who were our new stars, and they gave me confidence. They were hard-nosed ball players, and I think they gave the other players confidence too. Just before the game, the coaches prepped us one more time as we gathered around in the locker room. Players quietly fidgeted to get their pants and shoulder pads in place. The coaches then left the room and the captains were allowed to speak. Dutton spoke first. He was typical John, brash and bold. He was always outspoken, so we weren't surprised by anything he said. But Daryl, who was usually real quiet, took his turn and spoke in an uncharacteristic fashion. He was emotionally charged, which fired us up even more. His last words were on the order of "Let's just go out and kick their ass." We all cheered. The coaches came back into the room. Coach Osborne gave us a moment of prayer. We didn't give him a chance to talk again; we were out the door. Like a conquering horde, we ran out the tunnel. Confident as I passed through the red doors leading out the tunnel, I reached up and tapped the old horseshoe that was attached to the wall. It was a tradition that went all the way back to the mid-1940s. As we made our way through the rope-enclosed walkways to the southwest corner of the stadium, fans cheered and stuck their hands out to touch us. I was up near the front. We waited for Coach Osborne to lead us out, then I floated toward the field. The goose bumps rushed up my back. The adrenalin release was enormous. The band played "Hail Varsity" as seventy-six thousand red-clad fans, on an overcast day, cheered. Then the crowd chanted, "Go Big Red! Go Big Red!" Once we reached our sideline, we piled on one another in a human circle. This book doesn't do justice to the excitement; you would have to be there. Players at Michigan or Oklahoma or Alabama would know.

Since I was on the kickoff team and a backup, I could be called into the game at any time, so I stood on the sideline watching the game intently. I was no longer a fan. Now I was a player.

That September 8, 1973, a rout took place. Steve Runty, filling in for an injured David Humm, handled the team superbly. Duck, as he was called, completed nine of eleven passes for 105 yards and scored a touchdown on a 1-yard sneak, which signaled the release of thousands of red and white balloons by fans. He wasn't supposed to be a very good passer, but he showed people what had happened many times before in Memorial Stadium. Put a Big Red uniform on a homegrown kid, put him out in front of seventy-six thousand screaming fans, and he'll get the job done. Randy Borg, another homegrown, returned a punt 77 yards in the first quarter to give us a 14-0 lead. But it was Tony Davis who epitomized our effort. In typical blue-collar fashion, he slammed his way for 147 yards rushing in twenty-four carries. After a 43-yard scoring burst in which he broke several tackles, he ran to the back of the end zone and punched the fence. He was jumping and hollering. It was great. His enthusiasm was what our team was all about that day. Our defense also played inspired ball. Dutton was the game's outstanding defensive player. Bell showed what he could do. Our two linebackers, Bob Nelson and Tom Ruud, played with poise and intensity.

As the game progressed, I watched sophomore defensive tackle Ron Pruitt and defensive end Bob Martin. I was amazed and a little jealous at how well they performed. But those weren't strong emotions. I was more concerned about winning. Aside from several kickoffs, my turn to play came in the fourth quarter. The jog out onto the field was scary. This was it. I got into place in the defensive huddle and waited for the defense to be called. There was very little talking except for a few "Let's go's" and "Let's keep hustling." UCLA broke huddle. I sized up the huge six-five, 260-pound tackle who jogged toward me. UCLA was a really big team, bigger than we were. I lined up on his outside shoulder and the action started. Everything happened quickly. In an instant, gold-and-blue bodies were firing out hard and low in every direction, accompanied by crashing pads and grunts. Just as fast as it started, it was over. My man down-blocked and I jammed him; the play went the other way. He didn't play as menacingly as he looked. In fact, I thought he was kind of slow and mushy compared to the guys I went against in practice. I was impressed at how business-like we were and surprised how quickly everything happened. The pace seemed much quicker than our practices. All decisions and reactions were split-second ones. The crowd noise I heard on the sideline seemed muted on the field. I heard only the linebacker calling the defense, the brutish sounds of colliding bodies, and the refs blowing their whistles. On the sideline, Kiffin asked me questions about UCLA's blocking schemes. I was so hyped up that I couldn't answer him. Everything was like a blur on the field. The short time I played seemed longer than it actually was. When it was over, I had made one tackle and been in on an assist. I had also lost a contact lens, which the ref briefly stopped play to look for. It reminded me of the schoolyard when someone's glasses fell off and we'd all stop playing, but this was in front of the nation on television.

The final score was Nebraska 40, UCLA 13. As I wandered around shaking hands, I thought to myself that I had done all right. The UCLA players were nice guys. It was weird that a minute before we had been enemies attacking each other at full force and now we were shaking hands like old friends.

As I jogged into the locker room and began to strip off my combat gear, I felt a letdown. I had been so emotionally charged that everything after the game was anticlimactic. Coach Osborne came in and we all gathered for another moment of prayer. He congratulated us, and it became a winners' locker room, with smiles, reporters, laughter, and music. There were people everywhere. Position coaches went around shaking hands, congratulating everyone. Kiffin came around to all of the defensive linemen. Guys like Tony Davis and Steve Runty sat half-naked and gave interviews. I didn't know what to do. I sat there and took it all in for a few minutes, then dodged the piles of tape and equipment and showered. When I left, fans, families, reporters, and players were still savoring the victory.

I was feeling pretty good about myself and the team. After the game I went out with my roommate, Donny. Donny was good for me to be with after a game because he'd never carp. Instead, he'd be complimentary and say things like "You guys looked good." I'd say, "Did you see that good play I made?" He'd say, "Yeah, it was a good play." "Did you see my bad play?" And he'd say, "I missed that one." He'd just listen and be a friend. He'd always have a party for us to go to. That night at the party everyone was talking about the game. I felt special and important, even a little cocky. I was also preoccupied. Every moment I wasn't involved in a conversation, my mind would drift back to the game. I'd play each play over and over, evaluating as I thought Kiffin would. Some plays were hazy, some I remembered distinctly. At first I thought mostly about the one tackle and assist I'd had. Eventually I went over all my plays, kickoffs included. The bad plays brought a rush of anxiety, for I knew they'd bring criticism from Kiffin. When I tried to sleep that night, I tossed and turned in bed, still thinking.

Sundays during the season were always reserved for treatment of injuries, a little running, and a film session. All injured players reported to the field house early in the morning for treatment. Later in the day, the traveling-squad players reported for some light running. Before we started, we'd all goof around throwing the football. All the defensive linemen would take turns going out for passes. Just as when I was a little kid, everyone wanted a turn at being the quarterback. We'd stretch out and run a few laps, then run ten forty-yard dashes. The first few dashes were at half-speed, and gradually we increased our effort until we ran the last few at full speed. Then we'd head inside to watch the films of the kicking game. The entire kicking game of punt returns, punts, kickoffs, and kick returns would be strung together on one reel. All the players sat in the large auditorium of the new locker room. The coaches responsible for those particular areas of kicking would make comments about the overall effort of the team. During the showing of the film, a position coach would comment on good or bad plays and effort. On Randy Borg's punt return, John Dutton had made a nice block. Kiffin told everyone to watch Dutton as he showed it over and over. "Nice block, Dutton," he exclaimed. Anytime anyone made an unusually vicious block or tackle, it would be shown again amid the cheers and jeers.

After the kicking-game film, we'd break up into groups. Each position coach would take his particular group into his office. I couldn't wait to see myself make a tackle on film. I imagined all the praise I was going to get. I sat there watching intently. Kiffin was full of praise for Dutton and Bell. Pruitt too received some compliments, but he had made some sophomore mistakes. Yet Kiffin's voice gave the impression that he was real happy with the job Pruitt had done. When he finally got to the part of the film that I was in, I could hardly stand it. There I was, No. 75, a familiar figure on a black-and-white film of quickly moving bodies. I studied every move I made, just hoping Kiffin would throw a little praise my way. The action seemed different from what I had imagined the night before. It became apparent after his first few remarks that I hadn't played as well as I'd thought. Kiffin's overall evaluation was that I'd had some good plays but more bad plays. He said I needed to work on reading the head better and taking on the blockers tougher. It was disheartening. When he finally turned on the lights, I was glad. I'd had enough of films and football for the day. It was Sunday, so I went to my room to relax.

As a player I was becoming accustomed to being evaluated by Coach Kiffin. He was usually extreme with both praise and criticism. He was always trying to take his players to a higher level of intensity. I was used to being criticized by him, but ever since I had been named to the traveling squad, he seemed to ease up on me. I think he was more interested in getting the first-teamers ready to play, but now it was evaluation time again. Every game I'd play in would be a source for him to critique my performance. Being the nervous sort, I worried about it all the time. After my lackluster performance in the first game, I figured he'd replace me with someone else. He didn't, but he did start monitoring my progress closely again. He really watched the next week at practice. He stood behind me during the read-the-head drills and yelled, "Not good enough, Mills. You gotta deliver more of a blow and stand the blocker up." Every mistake I made was pointed out. It was apparent that he was now going to get the second-teamers ready to play. I used to hate that part of practice because I knew I'd get yelled at. I knew he was only doing his job the only way he knew how. He wanted more out of me, and his method was to yell to get it. He had designed the defenses that had led to two national championships, so why should he change? But I was trying my best. I'd deliver a forearm blow as hard as I could, but the result he wanted wasn't there. Because I was trying my best and couldn't do what he wanted, I began to resent him again. He had the power to make me feel good with praise or make me feel bad with criticism. I feared him yet admired him; he became the central figure in my life. With no game that week, I anxiously escaped home to Omaha.

By now I was used to the celebrity status back home, and I was eagerly anticipating the praise, since I had played on national TV. It was kind of funny, though. Instead of talking to me about my tackle and assist, everyone mentioned how they had stopped the game to find my contact lens. One friend named Subby Consentino said, "Mills, you big ham, you lost it on purpose just so they'd put the camera on you." My cousin Tom Lalley said, "Here's a guy who gets on national TV for losing a contact." It was typical neighborhood raze. Everyone laughed; it was great. After a while, though, they discussed serious topics like "Mills, did them guys hit hard?" or "That guy you were playing against looked huge." The older guys, who were into gambling, wanted to know if we were for real, what Osborne was like, and would there be a letdown for North Carolina State, our next opponent. They'd tell me what the betting line would be and ask if I thought we could win by the point spread. I went along and played the part of an expert and told them what I thought. They ate it up, even though I didn't know much more than they did. I represented inside information to them.

Back on campus I continued with my role as a big-time college football player. I walked around campus a little taller, more confident than I had been the year before. Why not? I was a playing member of the second-rated team in the country. I figured, except for a few inconveniences, I had life on a string. Granted, I dreaded practice and Kiffin's yelling, but the only really hard practices were on Monday, Tuesday, and Wednesday. By Thursday they were relatively easy polish practices, and on Friday we didn't go over anything except the kicking game. I could handle it.

For the most part, football took up the entire afternoon. I'd be at the field house by 1:30 to get taped and left again at 5:30 or 6:00. After a heavy meal at the training table, I usually didn't feel like studying. Most of the time I'd fall asleep for an hour, then try to read. Sometimes I could force myself to study, but most of the time I'd go out with my friends, who had studied earlier in the day. The fear that I'd miss out on something was too great. I just tried to make it to class and take some notes figuring I could catch up on the reading before the test.

One of the benefits of being on the traveling squad was that I'd get six free tickets to all the home games. Lettermen would also get an extra ticket for every year they lettered. Some seniors were getting as many as nine tickets. I sold mine to relatives or friends back home for around thirty dollars a ticket or whatever they'd be willing to pay. They were glad to have the tickets, plus they realized that as a college student I was broke. The fifteen dollars our scholarship allowed for laundry money didn't last long. Heck, I'd eat more than fifteen dollars' worth of snacks during the week. I'd always get hungry at night. At the South Street Palace, we had a refrigerator and our moms would send food down each weekend, but with our appetites, it didn't last long. Consequently, I'd usually go out at night and get a burger. I also liked to socialize downtown with a beer. I went on dates to movies, and I got tired of wearing just a white T-shirt, Levi's, and tennis shoes.

I remember a girl telling me she knew me because "I was the big guy who always had on the white T-shirt." I went out and bought some cowboy shirts and a pair of tan, calf-high boots with the big heels. I also had to pay guys gas money, but usually I hitchhiked. I rode my bike until it got cold (we lived three miles from campus). So despite having my room and board paid for, I always seemed to need some extra money. My mom helped by sending me some once every couple of weeks, but as I said, ten or fifteen dollars didn't last long. Having money from the sale of my tickets made my life more enjoyable.

Despite our No. 2 rating, we had to come from behind twice during the next two games, against a Lou Holtz–coached North Carolina State and Wisconsin. We had shown character as a team coming from behind, but we weren't playing up to our potential. I played on kickoffs and a few goal-line situations. David Humm, Tony Davis, and Frosty Anderson had established themselves as our clutch performers. The youth and inexperience of some of our defensive players were evident, but Coaches Kiffin and Powers kept pushing us, striving for the excellence that they had been used to. Kiffin would say, "We're not there yet, but we're still gonna have a great defense."

The Minnesota game marked a first for me in that it was an away game. I loved to fly, and boarding the plane with the other team members was special. We stayed at the Leamington Hotel in Minneapolis. It was a large building several stories high. We had some free time after we arrived, and that proved to be a downfall for me. While other players were relaxing in their rooms or playing cards, I went to investigate the hotel. Sitting in the lobby, I ran into a college coed who was in town to visit relatives and go to the game. We started talking. I must have been crazy when I asked her if she wanted to drink some beer up in my room. I went down the street to a package liquor store and bought a quart of beer. We sneaked it up to the room. I checked to make sure Dutton was gone, and then we drank the quart hurriedly for fear of being caught. When we finished, I realized how stupid I was. I checked the hallway to make sure it was clear and quickly got her out of the room. When we got to the lobby, we parted, and I was relieved I hadn't been caught.

That night we followed our usual routine of dinner, movie, and meetings. The next morning at breakfast, the team was unusually light. We were a several-touchdown favorite over Minnesota, and I think most guys felt it would be an easy game. As a result, we were in a relaxed mood. I don't know who started it, but someone began to make fun of the breakfast. The toast was soggy and the bacon was cold—nothing serious, but I got in my two cents' worth and made a couple of cracks to get a laugh. After the joking, we were off for a scenic ride to the stadium on a colorful fall day.

Coach Cal Stoll's Gophers came ready to play, at least in the beginning. They had a very stubborn defense. It forced us to go to the air. David Humm was ten of nineteen for 204 yards. Frosty Anderson caught two touchdown passes of 19 and 67 yards. We beat them 48-7. Because of the lopsided score, I got to play the entire fourth quarter. I had some problems, though. Minnesota had a gigantic offensive lineman. I fired out one time to deliver a blow, and I got my bell rung, which dazed me for several plays. Besides that, it was a cool, drizzly day, the kind that numbs your body and intensifies the pain of contact. My heart wasn't in the game at all.

Running back John O'Leary made his debut in the NU limelight in that game. He scored two touchdowns, one of which was a 66-yard punt return. He also took a hit that cracked his jaw, which later had to be wired. I remember how all the reporters swarmed around him after the game. As I stood there stripping my tight red game pants off, I could feel John's enthusiasm and excitement. He beamed and happily answered reporters' questions. There I was in my customary observer's role; I was content to travel and play sparingly. On the plane ride home, I played out my performance and realized I'd be in for a long afternoon during films on Sunday. I couldn't think of one good play during the game.

The film session began like it always did, with Kiffin smoking and talking, running plays over and over when he wanted to make a point. The first unit had played pretty well and the film was entering the fourth quarter. As usual, I was nervous, especially so this time because I knew I hadn't played well. On one particular play I was pursuing the ball carrier. Kiffin felt I wasn't going at full throttle. He showed it once and said, "Mills, see yourself here. You think you're going full speed?" It was a rhetorical question as he showed it again. "Shit, you aren't selling out," and he proceeded to work himself up. He went on how I was letting the team down, that I was loafing. Now I didn't see it that way. I knew I'd played badly, but I certainly didn't feel I was loafing. The basis for his accusation was that on one play I rounded a turn in my pursuit of the ball carrier. His experience told him a man hustling cuts corners sharply when going full speed in pursuit. He was right. It did look like I rounded a turn, but I had been standing on the sidelines for three quarters on a cool, wet day with my ankles and knees taped tight. I stared at him through the dark in disbelief. I felt safe because I was seated behind him. But he sensed my stare or maybe had eyes in the back of his head because he barked, "You don't like that! Well, we don't like you bringing those damn sluts up to your room, and we don't like you complaining about the breakfast. You got that, Mills?" Then he went on showing the film. His tone returned to normal. All the time I boiled and wondered, How did he find out?

When I got outside, a couple of the other players came up to me and said to forget about it. They felt sorry for me because I had just caught the full wrath of Monte Kiffin. All the way home I steamed. I thought about cussing him or even punching him out. I was still angry on Monday. I decided that if given the chance, I'd respond to him. Well, the chance came one sunny day in front of the training table. He and I were both walking in for lunch. He spoke to me: "Hi, Mills." For him, chewing a player out was all a part of the business. I conceded that maybe he was right, maybe I was loafing. I shouldn't have joked about the breakfast or brought a girl into my room. I guess I felt that the punishment of public humiliation didn't fit the crime. So I said to him, "Hey, Coach, can I talk to you?" And we got face to face. I was so nervous that my entire rehearsed speech came out in one long uninterrupted burst. I said something to the effect that it wasn't right to call that girl a slut because it could have been my girlfriend and that as far as my complaining about the breakfast, the other guys were also doing it. I told him why I rounded my pursuit angle but the important thing I told him was that his yelling made me nervous. I said it was hard to concentrate when he was standing right behind me chewing me out. I told him a lot of the times I goofed up was because I got too worked up about trying to please him. I ended it by saying if he didn't think I could do the job, he should get someone else. Well, he listened and said he'd try not to yell so much and that I should try harder. When I went in to eat, I felt drained but relieved. My body was wet with perspiration.

That afternoon at practice was too early to tell whether things were different with him. But as far as I was concerned, I had been given a new lease, and I was determined not to get yelled at again. I hustled like never before.

My personal battle aside, the team faced a real tough task. Despite beating Missouri 62-6 in Lincoln the year before, playing them on the grass of Faurot Field would be difficult. Coach Al Onofrio would have the Missouri Tigers ready. An omen may have come when the freshmen's fifteen-game winning streak ended on Friday with a 24-22 loss to the Missouri freshmen.

From the outset, the game at Missouri was a defensive struggle. I remember standing on the sidelines waiting for David Humm to throw a touchdown pass or Tough Tony to score on some tackle-breaking run. But it was not to be. Instead, we made mistakes. The biggest mistake came late in the game with only a couple of minutes left when we fumbled a punt and Missouri recovered it at our 4 yard line. They scored to take a 13-6 lead. Dave ("The Dealer") Humm, as announcer Lyell Bremser called him, responded with a 13-yard pass to Ritch Bahe and a 22-yarder to Larry Mushinskie. Humm finished the drive with another pass to Bahe for the touchdown. My teammates and I went nuts. Coach Osborne then elected to go for two points and the win instead of the extra point and a tie. I held my breath as The Dealer received the snap. The ball was in the air, and in an instant the play was over—an interception. Missouri fans exploded as I jogged slowly into the locker room. It was quiet. We said our prayer, Coach Osborne spoke a few words, and we showered. Losing a game like that eats at your insides. We were the better team. On any given day, a team can rise to the challenge, and that day Missouri did. In victory our celebrations were short lived because we'd have to look to the next game. Losses are different because they linger, because the pain won't let you forget, and because the game will be scrutinized a little more intensely to see what went wrong—to ensure the fiasco does not happen again.

Coach Osborne experienced his first loss as a coach. By going for the win, he established himself as the consummate competitor; it would separate him from many of his contemporaries. He wasn't a politician playing to the sentiments of fans or the rating polls. He was instead an athlete, a fighter, a guy who never quits, a guy who plays the game to win. In that way he was just like Coach Devaney. But slowly he was finding his way and developing his own distinct style. I sensed greatness from him as a coach.

The next week at practice, I continued hustling and trying and Coach Kiffin was still intense, but there wasn't that explosive friction between us. He did his job, and I tried to do mine. The result of our team's hard work produced a tough 10-9 victory over a Kansas team led by quarterback David Jaynes and running back Delvin Williams. It wasn't a very impressive win, but nonetheless we were rated No. 10 in the AP poll going down to Stillwater to play Oklahoma State.

Playing at Oklahoma State is truly like playing in a pit. The closeness of the fans to our bench was uncomfortable. They were right on top of us, booing, hissing, and cussing. I couldn't believe how crazy their fans were. Some of us, including myself, responded in kind, with hand signals. Unsportsmanlike, I know, but in the heat of the competition, tempers are often lost. Just like the Missouri game, this game came down to a call by Coach Osborne. With two minutes left in the game and the score tied 17-17, Coach decided to go for the touchdown with the ball on the 6-inch line instead of attempting a field goal. The logic was simple. Oklahoma State quarterback Brent Blackman had been moving their team all day and there would still be plenty of time for him to move the length of the field and score. To avoid a possible tie, Tough Tony was given the ball on fourth down. Cleveland Van, their super linebacker, made a great play and stopped him short. End result: tie game. Again a crummy feeling set in that we were better and should have won.

With a lot of bowl officials present, we rebounded and defeated Colorado 28-16 the next week, playing our best all-around game since UCLA. The following week we routed Iowa State 31-7. After the game there was speculation that we'd be headed to Dallas to play Texas in the Cotton Bowl. Bowl games were a reward for a good season. We were rated No. 11 and had a 7-1-1 record. We thought we deserved a bowl. It was so exciting to be a member of the team. Plus, Coach Kiffin had praised me during films. Before the Iowa State game we had been practicing coming out of a slant technique. In a couple of our defenses, the defensive tackle was supposed to slant down toward the center into the area where the quarterback got the ball from the center, but if the play went in the opposite direction of our slant, Coach Kiffin wanted us to change directions, come out of the slant, and work back toward the ball carrier. In the game I slanted, read the play going the opposite way, changed directions, and made the tackle. Kiffin showed the play over and over. He was all smiles to me. In fact, he said to me privately that I just kept improving.

The next week we played at Kansas State at Manhattan. We all knew that if we won, we'd get an invitation to the Cotton Bowl. That was on our minds. Also, an awkward thing happened to me getting off the bus at our hotel. I was one of the last guys off and noticed some Nebraska fans standing around watching us. I was used to that by then because on game day fans would be everywhere. They usually didn't talk to me except to ask where the stars, like Tony Davis, John Dutton, or David Humm, were. Your typical fan is interested only in the stars of the team. As I walked by a middle-aged couple, the woman asked me if I was David Humm. I hesitated, then couldn't resist. "Yes," I said, and smiled. She got all excited and began banging me with questions: "Are you guys going to win? Are you going to Dallas? Are you going to throw a lot today?" I answered her by doing my best Dave Humm impersonation and after a few minutes I said, "Excuse me, I have to go to a meeting." I was six-four and pretty light for a defensive tackle and I had long, dark hair like Dave, so I could see how she'd mistake me for him. I loved it because I now knew what it was like to be addressed by the fans as a star. As I walked away, I had to hold back the chuckles.

The outcome of the Kansas State game was 50-21. We gained 612 yards on offense. I got hurt that game, a strained left knee, while lining up over the offensive guard in a Husker defense. Their center, executing a cross block, fired out and took my knees out from underneath me. The pain was severe as I was helped off the field. One thing about Nebraska, the trainers really cared; George and Paul always looked out for us. I was taken to the locker room for treatment. Fortunately it was only a slight strain and I would be ready to make the trip to Norman the following week.

It was an exciting time. We were going to Dallas to play Texas in the Cotton Bowl. We were rated tenth, we were 4-1-1 in the Big Eight, and we were going to play 5-0 Oklahoma. If we beat them and they lost their last game, we'd win the Big Eight title. Although it was going to be difficult, we did have a chance to win the Big Eight, and that was one of our team goals.

The Friday before the game, we had a short workout at Owen Field in Norman. I felt a part of a great tradition. It was this very field on which I had seen the Game of the Century on TV two years before. It was different from Memorial Stadium. In comparison to the height of Nebraska's stadium, Oklahoma's was kind of flat. Plus, it didn't seat as many people—only about sixty-two thousand.

The entire week prior to the game was one of intensity. It is always intense when Nebraska plays Oklahoma. Despite name calling by some of our players, there was a genuine respect for Oklahoma and also a little competitive fear because they were a great team. They were 8-0-1 at the time, the 7-7 tie coming against Southern California in September. In fact, Kiffin, in an uncharacteristic move, showed us films of their defense. I'm not sure for what reason. In any case, I saw them on film. Kiffin pointed out the Selmon brothers, Lucious, Dewey, and LeRoy, who anchored their defensive line, and Rod Shoate, who backed them up at linebacker. They were dominating. As any defensive coordinator would, I think Kiffin admired them, for they were the basis of a truly great defense.

Coincidentally, that night while we waited to go into the movie theater, the Oklahoma players were coming out and I saw the Selmon brothers up close. I sized them up. They were impressive-looking athletes. Sophomorically, I started making Selmon-brothers jokes, but on Saturday they got the last laugh. The Oklahoma defense completely dominated us. We never crossed the 50 yard line. They beat us 27-0. Not since 1968 had Nebraska been shut out, and then it was at the hands of Oklahoma. As I stood there on the sidelines, I cringed every time they scored, their men's spirit group fired its shotguns, and their band played "Boomer Sooner." Whenever we started moving, they'd intercept a pass—three in all. Quarterback Steve Davis stole the show offensively by scoring three touchdowns while gaining 114 yards on eighteen carries. I finally got into the game in the waning seconds, and I had vengeance in my heart. I tried to smack whoever was over me as hard as I could. I wanted to inflict damage. But he just fired out low, machinelike, waiting for the game clock to signal the end of another day's work. So much for Oklahoma.

11

Cotton Bowl

With the regular season over, I began to concentrate on passing my courses, particularly Spanish, which was a five-credit-hour class. If I flunked it, I would become ineligible for football and would have to make up the hours either next semester or in summer school.

My taking Spanish was a mistake. It was a difficult class for me because there were daily assignments. I was not the type of student who could study every night, and I was concerned that I was going to fail. I took the class only because I was in the College of Arts and Sciences and a foreign language was a requirement. I had enrolled in the College of Business my freshman year, but I soon transferred to Arts and Sciences when I found out that introduction to accounting had daily assignments. I tried it for a while, but I was kidding myself to think that I could come back to the dorm every night after classes and football practice and make entries in a ledger. I was not that disciplined.

My goal was to get a degree in any subject but physical education. I was keenly aware of the dumb-jock stereotype. In fact, more than once someone jokingly asked if I were a PE major. Since the Business College had the kind of classes that called for daily assignments, I consulted with an academic adviser in Arts and Sciences and switched colleges, planning on a history degree. Spanish was a requirement, unfortunately. Realizing how hard it was going to be for me, I took the class pass/fail. This meant I'd either pass or fail but wouldn't receive a grade. I figured I was going to get a *D* otherwise. Even though I wasn't the greatest student, I did want to maintain a respectable grade-point average.

The sad thing was that I'd had two semesters of Spanish in high school. I hadn't learned anything, though, and now I was paying the price. I had a definite linguistic deficiency, but it was too late to worry about that now because it was finals week and I was not ready to pass a comprehensive Spanish exam.

Unbelievably, I'd been through a semester of Spanish and didn't know anything. The only reason I was passing was because the guy I sat next to helped me. He was a big football fan and knew I was a player. Before and after class, he'd always ask me questions about the team. When the teacher asked me a question in class, my friend whispered the answer to me. I didn't ask him to, he just started doing it one day. Whenever we'd take a test, he'd make sure he wrote big and kept his paper where I could see it. Not once did we discuss the fact that we were cheating. It all happened as if it were a normal, everyday occurrence. I disliked going to class because I'd always leave feeling guilty.

I did study for the final, but you can't make up a semester of Spanish in a week. The day of the test I got to class a few minutes late. I entered the room to take my seat and was stunned. Somebody was sitting in the seat next to my friend. The teacher said, "Señor Mills, please come and sit here," pointing to a desk directly in front of her. My legs and stomach felt like I had just gotten off a fast elevator. I picked up a test paper and sat down. I read it over and tried to answer a few questions. It was literally a foreign language to me. Nothing seemed familiar. I began to sweat and feel nauseous. Realizing the futility of my situation, I got up and handed the test to the teacher and told her I was sick. I left the room in a panic.

What happened after that was almost miraculous. I had gone home resigned to the fact that I had flunked and would be taking extra classes and going to summer school. The next day, the teacher left a message at my dorm to call her. When I called her, she wanted to know how I was feeling and said I could retake the test in her office. Immediately I began trying to remember what was on the test. I got all excited and thought I was going to pass, but after a few more hours of studying, I decided that I was still going to flunk. I could remember only a few questions, and cramming for a comprehensive Spanish exam when I hadn't studied all semester was useless. It was official; I was going to flunk Spanish. No big deal. I'd just take it again during summer school. Why worry? I kept telling myself. With that thought I went to her office in a lighthearted mood. I was joking with her and just feeling glad to be getting it over with. She surprised me by asking if I had time to go get her a hamburger before I took the test. "Sure," I said. My mind began to click. Maybe she was going to let me pass, no matter how I did on the test. She certainly was treating me nice; she seemed almost sympathetic. After I returned with her lunch, she escorted me to a little office and handed me a test. She closed the door behind her. I immediately took out my Spanish book and made it an open-book test. An hour later I was done. Even with my book the test was hard. I left with a sneaking suspicion that I'd passed.

I did pass, and to this day I don't know whether that teacher purposely put me in the room alone, knowing I would cheat, or whether she passed me regardless of a failing score. In defense of the teacher, she may not have known that I cheated. I say that because I don't want people getting the idea that it was a routine event for professors to give football players special consideration so they could pass. It may have happened, but it wasn't widespread or institutional. Typically, a football-fan professor, sympathetic to all the time and effort a football player puts into playing, might give that individual more time to turn in an assignment or allow him extra time on a test. If the player didn't have a high-enough grade average to pass but was close and was trying hard, the professor might give him the benefit of the doubt and pass him. The professor may have joked and kidded with the player more than the other students, thereby putting the player at ease, which in turn would make the professor appear more approachable for help in case the player was having a difficult time in the class. On the other hand, there were professors who didn't like football players and resented all the attention the football team received at the expense of the university as a whole. Those professors felt that the football team's notoriety detracted from the true mission of the university, which was education and research. Given the opportunity, those professors never passed up a chance to put ball players in their place. In fact, some went out of their way to do so. I know more than one player who came out of a class red-faced from a tongue lashing by a football-hating professor.

If there was a problem with cheating, it was with the other students. It was not uncommon for football groupies to let athletes copy their notes, write and type papers for them, or let them copy during tests. A certain percentage of the players took advantage of this opportunity. Some players cheated all the time, some cheated part of the time, and some never cheated. Overall, the majority of the players did their own work. If someone was cheating all the time, common sense would tell you that eventually it would catch up with him. Those individuals never made it through school. The players who did graduate had to earn it just like everyone else.

Next on my college agenda was the Cotton Bowl. Unlike the previous year, I knew I was going to make the trip to Dallas, and the thought of another bowl vacation was exciting. We started preparing for the game after finals, which were earlier than in previous years. The workouts were hard, strictly conditioning drills. Apparently some of the older guys, who were accustomed to Coach Devaney's more laid-back approach to bowl-game preparations, were upset with the extra conditioning work. Our captain, John Dutton, was the most outspoken. One day after the workouts, John was sitting by his locker complaining. "You know, I heard Ohio State starts practice for the Rose Bowl about a week or so before the game," he said. "Bowl games are supposed to be a reward, not a punishment. All this conditioning stuff is bullshit." Being the reactionary I was, I said, "Yeah, Dutton, this extra conditioning is a bunch of garbage. We ought to protest. Seriously, let's protest." Many of the players felt the same way, and it was the topic of conversation that week. Disgruntled players let Dutton know how they felt. John wasn't one to let an issue die. After a workout, he called all the players into a circle for a meeting. He expressed his views about the practice schedule. He wanted the coaches to ease up and use the game as a reward instead of punishment. The coaches looked over at us, stunned. Everything was getting way out of control. John aired his views and asked for the support he had gotten all week. With the coaches looking on, no one would speak out against the practices. John said helplessly to those of us circled around him, "Come on, some of you other guys speak up. I'm not the only one who feels this way." I shrank into the back of the crowd. None of us would support him. He stood there alone, humiliated.

The next day, Osborne met with Dutton. For the next three days everyone speculated about John's fate. Would he be kicked off the team? I was absolutely freaking out. If he got kicked off the team, I'd start in the Cotton Bowl against Texas. I was confident, but not that confident. Plus, I felt bad for Dutton because none of us complainers stood up for him during his hour of need. He'd been left alone to face the consequences. I thought he was being a good captain by expressing the concern of his teammates. Coach Osborne met with the seniors on Saturday to get their views and then thought about it over the weekend. On Monday he said Dutton could play in the game but that he'd be stripped of his captain status. I was glad that little episode was over and grateful that Big John hadn't been kicked off the team.

Our practices in Lincoln were hampered by extremely cold weather. It was so cold that we had to conduct most of our practices in Schulte Field House. I kept thinking about how nice Miami had been the year before. Coach Osborne described Dallas to us and told us about the climate. Nevertheless, I had visions of a warm oasis like Miami. Boy, was I shocked when I stepped off the plane in Dallas to be welcomed by a fifty-degree blast of cool air. Other than the temperature, it was just like the Miami welcome, with reporters, cameras, Cotton Bowl officials, and fifteen pretty girls in cowboy hats. They were there to escort us to the Marriott Hotel, where we'd be staying.

Once we were at the Marriott, the girls walked us down a long hallway to a room where we were given white nylon jackets with the Cotton Bowl insignia on the chest. As I walked down the hall, I began talking to one of the escorts. Her name was Cindy. She was a sophomore at SMU, and she was cute. By the time we reached the end of the hallway, I had her name and phone number and a tentative date set up for the next night, which was, according to our schedule, a free one. As usual, we were on a tight schedule. I had to get up to my room to unpack because practice was in two hours. I couldn't wait to tell my roommate, Big John, about my date. He laughed and told me I was a wild man.

As our buses arrived at the Cotton Bowl, I was struck by a sense of history. Nine years earlier, I'd watched Arkansas beat Nebraska

10-7. Now it was my turn. I, George Mills, actually playing in the Cotton Bowl. How ironic, considering that less than nine months ago I had quit the team. I was really caught off guard when Coach Fischer said during the ride, "Well, Mills, I thought we lost you. You've really come around. Keep it up." His compliment signified how different things were for me from last spring. Now it was hard for me to relate to the frame of mind I was in when I quit. I guess I had made up my mind to be a good player and just tried harder. Playing was still a struggle, the hardest thing I ever did, but somehow I managed. In any case, I was glad I hadn't quit.

During practice that day, we focused on contact work. It was our last day of hitting before the game, and everyone was fired up. I was feeling especially cocky because of all the good things that were happening to me: a possible date, playing in the Cotton Bowl, and Coach Fischer's compliment. During a tackling drill with the defensive linemen, I was going all out. We took turns being the ball carrier. Coach Kiffin wanted us to juke—put a fake on the tackler to make the drill more realistic. When it was my turn to be the ball carrier, John Dutton was the tackler. Well, he might have been an All-American, but I knew I was quicker than he was. I wanted to impress Coach Kiffin. As I ran at Dutton, I stuttered my feet and faked right then went left. He missed. "Do it again," Kiffin said as he bent over, putting his hands on his knees. "Concentrate!" I was in the height of my glory. I had faked him out and made him miss. I'll do it again, I thought. I ran at him, stutter-stepped, faked right, faked left, then burst past him to the right. "Dammit, Dutton, do it again!" Kiffin screamed. By now I had come to recognize all of the underlying moods that corresponded with Coach Kiffin's yelling. Sometimes he'd yell because he was in a bad mood, sometimes he'd yell because it was just habit, and sometimes he'd yell pretending to be angry. There was one yell, though, that when you heard it, you just responded to whatever his command was because he was genuinely angry. I unfortunately had heard it a few times, this being one of them. Problem: How do I let Dutton tackle me without appearing to be going less than full speed? I didn't even want to think about what would happen if he missed again. I bolted toward him, stutter-stepped then planted my left foot and ran right, but making sure he wouldn't miss while preparing my body for the ferocious hit I was about to take from an angry six-seven, 260-pound All-American. I felt his helmet rip into my jaw, and then I blacked out. I lay on the ground for a minute and got up. Kiffin asked, "Mills, you OK?" "Yeah, yeah, Coach, I'm OK," I said. "Take your helmet off a minute." My bell had been rung. After practice, Dutton and the other guys asked if I was OK, then they all kidded me about it, saying things like "Hey, Mills, what day is it?" or "Knock, knock, is anyone home in there?" as someone reached to knock on my head.

Dutton was a unique athlete, a true thoroughbred. He was extremely big, strong, and amazingly fast, 4.8 in the forty, for a man his size. He was also a stone animal. When he was on the field, he left his mark by manhandling opposing offensive tackles. One game I watched him literally turn a big offensive tackle in a circle while rushing the passer, and then Dutton threw him helplessly to the ground. With his size and unusually long arm span, he must have appeared wall-like to opposing offenses. In addition to that, he was tough and never got hurt. John ended up being All-Pro and playing fourteen years in the National Football League.

Another guy equally as tough as Dutton was our middle guard, John Bell. Bell wasn't that big, six feet and about 222 pounds, but he was extremely strong and quick. He was also a member of the wrestling team. Bell's great assets were his toughness and his desire to prove he was as good as Rich Glover. That was his motivation. He had an attitude like Tony Davis: he was the best and he wanted to prove it to the world. He was also one of the more interesting guys on the team, definitely a free spirit, a true Californian. John and his wife lived in an apartment that looked like a barn. Once I visited him and was startled to be greeted by two very large Doberman pinschers. From the time I entered until I left, they sat by my feet and watched me. I was nervous and wouldn't move from the couch. Bell laughed and said, "Loosen up man, they won't bite unless I sic them on you." He also had a ten-foot python that he kept in a large aquarium.

Occasionally Bell had parties at his red house-barn. Sometimes he and Jeff Class, who also was a member of the wrestling and football teams, would start punching each other or slap-box. They would do it off and on all night. Then one of them would hit the other one too hard and the punching would escalate until they'd lose control and it became serious. They'd tee off on each other and then wrestle as partygoers looked on. I'd watch and think, Man, these guys are crazy. Whenever I'd see either of them at the training table with bruises or a black eye, I knew what had happened.

Bell and I lockered close to each other and became friends. We'd always joke around at practice. He'd make fun of me, and I'd make fun of him. One day he came to practice after eating something with onions or garlic in it and his breath was strong. I let him know about it. Whenever I had a chance during practice, I'd call him names like Dog Breath, Onion Mouth, and Garbage Can. I'd say things like "Hey, Bill, you ever hear of a thing called mouthwash?" and "Boy you have got to brush tonight." He laughed and countered with his own jokes. I kept it up in the locker room after practice. I had just cracked a good one and was laughing when all of a sudden I saw Bell throw down his shoulder pads, saying, "Mills, I've had enough." He started walking toward me with a crazy look in his eye. I'm in trouble now, I thought. I wanted to calm him down, but before I could get two words out of my mouth he grabbed me and put an awesome takedown move on me. We clenched and I struggled to get free. Each time I'd move or jerk away, he'd maneuver to a better position. Within a minute he had me tied up in knots. He had me face down with my arms locked behind me, bouncing my face off the floor. He was killing me. I screamed for him to let up. Despite the pain I was in, I was laughing. He finally let me go, and after that I didn't joke with him as much.

Because they were both star senior linemen, I compared myself with Dutton and Bell. Dutton was great because he had it all: size, strength, intelligence. But it was his dominating size and toughness that separated him from the rest of the college players. Bell didn't have the physical attributes that Dutton had, but he made up for it with an ardent desire to be the best. Dutton had great size. Bell had great desire. I asked myself what I had that was great and decided that I'd have to get bigger, stronger, tougher, and faster, plus, I'd have to keep improving on my attitude and desire. Oh well, I was still only second team. I'd work on it in the spring. I had a bowl game to enjoy.

That night we attended a party at a dude ranch. There was an ocean of Texas barbecue, ribs and steak, people everywhere, and a rock band, all under the stars. It was a great party, but it was the last evening event I'd attend with the team. From the next night on, I went on dates with Cindy. She showed me the town. We went to some SMU hangouts. We went to her parents' home for dinner one night. I took her out to eat at a fancy restaurant, using my bowl money. Along the way, I got to meet some of her friends and got an inside view of collegiate life in Dallas.

During all of our dates, I felt slightly intimidated because Cindy was from a well-to-do family. She was in a sorority and generally much more sophisticated than I. She drank Scotch and water; I drank beer. She wore nice dress clothes; I wore Levi's and flannel shirts. There was definitely a class distinction. I remember the night I took her out to eat. We were getting up to leave, and I left what I felt to be a generous tip. She said nonchalantly, "Leave him some more." I got hot. She insulted my tip. We argued a little, and then she cried and we made up.

On another night she took me to a classy little pub where all the SMU people hung out. She introduced me to Doug English, the star defensive tackle for Texas. Apparently he was dating one of her friends. He was six-five, about 250 pounds, and really well dressed. I couldn't wait to tell my teammates I had seen one of the Longhorns.

Although I was having fun, Dallas was nowhere near as much fun as Miami. Miami had the beach and sun. Plus, Coach Devaney had scheduled lots of interesting things for us to do. The itinerary for Dallas was limited and controlled. It reflected the personality of Coach Osborne. He had said the year before that things would be different next year at the bowl game, and they were. If Miami was like a wild party, Dallas was like a luncheon.

As far as bowl games go, ours was a dull matchup. Texas was rated eighth and we were ranked twelfth. Both of us had been demoralized by Oklahoma, which couldn't play in any bowl game because of its NCAA probation for rules violations. The press was trying to create interest in our game, so there were lots of human-interest stories about players. I was interviewed one evening by *Omaha World-Herald* sports columnist Conde Sargent. I never thought he'd put the interview in the paper, but he did. Tuesday, January 1, 1974, my first college football interview appeared in the New Year's Day paper as follows:

Pressure

Nebraska usually seems totally prepared for bowl encounters. The starters know their assignments inside and out.

I had always felt the first stringers have an advantage in that they are out there every minute and involved in the game.

Conversely, I've wondered how you'd like to be Rich Sanger and see your first action punting out of the end zone.

How would you like to be Willie Thornton, playing sometimes only when the foe is punting and when a good rush might turn things around for your team?

How would you like to be George Mills, the sophomore defensive tackle, and play only as the sixth man in the line when N.U. shifts to a goal-line defense?

Black Shirt Dreams

Meet Mr. Mills, a 6-5, 220 pounder out of Omaha Ryan High.

The situation is generally desperate when he's in a game. The defense is either backed up inside the 10-yard line or the foe is third down and two yards or closer to a first down. "The only thing I worry about coming in fresh off the bench is that I might jump too soon and be offsides," said Mills.

"It's always going to be short yardage or inside the ten when I come in," said Mills, the backup man for All-America John Dutton in N.U.'s depth charts.

Mills is the lightest interior lineman, a couple pounds short of middle guard John Bell's weight.

"Sure, I'd like to put on weight. I have gained ten pounds since spring practice. But speed has as much to do with playing at Nebraska as size."

Is there any assignment Mills would rather have than being a goal-line defensive specialist? "Yes," he said quickly, "I'd give it up for a black shirt." N.U.'s defensive starters wear black shirts in practice.

Watch for George Mills today. He's No. 75. You'll likely see him almost any time Texas' wishbone gets to third down and two.

The day of the game was cold and overcast, with intermittent drizzle. I stood nearly frozen on the sideline for the first half and watched a defensive struggle. The score was 3-3 at halftime. In the third quarter, we put thirteen points on the board. At that point it was obvious that we'd win. Our defense had kept their star fullback,

Roosevelt Leaks, who was hampered by a leg injury, in check. Coach Kiffin began to substitute. I trotted into the game toward the end of the third quarter with the score 16-3.

Knowing I was on national TV, I warmed up in a hurry. Trying to come from behind, Texas began passing. For a wishbone team, that means doom. The guy I was playing over wasn't a very good pass blocker. He set up on one play to do it and I was on him before he could react. I slipped by him, reached out and grabbed quarterback Marty Akins's jersey, and pulled him down as he tried in vain to pass. A sack. Two plays later, I beat my man again and, along with a couple of other players, sacked the quarterback. On the sideline I grimaced in pain. Despite taping my little finger, I had dislocated it again. It slipped back into place, but it hurt.

The final score was 19-3. Tony Davis was voted the game's outstanding offensive player. He rushed for 106 yards and scored a touchdown. Quarterback Steve Runty came off the bench in the second half to relieve Dave Humm and did a good job leading the team. Middle guard John Bell played an outstanding game on defense. Everyone contributed to the win, including me. It was only fitting that my cousin Tom Lalley was at the game. It was he, after all, who had coaxed, encouraged, and even at times belittled me into playing football when I was little.

I spent my last night in Dallas at Cindy's parents' home. We watched the other bowl games and ate dinner. They treated me like a celebrity. It was strange watching the other bowl games on TV. Bowl games and players were always something very special to me when I was growing up. They were larger than life, almost like fantasies. My reality of playing in a bowl game was not as great as dreaming about it when I was little. I wouldn't let anyone know I felt that way, though. I kept playing my part.

Back in Lincoln, there was a foot of snow on the ground. My cousin Tim picked me up at the airport. I was shocked when he told me that the play in which I sacked quarterback Marty Akins was shown on instant replay. He also told me that the CBS announcer Lindsey Nelson said some positive things about my performance. Unbelievable. If I was a small celebrity before, I was now a superstar. Everywhere I went, people asked me about the game and the quarterback sack. But the biggest surprise came shortly after second semester started. I was in the coaches' office picking up my room allowance. I was walking out and Coach Warren Powers, the secondary coach, spotted me. He said, "Nice game, Mills. You got two quarterback sacks." Then he chatted with me a moment and said I'd start out No. 1 at right defensive tackle in spring ball. There was an explosion of emotion in me; at once I was proud, excited, and nervous. Whether I was ready or not, I would wear a black shirt come spring.

12

Pain and Injury

The first thing I did when I returned to school for second semester was to go to Gerry's Sporting Goods Store and pick up my letterman's jacket. The jackets were reversible; one side was brown suede and the other was red cloth with tan arms and a big white N on the left chest. There was no bigger status symbol on campus than a letterman's jacket, especially if you lettered in football. For two and a half years I had longed to wear one. At first I was tentative about wearing it, fearing some of the older player might say something sarcastic; then I wore it everywhere. Later, when the novelty wore off, I wore it because it was warm and the best coat I had. It was my most prized possession. Wearing it, however, did not ensure respect from other players, especially players I'd been competing against.

One day after winter conditioning I was in the weight room doing bench presses. I felt a set of eyes examining me. It was Mike Fultz, a black freshman defensive tackle. He was six-five, 255 pounds. He was at the next bench station doing sets with much more weight than I was using. I felt he was sizing me up. He looked more like a first-team Big Eight tackle than I did, and I think we both knew it. It made me feel uncomfortable.

Big John Dutton was gone, a No. 1 draft pick by the Colts. Now his right-defensive-tackle spot was wide open. Knowing I would start out at first-team right defensive tackle was a real motivator for me. My workouts were vigorous. I tried desperately to gain weight and get bigger. I knew spring ball was about to begin and I would have to defend my prized black shirt against a host of players who also wanted to wear it. Away from the practice field, I was confident as I imagined myself starting and playing well, but around my competition, I didn't feel as confident. I felt helpless somehow. People wanted what I had, and if I didn't play better than they did, they'd take it. Nothing I had done in the past mattered now; not a letterman's jacket, not the quarterback sacks in the Cotton Bowl, not Coach Powers's praise. It was all history. I could only hold on to my No. 1 spot by outplaying my competition on the AstroTurf of Memorial Stadium. Everyone would be watching me; they'd all know whether I deserved it.

Before the first big scrimmage that spring, I was jittery. I thought that wearing the black shirt would somehow help elevate my play. It didn't. I did have some good plays, including a quarterback sack, but as usual I didn't look good on many of the running plays. I'd also sprained my ankle. After the scrimmage, Conde Sargent interviewed me. This is how it appeared in Sunday's paper:

NU Gridders Are Intense During Drills
By Conde Sargent

The hitting at Nebraska's first spring football scrimmage was intense Saturday at Memorial Stadium.

George Mills, a junior-to-be defensive tackle, said the explanation was easy.

"I couldn't sleep last night," Mills said. "I kept rolling over and thinking about what I would do today. Now I'll probably have a hard time sleeping tonight because I'll be thinking of the things I did wrong."

Coach Tom Osborne, who was generally pleased with the scrimmage, acknowledged spring practice puts "a lot of heat on the individual players. They know we have to evaluate them. Their performance each day is going to be important."

Mills, the 6'5", 220-pound Omaha native who can run forty yards in 4.7 seconds, is a member of the first defensive unit, an outfit which had a slambang session with the first offense, being nicked for a touchdown by fullback Tony Davis on the last play of the showdown.

"I'm a junior," Mills said. "This is it for me. I have a goal of starting. If a junior is equal with a freshman, that's not good enough. I'll have to be better than the guys under me."

That accounts for much of the intenseness: older players trying to keep jobs and younger players trying to work up the ladder. . . .

"They're looking for the hitters," tackle Mills said. "Coach Kiffin (defensive specialist Monte) is a perfectionist. My technique wasn't perfect today, I got hooked (blocked) too much."

After three practices, nobody was perfect. They were simply trying to be.

I had spoken truthfully. In short, I was in a battle with some younger guys and had to play better than they did. The unwritten rule was that if a junior and a sophomore are equal, coaches generally preferred going with the younger player. Three-year starters were prized commodities.

I was rattled, but I was intent on keeping my black shirt. My immediate problem was to get the swelling down in my ankle so I could practice again. I started hot-and-cold whirlpool treatments. On Monday I thought I could practice, so I had the trainers tape my ankle as tight as I could stand it. It was useless; whenever I pushed off on it, the pain was severe. I watched practice from the sidelines. For the first time I was angry that I could not practice. It was frustrating to watch, knowing that the two guys below me, Stan Waldemore, a six-four, 240-pound sophomore from New Jersey, and Mike Fultz would be energetically trying to take over my spot.

The real disappointment came on Wednesday when a new depth chart came out: Stan Waldemore had been moved to first team. I couldn't even hold my black shirt a week. In the newspaper on Thursday I found some small consolation. It quoted Coach Osborne as saying that Stan Waldemore's promotion was "partly because George Mills is injured but also because he had graded high in the last week's scrimmage." I made up my mind that no matter how my ankle felt, I was practicing Friday.

The grading system Kiffin used that spring was simple. He evaluated each play by the middle guards and defensive tackles as either a good play, average play, or bad play. He graded every play during filmed scrimmages, then posted the results. Even though I felt pressure from being constantly evaluated, I liked it because I always knew how I stood in relation to Waldemore and Fultz. Kiffin always gave us a copy of his evaluations. I'd study it and figure out how many good plays I needed to regain the top spot.

All spring I tried fiercely and never missed another practice, despite several more injuries. At various times I had a hurt rotator cuff in my right shoulder, a dislocated little finger, a twisted knee, and a hip pointer, plus my ankle always felt a little weak. Nevertheless, I wanted to start and was willing to pay the price.

Back at the South Street Palace, my roommates encouraged me. My cousin Tim was especially supportive. I really thought I was better than Waldemore, and I wasn't even worried about Fultz, who was listed on the third team. He was big but seemed to have a hard time adjusting to playing in a three-point stance with his left hand down, as right defensive tackles were taught. Every day in practice I tried to outplay Waldemore, who, by the way, was a great guy, as was Fultz. I liked them both, but this was competition, so all of us kept our distance, shelving potential friendships for another time.

I kept telling Tim that I was better than Waldemore. One day Tim came out to watch us practice to verify what I'd been telling him. He followed us around the practice field. It was a great inspiration to me. I played hard and I tried to dominate Waldemore and the other tackles in one-on-one drills. Tim agreed with me: I looked like the better tackle. But the only way to move up on the depth chart was to grade well in the filmed scrimmages. I just never had a great scrimmage. I had some good plays, but I was never dominant like Dutton was. In fact, none of us was playing great because toward the end of spring ball, Kiffin tried moving Ron Pruitt, who was the starting left tackle, over to the right side. Six-foot-eight Dean Gissler, who was Pruitt's backup, was playing well, but then he got hurt and Pruitt was moved back. It was frustrating. I felt I was the better athlete, but for whatever reason, I couldn't get the black shirt back.

Although I was frustrated, I felt good about myself because I was finally giving an all-out effort. In fact, Tony Davis complimented me during one scrimmage in which I beat a block and tackled him for a loss. "Nice hit," he said as he got up. Then, after the scrimmage, George Sullivan said, "Georgie, I'll be glad when spring ball's over so you can get healed up." Their comments supported my belief that I was giving it my all.

In the spring game the Reds defeated us 41-40 in a real shootout. I was disappointed that I had to play on the White team again but was excited that spring ball was over. I figured I'd concentrate on lifting weights during the summer and pump up. I'd get bigger and come back next fall to win my black shirt back.

I also had to make myself eligible again because I had flunked an economics class. Actually, I just quit going to class because it was extremely hard for me. Nor did I like the professor. Plus, for the first time, I was totally engrossed in football. Economics was the only class I had ever flunked in college. To be eligible in the fall, I'd have to make up one hour. I passed twenty-three hours for the year and needed twenty-four to stay eligible. Since I was going home for the summer, I couldn't attend summer school, so I had to take a correspondence class, English composition. I figured it would be easy, but I was wrong. It was work. I had to read three books, plus do weekly written assignments. The worst part was getting motivated to do the work. By the end of the session I was sick of doing the assignments. The professor grading my work wrote me some short, nasty notes suggesting I try harder or else. I finished and received a *B*.

My schedule during that summer reflected my dedication to achieving my goal. I ate a big breakfast, lifted weights for two hours, then ran two miles and did agility drills. I'd come home after that and work on my correspondence class and then my mom would make me a huge supper to help me gain weight. After supper, I drank a gain-weight concoction consisting of two eggs, a protein supplement, one banana, and ice cream. In the evening, I'd go to my bartender job at Theodore's Bar and Grill.

Working at Theodore's was an experience. The place was on the corner of Tenth and Jackson streets in the east Omaha warehouse district. My aunt Adelaide Lalley, who ran the kitchen, got me the job. By 7:00 P.M. the streets were empty and by dusk the crazies would start coming in. Much of the clientele consisted of winos, who purchased cheap wine to go, and an assortment of other heavy drinkers who, after a while, would begin telling me their troubled life stories. Sometimes when they were drunk and obnoxious, they'd want to fight me or arm-wrestle. "Where'd you get them muscles?" they'd say. When I was in a bad mood, I'd ignore them, and when I was in a good mood, I'd humor them. One time a guy bet me ten dollars I couldn't lie on my back with my arms outstretched and lift him up. I took him on. He stood on my hands, and I easily hoisted him over my head. He couldn't have weighed more than 150 pounds. When the place was empty, I'd exercise by doing dips between an opening in the backbar, and I'd make myself colossal-size cheeseburgers. Whenever I could, I'd close by 10:00 P.M.

All my friends and relatives knew I was battling Stan Waldemore and Mike Fultz for a starting spot, and they were all supportive. I told my dad about Kiffin's grading system and what I had to do. My mom helped by cooking big meals. Friends would say, "Keep working out, Mills. You got to do it." Even when I jogged on the streets, people I knew who drove by yelled encouragement.

By the end of the summer, my weight was up to around 230 and I was bench-pressing more than 320. I was in shape. One of the first players I talked to after reporting to fall camp was linebacker Bob Nelson. He said, "Mills, how much you weigh? How much you benching?" He had noticed how much bigger I had gotten. It made me feel good. I was on a mission to start at right defensive tackle for the University of Nebraska.

As usual it was hot that August and the heat took its toll on me. By the end of the first week my weight had dropped down to 223, but I felt great and was practicing hard. I went into the first scrimmage with confidence as I lined up across from my man. I thought, I'm going to beat you every play. The first couple of plays went to the other side of the field. I delivered a blow and pursued. I was getting anxious; I wanted to make a good play. On the fifth or sixth play, I had a chance to show what I could do. It was an isolation play where I was one-on-one with the tackle. I beat his block and moved to his inside. On the heels of the blocking fullback came the I-back. I slid into the hole and hit the I-back. It was a forceful hit, but I hadn't locked my arms. Instinctively, he began to bounce off, so I wrapped my body around his; as I did, I planted my foot in a pile of bodies. Tangled, we fell to the ground. There was a queer sensation in my left knee. Something had stretched, and then there was numbness; within seconds there was excruciating pain. I rolled on the ground moaning as the players unpiled. George Sullivan trotted over and knelt down over me; with a calm voice, he asked a few questions as he briefly examined my knee. He instructed two student trainers to help me into the training room to ice it. As they helped me off the field, I didn't want to believe I had been injured. I kept telling myself that it wasn't going to be serious, but within minutes my knee had swollen up like a grapefruit. The pain was pulsating. I knew it was going to be serious. How untimely! I was in a battle to earn a starting spot and now I'd certainly miss a week or more of practice. Stan Waldemore or Mike Fultz would start and wear the black shirt that I had worked for all summer.

I was sent to the Student Health Center for X-rays and was admitted as a patient. I had to remain there for a couple of days until the swelling and pain subsided and the doctors could make an accurate diagnosis of the injury. Lying there in bed, my throbbing knee numbed by pain pills, I broke down. All I could do was think about my lost opportunity and feel sorry for myself. I had worked hard for eight months to become a starter. It wasn't fair; plus, I felt I had let down everyone back home. It was one of the low points of my life.

After a couple of days I was released from Student Health. The diagnosis was that I had stretched a ligament but wouldn't need surgery. The doctor told me I could return to practice when the swelling was gone, and I figured I'd be back practicing in about ten days. Things were looking better.

I hobbled around campus the first few days with crutches and took whirlpool treatments before and after practice. First the cold water, then the hot, then the cold, then the hot, over and over. It was monotonous. I sat in the glass-enclosed room, leg in the whirlpool, and stared at the clock. At first the treatments were painful, but eventually I got used to them. Occasionally I'd share the whirlpool with other players who were rehabilitating injuries. I befriended several of them. The conversations would always start out with someone describing his injury, how it was received, and when he'd return to practice.

At practice I just stood around and watched. Kiffin would say, "Mills, when you coming back?" I'd say confidently, "In about a week, Coach." Ten days passed with little progress. The swelling was partly down, but I couldn't bend or extend the knee completely, nor could I push off it. My hopes were fading. I'd always felt I had total control of my body. I could run fast, jump high, and hurdle bodies, but I couldn't make my knee heal faster. Every day I kept hoping it would be the day I'd be able to run full speed again.

Eventually, Coach Kiffin quit asking me when I'd be back. His attention was directed at getting the starters ready: Ron Pruitt and Mike Fultz, who had won the battle to start.

When I finally started practicing, I did so at about three-quarter speed. I wore a gold shirt but didn't take any plays during team work. After the initial warm-up drills, which made my knee ache, I didn't do anything except stand around or sit on my helmet and watch. I usually had to flag down a trainer to cut slits in the tape on my knee because it was so tight. As I watched the team practice, I daydreamed about life outside football: school, girls, parties, girls. It was hard to feel like I was part of the team.

The first game was at home against Oregon. We whipped them 61-7. The next game was nationally televised and was against Wisconsin in Madison. I was on a date and watched the game from the TV lounge at Selleck Quadrangle, angry that I hadn't made the traveling squad. I still wasn't at full speed and wasn't ready to play, but I wanted to go nonetheless. The year before, I had grown accustomed to traveling with the team, and now it felt terrible to be left behind. More than one person stopped me on campus and asked me why I wasn't with the team. To make things worse, I had to watch underdog Wisconsin come from behind and beat us 21-20. The Badgers' winning touchdown came on a 77-yard touchdown pass with three minutes left in the game. I don't think I said two words to my date the entire afternoon. I just sat there, arms crossed, staring. At that point I had given up on my chances of playing.

The team rebounded by crushing Northwestern and Minnesota the next two weeks. I, in turn, settled into an observer role. The only time I exerted energy at practice was during the first ten minutes or so of agility drills and at the end of practice, when we ran sprints and Alpines. Occasionally Coach Kiffin would have me take a few plays during team work, but generally he was trying to get the first-teamers and their backups ready to play. I became a lifeless bystander. After I accepted my fate, my anger went away and I began to enjoy practice. I was still a fan, so I sat on my helmet and watched everybody. I talked with whoever was around, joked, and laughed. A couple of times I got yelled at for goofing around too much. I'd become unobtrusive until the heat died down and then return to my normal behavior of joking and laughing.

Not practicing much made me alert to other things. I wanted to know how everyone else was doing in school. While we stood around during team work, I'd ask guys what their plans were and what kind of grades they were getting. Mentally, I'd compare my plans with theirs. Some impressed me immensely. Guys like Rik Bonness, Tom Heiser, and Ron Pruitt were all good football players, but they were also excellent students. They knew what they wanted from school. I was amazed at how much motivation, determination, and stamina they had. They practiced hard yet had the discipline to study at night and get good grades. I admired them, and they deserved respect because they were accomplishing what few people could.

It made me angry when other students made negative comments about how easy football players had it. One time I got into an argument with a girl named Ruth. She said, "You guys got it made. All you have to do is practice a little football and you get a free ride. I have to get a part-time job plus take out student loans."

"Ruth, it's not as easy as you think," I said.

"Oh come on, you guys got it made. Tuition, room and board, plus whatever else Uncle Bob can do for you."

Warming up, I said, "You think it's easy practicing for two hours and going to meetings every day? Let me tell you something. When we come off the field after practice, we feel like we've been through a war. Your body is tired, your mind is tired, plus you're usually hurting someplace."

"Your mind's tired? Blocking those bags really tires your mind," she smirked.

"I've got a defensive playbook that's as thick as any lab manual," I said. "Learning a defensive or offensive scheme is just like taking another class, and if you goof up, the whole world knows it. How about pressure? You feel any pressure serving up those drinks? Get out in front of seventy-six thousand people on national TV and see what it's like." I also told her that if she didn't like her job, she could quit and find a new one, while I was stuck with football whether I liked it or not. She said, "Nice try, Jockstrap," and walked away.

People like her just did not understand how hard it was to play major college football while trying to earn a degree. I know it was hard for other students who had full-time jobs or families, but playing football took you to the limit of your energy level, mentally and physically. Just playing football without going to school would have been difficult; add school, and the task becomes extremely hard.

Imagine attending three one-hour classes and eating lunch between 8:30 and 1:30. Throw in time spent walking between classes, and that just about takes up the morning. At 1:30 P.M. the athlete heads for the field house to get taped and dressed for practice. At 2:30 there is a meeting with a position coach. By 3:00 the players are on the field, practicing. Practice is usually over by 5:00, but after practice there is a fifteen-minute in-season weight-lifting session, then a shower, and by 6:00 the athlete is in line at the training table. By 7:00 he's back in his room, supposedly ready to study. I can tell you that most guys at that point are ready to relax or even sleep. If the athlete does have enough energy and willpower to study for three or four hours, he's going to miss out on some socializing, which is also an important part of the college experience.

During the season, Saturdays are devoted solely to football. Then on Sundays there are stretching and short conditioning exercises, meetings, and film sessions. From mid-January to April, there are winter conditioning and weight lifting, followed by spring ball. During the summer, each athlete is expected to lift weights and run. Realistically, weight lifting is done year-round by an ever-increasing number of athletes. Players feel compelled to lift in order to get bigger, stronger, and faster, which will help them stay ahead of the competition. An average workout might last anywhere from one to two hours, depending on the time of year. Players normally lift weights less during the season, but that's not always true. Many guys lifted longer than the fifteen-minute in-season sessions. The addition of Strength Coach Boyd Epley to the football staff legitimized weight lifting; it had the effect of giving the players another job. Weight lifting is a separate sport. A great deal of effort is needed to make the kinds of strength gains that are needed to play major college football. It's no coincidence that a much-used slogan in the weight room is "No pain, no gain." I can also tell you that the weight-lifting gains made by All-Americans Rik Bonness and Bob Martin were done without the use of steroids. I knew of only one or two players who experimented with steroids, and they were not stars.

Players also spend time studying plays and thinking about games. Imagine a nineteen-year-old sophomore making the first start of his career in front of a huge crowd in a nationally televised game against Oklahoma. When he's at his early-European-history class on the Friday before the game, what do you think is going through his mind? Is he thinking about history or the game? On Monday after the game, in which he scored a touchdown, he's in class again. Is he thinking about the upcoming test or is he thinking about the touchdown he scored?

I don't want to make it sound like I was being exploited because I never felt that way. I was, in effect, working my way through school in a job that was more difficult and time consuming than I had imagined. I was attending school the hard way. The big games, notoriety, friendships, and the special feeling one has when he's a ball player were the things that kept me going. Even as a nonplayer I felt special. It was hard and I complained about it, but I was happy to be where I was.

Anyway, my diminished role in practice left me with more energy at night. That, coupled with my new role models—Bonness, Heiser, and Pruitt—put me in a different frame of mind. I now wanted to do well in school. I was no longer satisfied with just getting by. I wanted *A*'s, so I began studying more at night. Ursula Walsh, the athletic academic counselor, helped me a lot by developing a plan for me to graduate and by listening and being concerned. Eventually, I would get a B.S. degree from the Teachers College and major in sociology and have a minor in history. Graduating, which was once just a goal, was now my biggest goal. My injury forced me to reevaluate my life and what was important. I guess I was maturing a little.

I decided to make the best of my situation, which really wasn't that bad. I now knew that with more effort I'd graduate and that, even though I wasn't playing, I'd still get to go to a bowl game—provided we kept winning. Unfortunately, our team was struggling. Missouri came from behind to beat us 21-10. For the first time in a long time, we were 3-2 early in the season. We dipped from fourth to fourteenth in the ratings. At practice there was a rededication to effort because both of our losses were the result of fourth-quarter comebacks.

With improved effort, we reeled off three victories. We clobbered Kansas 56-0, struggled with Oklahoma State 7-3, and, in a regionally televised game, whipped Colorado 31-15. After the Colorado game, our record was 6-2 and there was speculation about a Sugar Bowl invitation. The rumor proved true, and a couple of days later we accepted a bid to play Florida. I still wasn't completely recovered from my injury and wasn't playing much, so going to a bowl game, especially a different one, was just what the doctor ordered. I had accepted my role as a nonplayer, but I still missed the thrill that goes with playing. When I was playing, my life was like a roller coaster. The highs and lows were extreme and depended on how I was performing at the time. In my nonplaying role, life was ho-hum, but my mood was much more stable. I needed some excitement. New Orleans, here I come!

We still had three games to play. We beat Iowa State and Kansas State. Our next game was against undefeated No. 1-AP-rated Oklahoma. We were 8-2 and rated sixth. Oklahoma was still on NCAA probation and banned from bowl games, and UPI omitted OU from its ratings. The game had its usual big buildup. Our practices were upbeat. If we beat Oklahoma, we could share in the Big Eight championship. We'd also avenge the humiliating 27-0 loss of the year before. For Oklahoma, the game meant a national championship; in effect, we became their bowl opponent.

The crowd, noise, and excitement of game day was overwhelming. I stood on the sideline in awe of the spectacle, mesmerized by the action on the field. We played them tough. It was 0-0 after one quarter and 7-7 at halftime. In the third quarter, we took the lead on a trick play. Dave Humm pitched the ball to John O'Leary for a seemingly end-run play. O'Leary ran a few steps and passed back to a wide-open Dave Humm for an 11-yard touchdown. The stadium erupted. Mike Coyle kicked the extra point, and we had a 14-7 lead. On the ensuing kickoff, we recovered a fumble on their 15 yard line. I ran down the sideline screaming and yelling. It was pandemonium. We were going to beat Oklahoma! Then we didn't score, and we missed a 21-yard field goal. It was as if their defense woke up and said, "Time to go to work." On offense they did what they did best: run the wishbone. Joe Washington was like a rabbit darting up and down the field. Their fullback, Jim Littrell, bulled into the line again and again. Quarterback Steve Davis was a magician, disappearing and then reappearing again for a 5- or 6-yard gain. They kept moving the ball, getting stronger and stronger as the game went on. They scored three more times and ended up winning 28-14, amassing 482 yards rushing. We gave it our best and lost to a superior team.

After the game I had two things on my mind: do well on my final exams and then enjoy a bowl vacation in New Orleans. My extra effort in school paid off with two *B*'s, a *C*+, an *A* in football (of course), and a pass in a course I took pass/fail. Also, during workouts for the bowl game, Kiffin surprised me by telling me I'd get to play in the game during goal-line situations just like the year before. I thought he had forgotten about me. Knowing I might get to play picked up my spirit. It was exciting to be going to New Orleans and a different bowl game. It was my third major bowl, and our team was shooting for a record six consecutive bowl victories.

We arrived in humid, seventy-degree New Orleans on Tuesday morning, December 24, 1974. This was our itinerary:

SUGAR BOWL ITINERARY

Tuesday, December 24

9:00 a.m.	Leave	Selleck
9:15 a.m.	Arrive	Lincoln Municipal Airport
10:00 a.m.	Leave	Lincoln Municipal Airport
		Lunch aloft
12:00 Noon	Arrive	New Orleans International Airport
12:30 p.m.	Leave	New Orleans International Airport
1:00 p.m.	Arrive	Fontainebleau Motor Hotel
2:45 p.m.	Leave	Fontainebleau
3:00 p.m.	Arrive	Tulane Stadium
		Workout
5:00 p.m.	Leave	Tulane Stadium
5:15 p.m.	Arrive	Fontainebleau
5:30 p.m.		Payment of player cash expense allowances at Fontainebleau
6:00 p.m.		Team dinner and team tie presentation with Santa Claus for the kids at Fontainebleau
		Free night

Wednesday, December 25

11:30 a.m.		Team Brunch
2:15 p.m.	Leave	Fontainebleau
2:30 p.m.	Arrive	Tulane Stadium
		Workout
4:30 p.m.	Leave	Tulane Stadium
4:45 p.m.	Arrive	Fontainebleau
5:30 p.m.		Team Dinner
		Free Night

Thursday, December 26

10:00 a.m.–12:00 Noon Ladies Walking Tour of French Quarters.
Bus leaves Fontainebleau at 9:45 a.m.
Eligible Personnel: Staff Wives
                              Team Wives
Dress: Casual
Bus leaves French Quarter at 12:00 Noon
for Fontainebleau

11:30 a.m.		Team Brunch
2:15 p.m.	Leave	Fontainebleau
2:30 p.m.	Arrive	Tulane Stadium
		Workout
4:30 p.m.	Leave	Tulane Stadium
4:45 p.m.	Arrive	Fontainebleau
5:30 p.m.		Team Dinner
7:30 p.m.–9:00 p.m.		"Your Father's Mustache"

Bus leaves Fontainebleau at 7:00 p.m.
Eligible Personnel: Team
                              Team Wives
Dress: Team—Coat & Tie
            Team Wives—After Five
Bus leaves "Your Father's Mustache" at
9:00 p.m. for Fontainebleau

Friday, December 27

| 11:30 a.m. | Team Brunch |
| 12:00 Noon–1:30 p.m. | Stag Quarterback Luncheon at Marriott |

Hotel. Cars leave Fontainebleau at
11:45 a.m. for Marriott
Eligible personnel: Staff
Dress: Coat & Tie

		Cars leave Marriott at 1:30 p.m. for workout
2:15 p.m.	Leave	Fontainebleau
2:30 p.m.	Arrive	Tulane Stadium
		Workout
4:30 p.m.	Leave	Tulane Stadium
4:45 p.m.	Arrive	Fontainebleau
5:30 p.m.		Team Dinner
9:30 p.m.–1:00 a.m.		Al Hirt's

Bus leaves Fontainebleau at 9:15 p.m.
Eligible personnel: Team
                                Team Wives
Dress: Team—Coat & Tie
                Team Wives—After Five
Bus leaves Al Hirt's at 1:00 a.m. for Fontainebleau.

Saturday, December 28

11:00 a.m.–1:30 p.m.		Ladies Seafood Luncheon at West End.

Bus leaves Fontainebleau at 10:30 a.m.
Eligible Personnel: Staff Wives
                               Team Wives
Dress: Casual
Bus leaves West End at 1:30 p.m. for Fontainebleau

9:45 a.m.	Leave	Fontainebleau
10:00 a.m.	Arrive	Tulane Stadium
		Workout
12:00 Noon	Leave	Tulane Stadium
12:15 p.m.	Arrive	Fontainebleau
12:30 p.m.		Team Brunch
1:00 p.m.		Payment of player cash expense allowances at Fontainebleau
6:00 p.m.–10:00 p.m.		Players Awards Banquet at Braniff Place

Bus leaves Fontainebleau at 5:30 p.m.
Eligible personnel: Entire party except children.
6:00 p.m. Team reception in Tulane Room
6:00 p.m. Cocktails for staff in Terrace Suite
7:00 p.m. Dinner in Grand Ballroom.

Bus leaves Braniff Place at 10:00 p.m. for
Fontainebleau

Sunday, December 29

11:00 a.m.–4:00 p.m.		Ladies Fair Grounds Luncheon
		Bus leaves Fontainebleau at 10:30 a.m.
		Eligible Personnel: Staff Wives
		Team Wives
		Dress: Casual
		Bus leaves Fair Grounds at 4:00 p.m. for
		Fontainebleau
11:00 a.m.		Team Brunch
4:30 p.m.		Team Dinner
6:15 p.m.	Leave	Fontainebleau
6:30 p.m.	Arrive	Tulane Stadium
		Workout
8:45 p.m.	Leave	Tulane Stadium
9:00 p.m.	Arrive	Fontainebleau
		Free Night

Monday, December 30

10:30 a.m.–1:00 p.m.		Ladies Tour of Garden District Homes.
		Bus leaves Fontainebleau at 10:00 a.m.
		Eligible Personnel: Staff Wives
		Team Wives
		Dress: Casual
		Bus leaves Garden District at 1:00 p.m.
		for Fontainebleau
11:00 a.m.–1:00 p.m.		Budweiser Seafood Stag at Royal Sonesta
		Bus leaves Fontainebleau at 10:30 a.m.
		Eligible Personnel: Staff
		Dress: Casual
		Bus leaves Royal Sonesta at 1:00 p.m. for
		Fontainebleau
11:30 a.m.		Team Brunch
5:30 p.m.		Team Dinner
6:15 p.m.	Leave	Fontainebleau
6:30 p.m.	Arrive	Tulane Stadium
		Workout
7:45 p.m.	Leave	Tulane Stadium
8:00 p.m.	Arrive	Fontainebleau

7:00 p.m.–9:30 p.m.   Dinner at Antoine's
                       Bus leaves Fontainebleau at 6:30 p.m.
                       Eligible Personnel: Staff
                                           Staff Wives
                       Athletic Only
                       Dress: Staff—Coat & Tie
                               Staff Wives—After Five
                       Bus leaves Antoine's at 9:30 p.m. for
                       Royal Orleans Hotel
9:30 p.m.–1:30 a.m.   Royal Orleans Party
                       Bus arrives from Antoine's
                       Eligible Personnel: Staff
                                           Staff Wives
                       Dress: Staff—Coat & Tie
                               Staff Wives—After Five
                       Bus leaves Royal Orleans Hotel at
                       1:30 a.m. for Fontainebleau
8:00 p.m.–10:00 p.m.   Team Movie
                       Bus leaves Fontainebleau at 7:45 p.m.
                       Eligible Personnel: Team
                                           Team Wives
                       Dress: Team—Coat & Tie
                               Team Wives—After Five
                       Bus leaves movie at 9:00 p.m. for
                       Fontainebleau

Tuesday, December 31

10:00 a.m.   Team Brunch
3:30 p.m.   Team Pre-game Meal
5:00 p.m.   Buses leave Fontainebleau for Tulane
              Stadium
7:15 p.m.   Kickoff of 1974 Sugar Bowl Football
              Classic
10:15 p.m.   After game all buses return to
              Fontainebleau
11:00 p.m.   Open house at Fontainebleau for
              entire party

Wednesday, January 1

No meals or events scheduled.

Thursday, January 2

8:00 a.m.		Luggage pickup
8:45 a.m.	Leave	Fontainebleau
9:15 a.m.	Arrive	New Orleans International Airport
10:00 a.m.	Leave	New Orleans International Airport
12:00 Noon	Arrive	Lincoln Municipal Airport
12:15 p.m.	Leave	Lincoln Municipal Airport
12:30 p.m.	Arrive	Selleck

Coach Osborne was more relaxed, and the reins seemed looser than they were at the Cotton Bowl. We had a 1:00 A.M. curfew until a couple days before the game, when it was changed to 11:00.

On the free nights or after scheduled events, I'd tag along with teammates to the French Quarter. We went to all the famous stops, such as Al Hirt's place and Pat O'Brien's. One night after stopping at a few live-music spots, I made my way to the Mississippi River. I just sat there watching it flow. I thought how lucky I was and started singing a popular Doobie Brothers song that seemed vaguely befitting:

> Well, I built me a raft and she's ready for floatin'.
> Ol' Mississippi she's callin' my name.
> Catfish are jumpin' that paddle wheel thumpin'.
> Black water keeps rollin' on past just the same.
> Old black water keep on rollin',
> Mississippi moon won't you keep on shinin' on me.

Although I hadn't played much all year, I was happy about the way things were going. Getting hurt was disappointing, but there were other things to look forward to. I was twenty-one, on schedule to graduate, in New Orleans on a free vacation, and getting ready to play in the Sugar Bowl, the last one to be played in memory-filled Tulane Stadium. I still had another year of eligibility, another chance to become a starter. Looking back to the beginning of the season, I probably put too much pressure on myself. This was college; it was supposed to be fun.

On the night of the game, it was warm and the stadium was alive. The large Nebraska following was vocal. We had partied in New Orleans, and now it was time to play ball. With a whistle by the official, the game started. We had been favored to win, but somebody forgot to tell Florida. They were a wishbone team and moved the ball on us surprisingly well. They scored a touchdown in the first quarter, then kicked a field goal in the second quarter. At the half it was 10-0.

In the locker room there was a frenzied, panicked look on everyone's face. It was the kind of look that comes when you know you're better than your opponent but they're taking it to you hard. The coaches huddled together and discussed adjustments. Players drank water, paced, and talked individual strategy. Position coaches then relayed the adjustments to players. Kiffin was animated while he talked. He was convincing us that if we kept Florida from scoring anymore, the offense would eventually score some points. Then it was time for Coach Osborne to talk. He gave his usual speech, but it was unusually emotional for him. His face red, he shouted, "Dadgummit, you guys are going to have to go out there and kick the hell out of them." That wasn't Coach Osborne's style, but it was effective. A charge of electricity surged through the room and went with us onto the field.

Something was wrong, though. We weren't able to stop them: five yards, six yards, four yards, they just kept moving the ball. Then our defense broke and Florida's halfback, Tony Green, ran eighteen yards down the sideline for a touchdown. But from across the field an official signaled that Green had stepped out of bounds at the 5 yard line. Florida ran another play, which lost two yards. They gave it to Green again and he ran six yards to the 1. Kiffin yelled for the goal-line defense. I sprinted out onto the field and lined up over the guard, crouched low. I was cocked and ready to fire. The ensuing dive play to the fullback was stuffed by our linebacker, Bob Nelson. In the defensive huddle, safety George Kyros said, "It's not over until they score." Fourth down. This was it. We lined up and the ball was snapped: a pitch play. I fired into the line low and hard, plugging a hole, scrambled up, and pursued the ball carrier. Out of nowhere shot 165-pound cornerback Jim Burrow, who beat a block and tackled the ball carrier. We ran off the field screaming and waving our arms and were greeted at the sidelines with slaps on the back and emotional words. Kiffin was screaming, "Nice job, defense!" We had done our job. There was no better feeling. Now it was up to the offense.

The offense, led by quarterback Terry Luck, who had replaced

Dave Humm, began to take charge. They ran dive plays, isolations, and quick pitches, many to big, 275-pound Mark Doak's side. Methodically, they moved up the field. Tony Davis kept hitting the hole and spinning after contact for extra yards. They drove 99 yards, with freshman running back Monte Anthony scoring from the 2. The score was 10-7 with thirteen minutes left in the game. We forced a punt, and again the offense moved the ball. With 7:20 left, Mike Coyle kicked a 37-yard field goal. Our defense held and we got the ball back at our own 25 yard line with about four minutes left. We moved the ball down to their 22. The big play on the drive was a classic 40-yard blood-and-guts run by Tony Davis. With a 1:46 left, Coyle kicked the go-ahead field goal.

I had forgotten what it was like to play in a big game. I had forgotten the bond that exists among teammates struggling to win. Instead of just being a member of the team, I felt like I was a part of it again. Although my part was small, I had contributed. My reward was to feel the heartbeat and breath of my teammates pulling for each other, acting as one, and the elation and pure joy of escaping defeat. When Mike Coyle kicked the winning field goal, ninety-seven NU players and about fifteen thousand fans and coaches rose into the air, propelled by the exhilarating emotion of the moment. As players, we lived for moments like this. It was what we would remember when we were old.

Tony Davis was the game's MVP. He rushed for 126 yards on seventeen carries. Defensive end Tom Pate was our best defensive player. Terry Luck gave us leadership, and Mike Coyle kicked two clutch field goals. Everybody contributed. For me, nobody knew I even got into the game back home. That was OK with me because I found my picture had been in the newspaper three times: once with Tony Davis, once with Tom Pate, and once with Mike Fultz and Monte Anthony. My cousin Mick Lalley said I was the most publicized nonstarter who ever played the game.

13

Roller-Coaster Ride

The beginning of the next football cycle came quickly and without much hope for me. Mike Fultz was named Sophomore Big Eight Defensive Player of the Year. I figured there was no way I'd ever beat him out for a starting position. Since I was a senior, it was important for me to become a starter. After all, that is everyone's goal, and I wanted to know what it was like. With my future at defensive tackle not looking so bright, I decided to try out for tight end. During winter conditioning I stayed after practice and caught passes with the other receivers.

Just before the start of spring ball I asked Coach Osborne if I could make the switch to tight end. He said no, he didn't think it was a good idea because there were already three good senior tight ends on the team. Intimidated because I was talking with the head man, I didn't argue. Disappointed, I then went to Coach Kiffin and said, "Coach, am I ever going to play around here?" He said, "Yes. All you have to do is work hard. Anything could happen." It was a patented response used when desperate lower-unit guys confronted coaches about playing time. He told me I'd start out on the second team behind Fultz during spring ball. Fultz was bigger, stronger, and as fast as I was. I'd also seen Fultz tackle a guy without his helmet, which had popped off, something I wouldn't have done. He was becoming another Dutton. How could I ever beat him out?

After several weeks of brooding, it was apparent that I had no other choice; if I wanted to be a starter, I had to outplay Fultz. I prepared myself mentally, and when spring ball started I was ready for a fight. I called on all my past experience and what I knew Kiffin was looking for in a player and used them to my advantage. I knew that promotions were based to a large degree on how I'd perform during filmed scrimmages. Kiffin would evaluate every play and then grade us. Knowing this, I made sure I hustled on every play because he always praised the guys who hustled. Whenever I was blocked, I'd get away quickly and sprint full speed with the correct pursuit angle toward the ball carrier, even if I knew I didn't have a chance at making the tackle. One time the ball carrier broke loose and was thirty yards downfield. Nevertheless I sprinted, arms pumping and at full speed, down the field chasing him. Sure enough, during films the next day Kiffin said, "I want you guys to see this." Then he showed the play. "Watch Mills there in the middle of the field. He's selling out. He's giving it everything he's got pursuing that ball carrier, and that's what you guys gotta do if we're gonna have a good defense. Good job, Mills." During the next scrimmage, in addition to hustling, I concentrated on using the proper technique. Kiffin was a perfectionist. He not only wanted us to make good plays, but do it with the correct footwork and proper arm movement. Every time I rushed the passer, I did exactly what Kiffin taught us. I'd fake inside, then grab the man's shoulder with my right hand and swing my left hand over his head. It was called the swim move.

The next film session had the same result. "Watch Mills pass-rush here. That's how you're supposed to do it. Nice job, Mills," Kiffin said. I didn't do everything perfect, but I was actually grading better than Mike Fultz during the scrimmages. Mike had been slowed a little by an injury, and fortunately I had none. It was the first spring I'd gone through practice without being hurt. Everything seemed to be going my way, but I never moved up.

For the last two weeks of spring ball, I continued to practice with intensity. I kept reminding myself that it was my last spring practice, my last chance. Finally, on the Monday before the spring game, Kiffin posted a new depth chart. I was listed at first-team right defensive tackle ahead of Fultz. If I hadn't seen it, I wouldn't have believed it. This is what I'd been working for. Now that it had happened, I didn't know how to act. I was elated but controlled. I went to his locker and said apologetically, "No hard feelings, Mike?" and exchanged my gold shirt for his black one. Although I was exploding inside with excitement, I felt bad for Mike because I knew how it felt to be demoted. All week long I was restless. I kept thinking I was going to goof up and lose my black shirt, but it never happened.

For the first time in my career, I started for the Red team, made up of first- and fourth-teamers, during the spring game. But my starting was undermined when the White team, which Fultz was playing on, beat us 20-6. After the game, I mentally replayed my performance, looking for good plays and I could think of only a few. I made myself stop thinking about it and figured that whatever was going to happen would happen. If they moved Fultz up in front of me, worrying about it wouldn't help. Instead, I basked in the glory of the moment. I was first team, at least for the summer, and I had just finished the best academic semester in my life: my semester grade-point average was 3.3 without cheating. I was absolutely thrilled. Although it had taken a long time to learn, I was realizing that worthwhile things don't come easy. My accomplishments were the result of hard work.

I went to the annual spring-game party put on by one of the boosters. There was unlimited food, drink, and beer. It was for players and coaches, but there were also friends and relatives of the guy throwing the party. I never liked wearing the name tags they gave us because people were always covertly trying to read the name on my tag. And always at these types of functions, someone would come up, read the tag, and, with a disappointed look, say, "Where's Tony Davis?" or "Where's Rik Bonness?" Most fans weren't interested in average players like me; they wanted to talk only to the stars. But this time I was feeling good about myself, and I had a good time.

The end of this spring semester was sad because the members of my recruiting class who hadn't been redshirted would be graduating. It would be the last time I'd see them. Not that we were the best of friends, but you can't help but feel close to guys who you've practiced and played with for four years. Graduating would be George Kyros, Ritch Bahe, and the Minnesota Twins, Tom Ruud and Bob Nelson. Both Ruud and Nelson had been starting linebackers for the last two years; both were great ball players. I remember Coach Kiffin saying in practice one day that they'd both be ten-year NFL veterans before they were through. Both were drafted that spring. Ruud, in fact, was a No. 1 draft choice and Nelson did end up playing a decade in the NFL. Thinking of them made me realize that my time at the university was almost up and I hadn't accomplished any great feat on the field yet.

I worked out that summer, running and lifting weights with dedication and intensity. I even felt guilty if I didn't do extra sets of lifts or run the extra sprints. I was working out to stay ahead of Fultz, who I knew would also be working out hard. I went through my workouts in a nervous frenzy. I gotta do this. I gotta do that. I gotta work hard. I told myself that this was it, that I was going into fall camp on the first team, something I had never done before. It was my last chance to start, and I had better not blow it.

I purchased a copy of *The Big Eight*, a football magazine. It had stories about players, predictions, and All-Star Team selections. I just wanted to see my name listed as a first-teamer. I found my name, and there was a quote from Kiffin: "Mills was one of the most pleasant surprises of the spring. He's shown he's ready to play Big Eight football. He's been banged up every year and this was his first full spring." Then I turned the page, and there was a full-page picture of Mike Fultz with the headline "Nebraska's next Outland candidate." The article described him as soon to be the strongest player ever to play for the Cornhuskers. He was also one of the biggest and fastest linemen ever. And Kiffin was quoted as saying Fultz was up with the likes of All-American John Dutton and Larry Jacobsen. I was stunned. The article made me more nervous about getting beat out in the fall, so I worked out even harder.

Being a senior didn't make fall camp any easier. The weather was hot and muggy, and the practices were as long and as hard as ever. I didn't grumble about it like I usually did; I concentrated on playing well, hustling, and doing my assignments. I zeroed in on one thing: starting the first game.

Disaster struck the first week of practice when Ron Pruitt, the starting left defensive tackle, broke his ankle. Pruitt was a two-year starter and a player everyone liked. The coaches were shocked. Before practice the next day, Kiffin called a meeting with Pruitt's backup, Jerry Wied, Mike Fultz, and me. He told us that it was his job to put the two best defensive tackles out there on the field and he didn't care who they were. He told Mike and me that in addition to practicing on the right side, we'd also practice on the left side. Coach told us that whoever looked the best playing the left side among us three would start. Kiffin told Jerry not to be offended or feel as if he didn't have confidence in him, it was just that he had to make sure he put the two best defensive tackles on the field.

I had been playing on the right side almost my entire career at Nebraska. Switching to the left side was hard. It meant lining up in a three-point stance with my right hand down when I was used to lining up with my left hand down. It was like trying to become a switch hitter in baseball during the middle of the season. In addition, I had a hard time with the defensive plays because I now had to do the opposite of what I had been drilled for so many years to do. Mike and I alternated with Jerry on the left side all week, and then Kiffin made up his mind. I would play on the left side, but Jerry would start the game and play the first and third quarters. I'd play the second and fourth. I'd also back up Fultz in case he got hurt. Kiffin told me I'd still wear a black shirt in practice and would be considered a starter. I was too naïve to realize it at the time, but Fultz was a foregone conclusion to start. What coach in his right mind would keep a talent like Fultz off the field?

Before I had time to think about what had happened, the story was in the newspaper. The article told how Pruitt had broken his ankle and how Wied and I would share playing time and replace him. It also had a picture of Jerry and me. About that time, Coach Osborne talked to me and said, "Keep your weight up, George, because we'll need you down the road." It was the first he'd spoken to me with reference to my helping the team. I was thrilled. So much so, in fact, that I didn't care about being switched or actually not starting the game. I wouldn't be a starter, but Coach Kiffin told me he considered me to be one, which was good enough for me. Kiffin knew how to handle his players. After five years he knew how to get my best. I responded to calm logic and rebelled at authoritative yelling. By talking to me and showing an interest in me, the coaches had won my loyalty. I was so emotionally involved with the team that I would have done anything they asked, even give up my dream to be a starter.

After Kiffin's reassurance, I wasn't thinking in terms of first and second team anymore. I was thinking only of winning. I wanted to do whatever it took to win. I was even running extra Alpines after practice. I had a good feeling about our team and I shared it with Mike Fultz as we descended from the top of the stadium. I said, "Just think, Mike, in ten weeks we'll be doing this and we'll be ten and zero." He laughed and said, "That's right. We're gonna win and kick some butt this year."

Our first game was at home against LSU. Several of our players were to be sidelined for it because of a minor NCAA rule violation. Quarterback Vince Ferragamo, backup tackle Dean Gissler, defensive starting safety Jimmy Burrow, and defensive end Ray Phillips all had to sit out because they had unintentionally been allowed to attend bowl games in previous years when they were ineligible. Plus, our All-American center, Rik Bonness, was out with an injured knee. Despite all those missing players, we still felt that we were a better team but that it would be a tough game. We won 10-7 in a defensive struggle.

After every play during the game, the announcer would say who was in on the tackle. I hadn't heard my name. It seemed impossible to get in on a tackle. Play after play, I'd deliver a blow, fend off the blocker, and sprint to the ball carrier. Just before I reached him, out of nowhere, red-jerseyed projectiles would explode into the runner and take him down. It was gang tackling at its best. There was literally no open space to sink a shoulder pad into. I found myself competing with my own teammates to get in on a tackle. We were like dogs fighting over a bone. We were a typical Kiffin defense.

The next game was against Indiana, and we waxed them 45-0. The following week we blew out Texas Christian 56-14. Then the University of Miami team came to town. They were coached by a former Husker assistant, Carl Selmer. Jim Walden, one of my freshman coaches, was their defensive coordinator. They knew our system well, so it was going to be a difficult game. We struggled in the first half but won 31-16. In that game, Vince Ferragamo came off the bench to relieve Terry Luck at quarterback. Vince had the looks of a young Greek god, plus he was calm and could throw the ball like a pro. Vince got the offense moving and for the first time played up to his potential. He went on to become an NFL player and lead the Rams to the Super Bowl one year. Next we beat Kansas 16-0. They were led by their great option quarterback,

Nolan Cromwell. At that point, we were 5-0 and rated fourth in the nation.

Everything was going great for me. There was another article with pictures in the newspaper about Jerry Wied and me. It told how we were doing a good job filling in for the injured Ron Pruitt and how, by Big Eight standards, we were both small for defensive tackles. The article also told how we were friends on and off the field, that we student-taught together and roomed together on the night of the game. I felt on top of the world. In addition, I had money. I had sold my football tickets to an attorney in Omaha for fourteen hundred dollars, to be paid in two seven-hundred-dollar installments, and at the time I had a single dormitory room across the street from the training table, which was convenient. I had a refrigerator to keep food and beer handy, and I was doing extremely well in school. Practice was still rough, but as a fifth-year senior, I was used to it.

The biggest thrill, however, was the attention I was getting. I was receiving letters from fans and girls, some of whom I'd never met. One girl wrote saying she had seen my picture in the program and thought I was cute. Others wrote and asked me for dates. Girls in my dorm were always leaving messages on my door. It was unbelievable. I loved it. The prizewinner, though, was a letter from a girl who had dumped me in the spring. Apparently, playing in the games made me more attractive to her. She wrote:

October 1975

Hi George!

I know this letter has got to come as a surprise to you, but it's just that I haven't seen you for so long I thought I'd jot you a line to see how you are.

I see you're doing very well this year in football. That's great! I listen for your name on the radio and [look for] your picture in the paper every week. Continued good luck!!

I'd sure like to start hearing from you and to know how you're doing in school, etc. It's been such a long time since we've seen or talked to one another, that it's hard to find a place to start. Worse than that, you probably don't even remember me. I hope that's not true.

I'm sorry about never getting back to you several months ago, but I was going through a really confusing time. Maybe you will understand, if I'm ever given the chance to explain.

I'll stop here in case you resent this letter for some reason, but I'd sure appreciate a letter from you—it would be great to start communicating again.

See you soon and good luck on next weeks game!!

Candy

As a player, I can tell you it was wonderful being appreciated so much by the fans, especially the girls. It added to the I'm-special feeling I had. The adulation wasn't limited to letters, either; there were also groupies who hung around the team. It seemed like every year there'd be a couple of girls who'd frequent the same bars the players did or show up at the parties we had. The groupies would date around, jumping from player to player. The girls would be labeled as being easy, and the word would spread. Then the dogs on the team, guys who'd chase anything in a skirt, would be seen in hot pursuit. The majority of the players, though, dated one girl at a time. Some were even dating their high school sweethearts, and many of the romances that developed in school ended in marriage.

I wasn't dating anyone, so every Thursday night I'd get shined up and head down to the Water Hole or the Brass Rail, two popular bars within walking distance of the campus. I'd walk in with my I'm-special attitude. People offered to buy me beers or invited me outside to smoke doobies (pot). It was prestigious for people to say they got high with a player. Cute girls would come up to me and talk; if they didn't, I'd go up to them. After drinking a while, I'd get loud and brash and my friends would respond by slapping me on the back and laughing. If there was royalty on campus, it was the football players during a winning season. By the end of the night, I'd be out of it, sweet-talking some girl in the corner. On the way home I'd stop and hog down some food, sleep like a log, and then get ready for another day at the factory.

My relationship with the coaches was at an all-time high too. I don't think it had as much to do with the fact that I was playing as it did with the fact that I was a fifth-year senior. Coaches treated seniors with more respect. Everyone knew one another well, and we had become like a family. Coach Kiffin and I were like old friends—he called me Millsy. We had survived our differences.

As with most of life's endeavors, situations change. Kiffin told me after the Oklahoma State game, which we won 28-20, that I wasn't playing very well. He said I wasn't making as many plays as I had made in the spring. He said if I didn't start playing better, he'd have to move Dean Gissler in front of me. Notice was served, and it hurt.

We beat Colorado 63-21, but I played poorly again. I missed a tackle and got blocked rather well by Colorado's huge offensive line. On Monday, Coach Kiffin told me Dean would move ahead of me. Although I practiced with the second team, I was really the third-team tackle. I was devastated. To make matters worse, one day I had to practice with the scout team because they were short of players. I had made history, the wrong kind, by being the first guy to go from wearing a black shirt to holding dummies in the same season. I was embarrassed, but I wasn't mad at Kiffin. I knew I was playing badly and deserved a demotion. I was even happy for Dean because he was a good friend and I knew he'd felt bad being a senior and not playing. I tried to figure out what caused my nosedive.

I decided my fall was a combination of things. First, I was partying too much and I had gotten out of shape. Plus, the attention had gone to my head, and I thought I was playing better than I actually was, which affected my motivation to the point where I wasn't trying as hard. What it boiled down to was that instead of trying to improve, I took playing for granted and became complacent, something you don't do at Nebraska. There's just too much talent around. I also realized that playing didn't solve all my problems. It didn't make me feel as good as I thought it would. What was important to me was being accepted by my teammates and friends, and I had that whether I played or not. Unknowingly, I'd shifted into neutral gear.

I had other things on my mind too. I learned that a former teammate, Tom Pate, had died. We had gotten to know each other pretty well during his senior year in 1974. He was a fellow Omahan and we had ridden back and forth from Omaha a couple of times. He had been playing linebacker for the Calgary Stampeders. During a game he was blocked and went into a coma. The doctors said it was the result of a congenital defect. I was saddened. I realized more clearly that football was not as important as I was making it out to be. It was only a game, and there were a lot more important things in life. Knowing that helped, but it was still very hard not traveling with the team to Missouri, which was our next opponent. I was a senior and I was left home like a common redshirt.

We beat Missouri 30-7 in a televised game and moved up to No. 3 in the national ratings. By this time I was convinced we were going to win the national championship. I decided I'd write a story about our quest to be No. 1 and began making written and mental notes about what was happening with the team. I also borrowed a tape recorder and began interviewing players and recording team meetings, pregame and halftime speeches, and locker-room talk. Whenever I had an opportunity, I discreetly turned on the recorder. Even though I was a benchwarmer, I was proud of our team. I was going to tell everyone about it in a great sports story.

I also started getting more involved with gambling. I had come from a gambling environment where on the weekends during football season people would bet. As a kid growing up, I would even bet a parlay. Nothing big, maybe a three-teamer for five dollars. It was just something to give me rootin' rights while I watched a game. Where I came from, gambling was normal. I continued to bet parlays occasionally while I was living in Lincoln. That fall I was betting with a friend named John. A couple of guys on the team found out that I had someone to make bets with and asked if they could bet with him through me. I said fine, no problem. As the season wore on, more and more guys called me to make bets for them. It was getting to be a hassle for me to make the bets and collect the money. John told me he'd give me a cut of the betting action if I kept it up. I looked at it as a part-time job. I started passing out football sheets, which listed games and point spreads, on Thursday to friends and players, maybe ten or so players when I first started. I'd also pass out parlay cards, which showed the approximate odds and payoff amounts for the number of teams and amount of money bet. Each week, more and more guys wanted sheets. Not all of them bet, though, and most of the ones who did would make goofy bets, such as six-teamers for ten dollars. I'd tell the novices that the more teams they bet, the more they'd win. There were some guys who knew what they were doing and they'd bet straight up, twenty-two or thirty-three dollars. Sometimes I'd get a fifty-five-dollar bet on the Monday night pro game. It didn't bother me that I was making money off teammates because I never thought about it. To me it was all just fun. Gambling represented a diversion. It was exciting to get down and sweat out the games. It was a real adrenaline shot to win or lose. Betting didn't affect anyone's play, and if a player did bet on Nebraska, it was always to win. Certainly no one was trying to throw games. It wasn't the type of gambling that scandals are made of.

By the end of the season I was passing out about twenty to twenty-five betting sheets. I remember one time I had to make extra copies so I used the copy machine in the sports information office. The coaches would have killed me had they known what I was doing. I guess I was impetuous and a little crazy, which, as college students, we all were from time to time.

I certainly must have looked crazy because I hadn't been shaving. It all started with our middle guard, John Lee. He had a skin infection and didn't shave for a couple of weeks. He looked like a black version of Bluto in a Popeye cartoon. The idea caught on, and Captain Bob Martin asked Coach Osborne if it was OK for the rest of the team to grow whiskers too. Coach told him OK, as long as we didn't lose. After that, practically everyone began growing a beard.

With our menacing new look, we went out and beat a stubborn Kansas State team 12-0 and then trounced Iowa State 52-0. The Cyclones' leading rusher was my old nemesis from high school, Creighton Prep's Jim Wingender. I always knew he was a tough player and he'd do well in college. That win gave us at least a tie for the Big Eight Championship because Oklahoma had been beaten by Kansas. We heard good news in the locker room after the game: Missouri was leading Oklahoma 27-21 late in the game. When we heard the score, everyone cheered and yelled repeatedly, "To the beach!" Then, a few minutes later, we heard the final score; Oklahoma had come back to win 28-27. A sigh was let out over the room, and for the first time our team appeared less than confident. It meant we'd have to beat Oklahoma in Norman the next week if we were to remain undefeated and go to the Orange Bowl, which the Big Eight was locked into by contractual agreement.

On Sunday, at films, we had to vote to decide where we'd go if we lost. Apparently the other major bowls we were looking at, the

Cotton and Sugar, had already made agreements with teams. People in Nebraska were angry with Alabama's coach, Bear Bryant, because they felt he was ducking us. Nebraskans thought Bryant was using his clout to play a lower-ranked team in the Sugar Bowl so he could finally get a win in a bowl game. His teams had lost six straight. If we didn't beat Oklahoma, we'd be left out of a major bowl. The Fiesta Bowl was courting us heavily. They said they'd take us even if we lost to Oklahoma to play against either Arizona or Arizona State in Tempe, Arizona.

At the meeting, Coach Osborne told us that because the Fiesta Bowl was a relatively new bowl with a smaller payout than the Orange Bowl, we would probably only be able to take eighty-five to ninety guys to the game. He said that it would be hot and we'd have to be in shape, which meant extra conditioning work. He cracked a joke about Dutton's protest two years earlier about working out hard before the Cotton Bowl and we laughed. He said if we didn't plan on playing hard and try to win, we shouldn't go. He said he was sick of the bowl talk and only wanted us to concentrate on whipping Oklahoma. He ended his talk by telling us we had fifteen minutes to talk it over and that we should end our discussion with a vote. The Fiesta Bowl officials wanted to know our answer that night.

Co-captain Terry Luck spoke first. He said the most important thing was that we go down to Norman next Saturday and kick Oklahoma's butt. Then everyone else got up and talked a little. Some guys spoke up for going, reminding everyone of our bowl-game winning streak of six in a row. Seven would be a new record. Some players talked about going as a needed reward for a long season. A few guys were worried about a letdown if we got beat by Oklahoma. They felt it wouldn't make much sense to go out and get beat again and end the season with two losses. Most players, however, felt snubbed at not being able to play in the Cotton or Sugar and were just angry. They felt we were a class team and deserved a major bowl. Terry spoke again, saying, "I agree with you guys. I feel we deserve more consideration than we've gotten, but I've been to the Orange Bowl, the Cotton Bowl, and the Sugar Bowl. Going to the Fiesta Bowl would be like going down to the Water Hole on Thursday night." Everyone laughed and we voted. It was Miami or nothing.

After the vote, we began an intensive week of preparation. The mood of the team was confident. Whenever two or three players were together, they'd be talking with pride about our team and the game. At practice the offense put in some new wrinkles: a couple of power sets for goal-line situations. The defense prepared as always.

Coach Kiffin loved big games. You could just see it in his walk and mood. He was lighter and funnier, cracking jokes. At films he said, "As far as their personnel goes, they have a good offensive line. They're just as big as Colorado. All I have to say is this: they're not any quicker than Colorado's line, so you'll have to beat them with quickness. They're big and strong, and they're slow! Shit, you don't play football big, strong, and slow. You play football big, strong and quick, just like I did when I played." We chuckled. He then gave us the Oklahoma scouting report. On paper they looked awesome:

OKLAHOMA

The way to beat Oklahoma is with team quickness and pursuit. This is our strong suit on defense and consequently, if we do this, we will stop them and win. They rely on the cheap touchdown a lot, just like last week in the 4th quarter against Missouri. Good pursuit and tackling eliminates this type of play. This is what Kansas did and we have a better defense and more quickness than they do.

Concentrate and learn your assignments in practice, so you can just react to what you see and not be thinking. We will give them enough looks so they can't sit and read us and at the same time we will keep enough carry over from each defense so it will be simple and you can learn your assignments and get after them.

In practice work hard at getting off your blocks and getting to the ball. They of course run a lot of options and what hurts them the most is when they cut back and there's that pursuit staring you in the eye.

We've come a long way. Oklahoma is not good enough to stop us. Remember—Oklahoma has some doubts about themselves, we don't.

OKLAHOMA PERSONNEL

LT—#67—KARL BALDISCHWILER 6'4", 262 lbs., Sophomore

LG—#75—CHEZ EVANS 6'2", 265 lbs., Junior

C—#55—DENNIS BUCHANAN   6'2", 230 lbs., Senior

RG—#66—TERRY WEBB   6', 247 lbs., Senior

RT—#79—MIKE VAUGHN   6'6", 282 lbs., Junior

TE—#80—VICTOR HICKS   6'4", 230 lbs., Freshman
                           Hicks is only a freshman. Good size
                           and speed. Can catch the football.

SE—#11—TINKER OWENS   5'11", 170 lbs., Senior
                           Great wide receiver. Excellent hands
                           and speed. Can catch the ball in a
                           crowd.

FB—#42—JIM LITTRELL   5'11", 205 lbs., Senior
                           Littrell hurt us last year with big 3rd
                           down runs. Good blocker for Washing-
                           ton. Had 147 yards against Nebraska
                           last year.

RHB—#4—ELVIS PEACOCK   5'11", 201 lbs., Sophomore
                           Has 4.4 speed. Likes to run wide.
                           Complements Joe.

LHB—#24—JOE WASHINGTON   5'9", 184 lbs., Senior
                           You all know what Joe can do! Every-
                           bodys All-American. Game breaking
                           moves and speed. Never let up on him!
                           Must be contained on punt and kickoff
                           returns.

QB—#5—STEVE DAVIS   5'11", 190 lbs., Senior
                           Outstanding Wishbone quarterback.
                           4.6 speed. Key man to stop in Sooner
                           offensive attack. Can throw if he has
                           to. Great team leader. Also capable of
                           long run.

The entire state goes crazy during Oklahoma week. The support
we were getting was fantastic. The fans really get involved. Some
guy named Leo Hill who owned a scrap-metal company had a

dinner for the senior players and their wives or girlfriends. It was an annual event. The meal was great: prime rib. Martin, Bonness, and I were the only ones without dates, so we sat together. Except for a few players, nobody really knew Leo, so we all acted formal and were quiet. Leo sat with his family. I recognized him because he was at every one of our practices. I especially noticed him one day when there were some guys up in the stands. Leo told the security guard to go check them out to see if they were spies from another team. I thought he was a school official because he acted with authority. Later I found out he was just a fan. At the end of the meal, he got up and told us how much he appreciated us and our efforts and said he was proud to be a fan. It was nice.

After a week of practice, the team boarded the plane and headed for Norman. Since I wouldn't be there, I asked one of my teammates to record the drama of the game. I told him just to put the tape recorder in his locker and click it on before the game, at halftime, and after the game. This was the big game, and it would be an integral part of my story of our undefeated season. I, in turn, headed for Omaha to attend my cousin Tim's wedding.

All through the wedding and reception I felt embarrassed at not being with the team. Whenever anyone asked me what had happened, I just said, "I got demoted." I ran into my uncle Tom ("Jeep") Abboud and told him how I felt. He said, "Don't worry about it. You've done more than any of them." But it was still agonizing not being with the team. Having to listen to the game on the radio was hard. I loved my team but couldn't be with them for the biggest game of the season. It was a tussle. We were leading 10-7 in the third quarter but, amazingly, we fell apart and got beat 35-10. All year long we hardly turned the ball over. During the game with Oklahoma, we turned it over six times in an otherwise statistically even game. Our fate was sealed. For days I had a sick feeling in my stomach. Oklahoma would end up being crowned national champion.

When I got back to school on Sunday night, I found out that the team had voted again and had decided to play Arizona State in the Fiesta Bowl. I was told that the older guys wanted the younger guys to see what a bowl game was like, plus everyone wanted to end the season on a winning note. The Oklahoma game had left a bitter taste in everyone's mouth. It was very had to accept. Even though they beat us 35-10, we still felt we were the better team.

The loss was the most disappointing one in the five years I had been at Nebraska.

We practiced for the Fiesta Bowl with the same intensity we had before past bowl games. Many had the feeling that we'd kill Arizona State, that we were going to take out our frustration on them. They were undefeated, but they played in a weaker conference. So when we arrived in Tempe, we were very confident. I think that for most of the seniors, though, we were more interested in having a good time than playing a game.

Arizona State had some good things going in their favor. They had two very fine receivers, John Jefferson and Larry Mucker, and a good running back named Fast Freddie Williams. We were playing on grass, which, after playing on AstroTurf, made you feel a step slower. We were overconfident, and it was hot; Arizonans were offering free drinks to Husker players at area lounges. And I think we had a huge letdown after we lost to Oklahoma. All this resulted in a 17-14 upset win for Arizona State. Like Oklahoma, it was a bitter loss, maybe even more so because we were supposed to win.

It was fitting that a beat-up Tony Davis was the last Nebraska player to touch the ball during a failed late-game march to score. He was, after all, our spiritual leader and our most gutsy player. Tony was the one who'd never give up, an example of what a Cornhusker should be. Watching him try so hard was always inspirational to me. Tony and Rik Bonness, Tom Heiser, and Bob Martin were all alike. They were homegrown guys who had dreamed since they were knee high of putting on a Nebraska uniform. When they finally did, they kept alive the tradition of pride and excellence. My fondest memory of the Fiesta Bowl was a bus ride to a restaurant at Camel Back Mountain. It was a beautiful, clear night. On the way there, we spontaneously started singing a song that was playing on the radio. It was an invigorating feeling, the kind you have after a win. We weren't the national champions, but at that moment we felt like we were.

14

Coming Down Off the Pedestal

The perpetual campus hero is not a young man but an old boy.
—Alexander Chase

For almost five years, my life, sometimes willingly, sometimes unwillingly, had revolved around football. Life without football was going to be a new experience, and I was not sure how I felt about it. I was excited about the freedom I'd have but was apprehensive about my future. The metamorphosis of going from player to former player was already beginning. I would learn the dynamics of it were such that for a long time I wouldn't be sure of who I was or where I belonged. It would be an unsettling time.

The only thing I was sure of was that I wanted to make my last semester at the University of Nebraska my best. I needed only nine hours to graduate, and since I didn't have to practice football anymore, I'd have an abundance of free time to do the things that ordinary college students did. I wanted to see what it was like to sit in the Union all afternoon talking to friends, reading, playing chess, or playing Foosball. I wanted to eat my meals in the dormitory cafeterias. I wanted to observe fraternity and sorority life to see what it was about. I wanted to make sure I didn't miss out on anything.

In order to experience everyday university life, I had moved back on campus. My place of residence, Love Hall, was surrounded by fraternities and sororities; it was the oldest dormitory on campus. I used to sit by my window and watch Greek life. It seemed like they were always doing something. Fraternities had lots of parties with various themes: toga, pool, cowboy. When they weren't having parties, they'd be stealing sorority pledge pictures. They'd even serenade the sororities. On Monday nights they'd wear suits and ties and have formal dinners. When it snowed, fraternities were always having snowball fights. Sometimes they got crazy and had huge bonfires in the middle of the street, and once they killed a turkey, which they proceeded to burn.

I always knew when the fraternity guys across the street came home drunk from the bars. They'd be loud and obnoxious, shouting at the top of their lungs. It was as if they wanted everyone to know they had been out partying; it was their signoff for the night. One time they woke me up from a sound sleep. I had a big test the next morning and I was furious. I opened my window and shouted for them to shut up and disperse or I was coming down to kick some ass. I figured I was a fifth-year senior football player and I could whip five skinny frat rats at once. Well, they quieted down and went inside. I felt manly. I'm bad, I thought. About ten minutes later, I heard some rustling and laughter, then a whistle and explosion. I looked out and saw that the fraternity guys were back and were shooting bottle rockets at my window. I couldn't believe the jokers had the guts to do it! I had to laugh too. I got to know some fraternity guys; they were OK, but I never wanted to join a frat because football was all the regimentation I could take. I just couldn't see myself putting on a tie every Monday night for dinner.

The dormies were equally fun loving. They'd play their music loud, fix their rooms up weird, and play pranks on one another. They'd have beer and pot parties and sneak girls into their rooms after hours. Don't get me wrong, there were plenty of serious students, but for a large portion of the student body, the campus was not much more than a young-adult funplex. Attend class then party was the theme. Not once in my five years did I ever attend a party where there weren't kegs of beer and somebody in a dark corner smoking pot. Every weekend someone had a kegger. There were off-campus parties, dorm parties, frat parties, and woodsies, which were held in wooded fields. Without any structure other than classes, students got crazy and had a ball. Life for them was uncontrolled.

In comparison, most football players by necessity were disciplined; they were also somewhat mild mannered and quiet because they were usually tired from practice or a game and wanted only to relax in their limited free time. Many were uncomfortable with the limelight and were withdrawn. We did have goof-offs on the team, but not that many. Of the 160 players in the program, there might have been 10 or 15 in any one year who fit the negative stereotype of a college football player by regularly engaging in any number of activities. Specifically, I'm talking about the players who used drugs, got drunk, were lecherously promiscuous, never studied, cheated, and bullied or intimidated other students to get their way. Some were very aggressive individuals who had a knack for looking for trouble and would have been doing the same type of things whether they were playing football or not. In other words, they arrived at the university with a propensity for deviant behavior.

The 160 players in the program were from all parts of the country and every socioeconomic stratum; they probably represented a good cross section of American life. It would be abnormal if a handful of them weren't troublesome individuals. In my opinion, the players' lifestyles were no worse than those of the general college population. The only difference was that when a player got caught doing something bad, it became news for the front page. That is the downside of publicity.

I was looking forward to playing on the senior basketball team. It was a big event for graduating football seniors because it was the last time we'd be together as a group, the last time the cheers would be meant for us. Playing against the faculties of high schools around the state was a good way to ease out of the sports program. We ended up scheduling about ten or twelve games, some in towns I'd never heard of. We'd get paid around $450 per game, which we'd divide equally. It amounted to about $30 a game, depending on how many seniors showed up. Knowing the fans wanted to see the stars, it was important for our All-Americans, Rik Bonness and Bob Martin, to be there, along with Tony Davis, Terry Luck, and Wonder Monds. Normally we'd have ten or twelve players show up.

The road trips were fun. We'd pile into cars and head for faraway places to be greeted by adoring fans and autograph seekers. We'd be silly during the games and try to make the spectators laugh. Occasionally, after the games, some high school girls would wait by our cars and ask to be kissed. It was like being a rock star. Then we'd drink some beer on the way home.

After a few games I began to notice a rivalry among some of the players, including me. Players appeared to be competing to see who could attract the most attention during the game. There would also be squabbles over playing time. Gradually, the bond that we had spent five years developing began to dissipate. Some guys were mad at me because I prearranged the sale of autographed balls at each game plus I set up a newsstand to sell a newspaper that reviewed our season. I had one of the faculty members from the school we'd be playing against sell them for me during the game for $1.50 each; the balls were sold for $35.00. Tony Davis called me Milski in reference to my entrepreneurial skills. The arguments continued and the dissension grew. Eventually a group of about eight guys scheduled a game to play on their own. When the rest of us found out, the sparks flew; we called them traitors. I had heard that in previous years things like that had happened, but I never thought it would happen to our group. We had been so close, and now it was every man for himself. We were literally fighting among ourselves.

After one game in a small town about a three-hour drive from Lincoln, Rich Costanzo, Jerry Wied, and I were drinking with some of the townspeople at a little party. I had a test the next day and was anxious to get back, but Jerry, who had driven, was having a good time and didn't want to leave. After about an hour and a half, my patience was gone. I repeatedly asked Jerry to go, but he ignored me. Finally I got belligerent and said, "What are you gonna do, Wied? Let's get the hell out of here!" He said, "I've had enough of you, Mills." We had a few more words and he said, "Let's go outside." I didn't wait; I punched him first. We fought maybe thirty seconds, and then Rich broke it up. I never felt so bad in my life. Jerry was my friend, one of the nicest guys on the team, and now we were fighting. Immediately I said I was sorry and wanted to make up, but he was still mad. There was another problem, since Jerry drove. How was I supposed to get back to Lincoln? Fortunately, he let me into the car, although he didn't say two words the entire ride home. Big Daddy Costanzo told us to forget it and tried to make peace. When we got back to Lincoln, I got out and told Jerry again that I was sorry. He didn't say much.

That fight was one of the most regrettably stupid things I did while I was in Lincoln.

About the time senior basketball ended, talk of the NFL draft began. I read a copy of the *Pro Football Weekly*, which had a list of draft ratings by a scouting service. I was surprised and honored when I saw myself listed. There were forty-eight defensive ends, and I was No. 44. All of a sudden I wanted to be drafted. I began filling out the questionnaires I had received from professional teams during the season. I also made a résumé about my few football accomplishments and mailed it to all the pro teams. I don't think I really wanted to play in the NFL; I just made myself believe I did. I was reacting to the fear of losing my identity. I had been Joe Jock for five years and now that was over. I feared for the future; I didn't know what I'd do after I graduated.

On the day of the draft, I stayed in my room and waited for a call from some professional team. It never came. Eleven of my teammates did get drafted, though. Rik Bonness was the first to go; he was the twenty-fourth player picked in the third round. Tony Davis and Wonder Monds, our uniquely named star defensive back, went in the fourth round and Bob Martin went in the sixth. It is interesting to note that Oklahoma, a team that my class had never beaten, had three players chosen in the first round, including the first player taken in the draft, LeRoy Selmon. It confirmed an old coaching adage: "You can't win without the horses." The team with the better players usually wins.

Jealous that so many of my teammates had been drafted, I was now determined to play pro football. I went to Coach Kiffin for advice. He said he'd talk to a coaching friend he had in the Canadian Football League. A couple of weeks later I was contacted by a representative from the Calgary Stampeders. He said they'd give me a tryout. I signed a contract for $17,500. What was more important was the fact that I now had a future. I was going to be a pro football player. So I started working out again with all the other guys who were drafted and learned another reason why Bonness and Martin were All-Americans: they lifted weights harder than anybody else. When the rest of us left the weight room, they'd still be doing extra sets. Although I had the free time to do anything I wished, every afternoon at 1:30 I'd head for the field house to work out. It was a habit.

About a week before graduation, I went over to the coaches' offices to say good-bye to everyone. I was sad. My five years were up, and I now had to venture out into the real world. Everyone was nice and friendly, especially Coach Osborne. He smiled and said, "Come back and visit sometime." I was getting ready to leave when I saw Coach Rick Duval. I panicked because he was the one guy I didn't want to see. In the fall there had been an incident which prompted me to avoid him. Coach Duval was always talking religion and Bible stuff to players. One day on the elevator he started in on one of the players. I got mad and said, "You know, that's not the way you win people over to God, by getting in their face with Bible talk." He looked at me with a big grin and said, "Would you like to talk religion sometime?" I was going to tell him that his excessive talk just turned people off, but I chickened out and opted to avoid him all year. Now it was just him and me in a hallway and he said, "Are you ready to have that talk now?" I couldn't escape. So I explained how I felt about his method of talking about God. He said he was just stirring up the water to get guys to talk and open up. Then he changed the topic to me. He told me that he knew what I was like, that I had gone around acting like a big man on campus. He said that was not the way to act and that I'd better start growing up. He said the only way I'd change was to ask Christ to come into my life. He said I literally had to say every day, "God, come into my life and help make me a better person." I was stunned, but I wasn't offended. I knew he really wanted me to be a better person. We ended by laughing and shaking hands. I even tried what he suggested.

On May 8, 1976, I graduated from the University of Nebraska with a bachelor of science degree in education. The president of the United States, Gerald Ford, spoke at the commencement exercises. I was proud of myself. I had completed 127 hours in five years and my grade-point average was 2.677. I had earned two letters in football and had attended four bowl games. Next stop was Calgary where I hoped to find fame and fortune.

I arrived in Calgary, checked into the dormitory where the team was staying, checked out my equipment, and was interviewed by some radio station. I found out I was the only recruit from a big-name school. I played my part, name dropping all the while. "As a backup to John Dutton, I learned a lot," I said confidently. Then I met some coaches and went back to my room to think.

I didn't like it. Compared to playing at the University of Nebraska, Calgary wasn't as nice. The stadium wasn't as big, the locker room wasn't as modern, nor was the equipment as nice. I even had to select my hip and knee pads from a big bin in which none of the pads seemed to match. At Lincoln, Gib always took care of that kind of stuff. Besides that, the Canadians had accents. Why that bothered me, I didn't know. All I knew was that I didn't like what I was seeing and I was already homesick and ready to leave.

I lay awake all night, trying to decide what I should do. If I quit, I'd disappoint people back home. If I stayed, I'd hate it. It was the same argument I had had at Nebraska as a sophomore. I kept telling myself to give it a chance. It didn't work. I was leaving. I figured I was in a foreign country and they'd never miss me. I was wrong. That morning on the radio talk show, they had an interview with a coach. He said, "There was one guy I was really impressed with. That was the big defensive end from Nebraska. He's very impressive looking, about six-four and two hundred thirty, and can run a four-eight forty. He backed up John Dutton at Nebraska, and backups at Nebraska can start at most other schools." I turned the radio off. That statement made it even harder, but I'd already made up my mind.

I decided to go back to Lincoln and stay with my old roommate, Donny Moriarty. I'd stay with him for a week and then return to Omaha. On the plane ride, I began thinking terrible thoughts. What if someone I knew saw me in the airport and asked me an embarrassing question about my Canadian football tryout? Even worse, what if I ran into Coach Kiffin? How could I ever face him? He went out of his way to get me signed, and I quit after the first day.

I walked out of the plane exit, nervous. The Lincoln airport was very small, so anyone who knew me could easily spot me. The first person I saw as I picked up my luggage was Coach Kiffin. There was no avoiding him. Blood rushed to my head. "Hi, George," he said. He told me he was there picking up a recruit. Then he said, "How you doing? When you heading up to Canada?" I lied. I mumbled. I looked away. I did all those things that guilty people do. Abruptly I said, "I gotta go, Coach," and walked away. About a week later I sent him a letter explaining what had happened and I apologized. It was not a good way to end a relationship with somebody I had grown to respect a great deal. It left me with a sick feeling.

When I returned to Omaha a week later, no one asked what happened. I think they all figured I got cut and felt sorry for me. From then on I concentrated on getting a job. I had thought that as long as I had a degree I could get a job anywhere, but what I found out was that teaching degrees were good only for teaching. I was disappointed that no one had offered me a salaried position. I ended up selling insurance and, on a part-time basis, real estate. Working on a straight commission was hard. If I didn't sell, I didn't get paid. It took three months to get my first paycheck. Along the way, I had to learn that in the business world everyone was looking out for their own interests. The days of people looking out for me were over.

To compete with more experienced salespeople, I began trying to use my football career to my advantage. Everyone loved Nebraska football, so I used the fact that I had played as a conversation piece to get my foot in the door. I wore my Big Eight championship ring, my Orange Bowl watch, and my Orange Bowl tie clasp on my blue Sugar Bowl tie. I was a walking piece of Nebraska memorabilia. To many people, I probably seemed silly. It took me a long time to learn that being a former Husker was a great conversation piece but did not ensure success in the business world. In order to make sales, I had to be knowledgeable and provide clients with a service. I worked hard at getting better; I studied and went to seminars. And I did get better. I qualified for a regional sales conference after only six months in the business. But this glory was not the same as the glory of football. I missed being a celebrity. I missed the adulation and the special feeling that goes with playing. I began to think about football; maybe I could try to play again. I started lifting weights for two hours every other day and eating heavily. My weight shot up to 248, my bench press to 375.

I ran into an attorney, Don Fiedler, who was interested in football. I had convinced him that I wanted to play again. He said he had contacts in the pros, and before I knew it he was trying to get me a tryout. I knew that if given the chance I could make it. I bought a tape of the sound track from the movie *Rocky*, which had just come out, and played it while I worked out. I was going to be the Rocky Balboa of football.

It was March 1977 when Don began calling and sending letters to pro teams, telling them about me. This is the letter he sent to Bobby Beathard, director of player personnel for the Miami Dolphins:

March 10, 1977

Mr. Bob Beathard
Director of Player Personnel
Miami Dolphins Football Team
Miami, FA [sic]

Dear Bob:

I have been devoting most of my time to my law practice since I saw you in San Francisco. However, a young man came into my office the other day that I feel might be of particular interest to you. His name is George Mills, and I'd like to tell you a little about him.

George is 22 years old, graduating from the University of Nebraska last year. He is a two-year letterman who, at graduation, stood 6'5" tall and weighed 228 pounds soaking wet. He played right defensive tackle and was known as the team's best pass rusher and for his exceptional speed for a big man, running the forty consistently in the range of 4.7 to 4.75. Nebraska was high on George from the onset. After being Red Shirted for one year, he played behind John Dutton, lettering as a sophomore. In his junior year, George was sharing the starting position with Mike Fultz until George strained his left knee which took him out of action until the last three games of the season. He worked very hard in Spring Ball and took away the starting position from Fultz in spite of the fact that Fultz had been named Sophomore Defensive Player of the Year in the Big Eight conference.

He held that starting position in fall camp until Ron Pruitt, the starting left defensive tackle, broke his leg. At that time the coaches tried to shift Fultz or Mills over to the left side to fill the vacancy left open by Pruitt's injury. George was moving better than Fultz, so he got shifted over and Fultz moved up into George's starting slot. He shared that starting position with another senior for the first six games. Then George got into Monte Kiffin's "dog house" for blowing a few assignments and eventually lost his starting position.

Scouts, who at one time had been very high on George, soured, and he was not drafted in the 1976 player draft in spite of being on the "The Hughes Draft List" which was published in *Pro Football Weekly*. However, several teams expressed interest in George to sign with them as a free agent. George did sign with the Calgary Stampeders in Canada. He went up there, all of twenty-one years old, got disillusioned with the program, and walked out of the camp after only being there two days. George never really has had a good look from any professional team.

George Mills now wants another chance. He has dedicated himself to being ready for it when the opportunity presents itself. He works out diligently at least once a day—running, lifting weights, playing racquet ball, basketball, and working on techniques with Lynn Boden, offensive guard from Detroit who winters in Omaha. His weight today is 250 pounds and it is a strong 250 pounds. He is bench-pressing 400 pounds and the amazing thing is that he has not lost any of his speed. However, this isn't what impresses me most about George; it is his attitude and dedication. I have participated in athletics all my life and I know a good attitude when I see one. George wants a chance to prove his ability as a professional football player. He is not so much interested in the money as wanting the opportunity to prove himself.

Please check your scouting reports on him, call his coaches, send a scout up to look at him, clock him and whatever else you may want to do. George is what you would consider a "sleeper" and he is worth a look.

I have only been in touch with one other football team, who is supposedly sending a scout up to take a look at George. The reason that I am contacting you individually is that I know that the Dolphins are looking to improve their pass rush, and this is one of George's strongest points. Frankly, I think that he would have a real good chance of making your football team, and that he is the type of player that the Dolphins could use.

Thank you for your time and consideration. If you are at all interested, please contact me by the end of the month, as I would like to give you exclusivity for signing him as a free agent, but you will understand that I cannot wait forever to know whether or not you are interested.

Good luck in the coming season, and I remain

Very truly yours,

Donald B. Fiedler

DBF:cgh

About a month later, a representative from the New York Jets said they would be willing to give me a look. I met a scout at the

University of Nebraska at Omaha field and did a short workout for him. I ran some forties and did some agility drills. About two weeks later, I received a one-year contract in the mail. I'd be paid $27,500 if I made the team; there was no signing bonus. The training camp was to begin in July, but before I'd be invited, I had to make it past the free-agent tryout session in May. I had to pay my own way to New York. It wasn't the kind of contact I had hoped for, but it was an opportunity.

My signing wasn't publicized, but it made me feel complete again. Ever since my NU career had ended, I had felt that something was missing from my life. Football was more than playing a game, it was a way of life and an identity. It was something I felt comfortable with. I had forgotten about the negative aspects of playing, such as practice and injuries, and remembered only the good things, such as the adulation and respect I got from other people. When I was a Nebraska player, other people made me feel that I was important, and I missed it. I wanted to feel it again.

I made it past the free-agent tryout and was invited to summer training camp. I reported to Hofstra University at Hempstead, New York, on July 7, 1977. The head coach was Walt Michaels; he had replaced Lou Holtz. I arrived in the afternoon and walked confidently around the campus, talking to the other players.

Two of the first guys I met were a quarterback named Matt Robinson and a big defensive tackle named Joe Klecko. We had time to kill before a 6:00 P.M. dinner, so we tagged along with some other guys and went to play pickup basketball in the gym. This was my first opportunity to prove to myself that I was as good an athlete as the guys who had been drafted. I played hard and did well. I thought to myself, I'm better than you, Joe Klecko. You might bench press 450 and you might be 265 pounds, but you're from Temple and I'm from Nebraska. However, we were playing basketball, not football.

After dinner we had a 7:30 meeting with the head coach and were given our schedules and a notebook of plays and defenses. There was also a sheet showing fines for various rules violations. Losing a playbook was one thousand dollars, so I guarded mine closely.

In the dorm that night, I listened to some of the second-year players tell how great it was to be a New York Jet. They'd walk into a restaurant wearing their green jackets and people would pay for their meals and drinks and women would ask them for dates. They said New York was the place to be if you were playing pro sports. My imagination was working overtime.

The next day we had a strength test and physicals. The strength test was composed of doing as many dips and chin-ups as I could. Then I did a standing vertical jump and ran a forty-yard dash. They also wanted to see how many bench presses I could do with 195 pounds. I was asked to do a minimum of eighteen; I did twenty-seven.

The physicals started with filling out a questionnaire asking about previous injuries. I listed them, then I was examined by some bone doctors. The day before we started practice, they wanted me to have my ankles and knees X-rayed; they were concerned about my past injuries. A couple of us were taken to a downtown hospital, where they did the X-rays, and then some doctor who had operated on Joe Namath's famous knees examined me. I felt very honored—Joe Willie and I looked after by the same doctor. I was definitely big time.

Just before the 2:45 afternoon practice, one of the trainers told me to report to the training camp director and bring my playbook. I was told I had flunked my physical because my ankles were weak and my left knee was loose; my legs wouldn't hold up to the strenuous rigors of the National Football League.

I wanted to delay going home a failure again for as long as I could, so I decided to visit my cousin John Grandinetti, who was now living in San Diego. I told the camp director I was broke, so he paid for my plane ticket and gave me five hundred dollars. On the plane ride I realized I was happy the ordeal was over. Instead of being disappointed, I was relieved that I flunked my physical. I wanted to feel special again, but being in camp made me remember how hard it was to play. I had fooled myself into believing I was willing to pay the price to play. I wasn't. I was a dreamer. But the dream was over. I could now end my bittersweet love affair with football.

After spending two weeks in San Diego, I went back to Omaha to begin my new life as a former Husker. There were lots of us around. One time at an insurance seminar, I met a guy in the parking lot. He saw how big I was and asked if I played football.

He told me he was a former Husker too; he had played on the 1955 team. I told myself I was going to get over this football ego trip and come down to earth. I didn't want to be hanging on to glory days twenty-five years after I played.

I did miss the thrill of competing, though, so I played in softball and basketball leagues. I found them to be extremely competitive. The guys playing took the games seriously, even going so far as to fight. But after playing in front of seventy-six thousand people, I had a hard time taking recreational leagues that seriously. I played because I liked the friendship of my teammates, but I was still looking for something.

I tried coaching. It was an opportunity to give something back to sports, since I had experienced so many good things during my athletic career. I started out coaching grade-school basketball, and it was a great experience for me. The kids looked up to me and I really liked teaching them about the game, but in the beginning I took the games too seriously. I think I was reliving my playing days. Once I drew a technical foul for arguing with the referee. I kept arguing and was kicked out of the gym. After that, I tried to keep things in perspective.

I stayed with coaching and eventually became a teacher and head high school football coach at my alma mater, Bishop Ryan High School. It was both exciting and rewarding. I received a great deal of support from the parents, players, and students. It was just like being an athlete again because I was treated special. In return, I tried to be the very best coach I could be. I think I was a cross between Coach Kiffin and Coach Osborne; I was animated and yelled like Kiffin, but I also tried to set a good example like Coach Osborne. I tried to teach the kids about the game and also about life. We attended Mass before each game, and we'd always say a team prayer before and after the game. Whenever I'd catch someone drinking or smoking, I'd punish them and tell them how bad it was. I spoke from experience. I knew that all the partying I had done in high school and college had definitely hurt my performance and had detracted from my having a good attitude. I told the players that alcohol and tobacco companies made glossy, slick advertisements because they wanted new consumers for their products. They got former athletes or attractive-looking people to advertise their products in the hope that teenagers would try to emulate them. I told them that whenever their friends wanted to do something illegal, they wanted someone to do it with them. I didn't want them to give in to peer pressure. I also told them to save sex for marriage, that cussing didn't make you a man, and that they should respect their parents and teachers. But the most important thing I told them was to use their talents to give glory to God.

What I found was that trying to set a good example was hard. Occasionally, after a game, my assistants and I would go out drinking, sometimes heavily. There were also times during the heat of the game when I'd use profanity. I'd always stressed academics, but when I had twelve players ineligible for a big game, I thought the rule was unfair, all of which made me feel hypocritical.

There was also pressure from parents. Some wanted their sons to get more playing time. When we lost games, people criticized my play calling. People who had never played the game were telling me what I should do. When we won, everything was great. All this made me reflect on all the things Coach Osborne must have gone through on a much larger scale. As a coach, I found it was impossible to satisfy everyone.

As the years passed, the need for recognition that had started when I was given a scholarship to NU faded. My association with the program was limited to going to games and occasionally answering questions from die-hard fans about what it was like to play there. I got married in 1986, and since then the focal point of my life has been my family: my wife, Diane, and our two sons, Aaron and Michael. Their health and welfare are the most important things in my life, and that's always been true except for one day: Sunday, May 27, 1990. I had signed up to play in a Nebraska football alumni basketball game against the San Francisco Forty-niners in Omaha. I hadn't noticed any publicity surrounding the game, so I figured not too many people would show up. I was tired that night and really showed up only out of curiosity. I wanted to see if any of my former teammates would be there. When I pulled up to the gym, I was surprised to see a long line outside. I told my wife to wait in the car with the kids, who were crying at the time, and I'd go in and investigate.

When I got inside, the place was packed with people. I had an immediate adrenaline release. I was late, and the players were already on the court warming up. I frantically tried to find the man in charge to get my jersey so I could go out onto the court. Warming up, I felt a surge of energy; I wanted to run and jump. Let's get the game going, I thought. Before we started playing we were introduced, and as I ran out on the court amid the cheering, I was magically taken back in time. I was a player again, and those cheers were for me. The feeling was staggering. Halfway through the first quarter, I remembered that I had forgotten about my family. I jogged out to the car and sheepishly asked my wife through the window if we could stay. With a halfhearted smile she said OK, and I found them some seats close to the court. At halftime I signed autographs for little kids. My wife looked on with amazement, wondering why anyone would want some second-team tackle's autograph fifteen years after he played. Later when she asked, I told her that's the power of Go Big Red. Finally, after the third quarter, tired and sore, I gathered up my family and left. The kids were tired, and I had had enough adulation for one night.

The game made me realize that one never really gets over the experience of playing college football. You go on with your life, but, given the opportunity, you readily plunge into reliving the experience. Satisfied after a short dip, the realities of life beckon: changing diapers, cutting grass, house payments, grocery shopping.

Coincidentally, Rik Bonness was at the alumni game. I found out that he had played several years of professional football and had gone on to become an attorney. He was married and had two children. He was getting on with life too!

Over the years I have tried to keep track of my former teammates. Mike Fultz, Stan Waldemore, Bob Martin, and Tony Davis all played at least five years in the NFL. Tony went back to Nebraska to get his degree and is currently working with the team in the computer film department. Ron Pruitt and Mike Fultz are teachers and coaches. Monte Kiffin became head football coach at North Carolina State and is now defensive coordinator for the Minnesota Vikings. Tom Heiser became a doctor and was one of the team physicians for NU until he was paralyzed in a surfing accident. He is rehabilitating with the same enthusiasm that made him an academic All-American. Bob Martin is a sales representative for a large company.

Playing college football is like getting shot out of a cannon. The flight varies for each player; some go high and some go low, but in the end, everyone comes down to earth with only an intense memory of what it was like. Perhaps F. Scott Fitzgerald sums up the experience best in *The Great Gatsby* when he describes one of his characters, a former player, as "one of those men who reach such an acute limited excellence at twenty-one that everything afterward savors of anticlimax."

A Note on the Author

George Mills, who played defensive tackle for the University of Nebraska Cornhuskers from 1971 to 1975, is a real estate agent. He lives in Omaha, Nebraska, with his wife and their two sons.

Books in the Series Sport and Society

Go Big Red!
The Story of a Nebraska Football Player
George Mills

Reprint Editions

The Nazi Olympics
Richard D. Mandell

Sports in the Western World, Second Edition
William J. Baker